Versicherungswissenschaftliche Studien

edited by
Prof. Dr. Christoph Brömmelmeyer
Prof. Dr. Helmut Heiss
Prof. Dr. Hans-Peter Schwintowski
Prof. Dr. Astrid Wallrabenstein
Prof. Dr. Jochen Zimmermann

Volume 51

Wenyu Qian

China's Insurance Regulatory and Supervisory Regime

Analysis and Advice Based on the Comparison with EU's Solvency II System

Nomos

The Deutsche Nationalbibliothek lists this publication in the Deutsche Nationalbibliografie; detailed bibliographic data are available on the Internet at http://dnb.d-nb.de

a.t.: Frankfurt am Main, Univ., Diss., 2018

ISBN 978-3-8487-6281-1 (Print)
978-3-7489-0390-1 (ePDF)

British Library Cataloguing-in-Publication Data
A catalogue record for this book is available from the British Library.

ISBN 978-3-8487-6281-1 (Print)
978-3-7489-0390-1 (ePDF)

Library of Congress Cataloging-in-Publication Data
Qian, Wenyu
China's Insurance Regulatory and Supervisory Regime
Analysis and Advice Based on the Comparison with EU's Solvency II System
Wenyu Qian
244 pp.
Includes bibliographic references and index.

ISBN 978-3-8487-6281-1 (Print)
978-3-7489-0390-1 (ePDF)

D30

1st Edition 2019

Preface

The research work was accepted as a doctoral dissertation by the Law Faculty of the Goethe University Frankfurt in January 2014. The legal acts involved in the dissertation constitute the legal basis as of the end of 2017 for insurance regulation and supervision in the EU and China. The dissertation was written over a span of four years, during which changes to the insurance regulations in the EU and China took place at times. The changes made to the regulations in the two jurisdictions by the end of 2017, including China's new solvency regulation system effective from 2016, are taken into account.

1. *New Regulatory Developments*

In March 2018, an institutional reform of the component departments of China's State Council, namely the central government of China, was announced. As part of the reform, China Banking Regulatory Commission (CBRC) and China Insurance Regulatory Commission (CIRC) will be merged to form a new supervisory institution: China Banking and Insurance Regulatory Commission (CBIRC). The prospective supervisory institution is charged with supervising banks and insurers in China. The merger means that the 'CIRC' mentioned in the dissertation will be replaced by the 'CBIRC'.

At the moment, the institutional reform of China's State Council is at a preliminary stage. The general arrangements for the reorganization of its component departments, including financial supervisory institutions, are made public in high-level schemes.[1] However, the implementing details of the reorganization are still being devised. On the basis of the relevant information available in the high-level schemes and an explanatory publica-

1 'Scheme on Institutional Reform of the State Council (Release Authorized by the 2018 Annual Sessions of the NPCC and the CPPCC)' *Xinhua News Agency* (Beijing, 17 March 2018). Yong Wang, 'The Clarifications on Scheme on Institutional Reform of the State Council' (the First Session of the 13th NPCC, Beijing, 13 March 2018) <www.gov.cn/guowuyuan/2018-03/14/content_5273856.htm> accessed 9 April 2018.

tion by the research chief of China's central bank,[2] the merger of the banking and insurance supervisory institutions will be accompanied by adjustments to their responsibilities – part of their rule-making powers along with their tasks of promoting the development of banking and insurance sectors will be assigned to China's central bank. With regard to the adjustment to the rule-making power, the scheme on the institutional reform of the State Council states that " the CBRC's and the CIRC's responsibilities of drafting important legal acts applicable in the banking and insurance sectors and formulating the fundamental framework of prudential regulations are assigned to the People's Bank of China".[3] Theoretically speaking, the prospective supervisory authority for China's banking and insurance sectors would have fewer regulatory powers than its predecessors. The regulations made by the prospective supervisory authority are expected to be completely of implementing nature. The central bank is supposed to take over the function of determining the essential principles and fundamental rules imposed on China's banking and insurance sectors. As for the second adjustment, the prospective supervisory authority would not be tasked with promoting the development of the banking and insurance sectors, as opposed to the case with its predecessors. It will likewise be assigned to China's central bank.

Although the responsibilities of banking and insurance supervisory authorities will be adjusted in the two aspects above, the impacts on the relevant analyses and views presented in the dissertation are limited. As a matter of fact, both of the two aspects are identified in the dissertation as part of the regulatory and supervisory weaknesses in China's insurance sector. The two aspects relate to the discussions in the dissertation, respectively on the legitimacy of the CIRC's formulation of essential regulatory principles and the appropriateness of making the CIRC responsible for promoting the development of the insurance sector. China's financial regulators must have recognized the illegitimacy and conflict of interests arising from the regulatory and supervisory work of the CIRC. They therefore decide to resolve the problems by shifting the assignment of the two tasks. But, assigning the two tasks from the supervisory authority to the central bank is not a good answer, because it only has the effect of transferring the same prob-

2 *See id. See also* Zhong Xu, 'Analysis of the Reform of Financial Regulation Based on the Scheme on Institutional Reform of the State Council' (*Caixin,* 13 March 2018) <topics.caixin.com/2018-03-13/101220637.html?sourceEntityId=101220731> accessed 9 April 2018.

3 *Supra note* 1.

lems – the illegitimacy and conflict of interests would again be created at the central bank. The reasons why the central bank's making the fundamental framework of prudential regulations and promoting the development of banking and insurance sectors will be deemed problematic are identical to the factors explaining why the CIRC's engaging in the same activities is considered inappropriate. The reasoning made in the dissertation with regard to the two areas of activity will be applicable, either directly or mutatis mutandis, to the judgment about the prospective role that the central bank will play in China's insurance regulation.

More importantly, it should be clearly indicated that the CIRC (the prospective CBIRC) will remain the primary regulator and supervisor for China's insurance sector. In effect, the regulatory role played by the CIRC will not be materially undermined by the abovementioned reforming measures. The reforming measures involve institutional and functional adjustments, but do not necessitate any changes in the existing regulations imposed on insurers and reinsurers. All the requirements related to the diverse aspects of insurance business, which are prescribed in the various types of legal acts made by the congress, the State Council and the CIRC, will continue to be in force. The essential principles and implementing details for most regulatory areas have been provided in the existing insurance regulations, which therefore leaves little room for China's central bank to formulate additional principles and rules of fundamental importance. In the event that a major change is needed for the insurance regulations to adapt to latest sector developments, the CIRC could amend its department rules and normative documents to serve such a need.

Apart from all the factors above, there exists another reason for the expected predominant role of the CIRC in insurance regulation after the reform. Before the reform, essential regulatory principles were supposed to be prescribed in the legislative act enacted by the congress, with implementing rules delegated to the CIRC. However, due to the lack of concrete principles and the insufficient coverage of regulatory issues in the legislative act, a large proportion of the essential regulatory principles are actually prescribed in the legal acts issued by the CIRC. The central bank, after the reform, will become a new insurance regulatory actor, formulating essential principles alongside the congress. In light of the regulatory culture and practices in China, the essential principles prescribed by the central bank of which the primary focus is on the conduct of monetary policies are liable to be consistent with those stipulated by the congress in terms of regulatory specificity and coverage. Since the reform does not involve any changes in the regulatory approach, the scope of the rule-making by the

CIRC will remain undefined, as is the same case with the regulatory arrangements before the reform. Eventually, it will be at the discretion of the CIRC, which is directly responsible for enforcing regulations and conducting supervision, to determine the need for supplementing the essential regulatory principles. The CIRC will continue to make both essential principles and implementing details that it deems necessary through its existing legal instruments - department rules and normative documents.

2. *Acknowledgements*

I am grateful to my dissertation supervisor, Prof. Dr. Manfred Wandt, for his insightful guidance and enduring patience. With his kind help, I was able to have the opportunity to further academic research after the completion of LL.M. study. I am really indebted to him. Over the course of the dissertation, he provided me with sufficient scope for shaping my own thoughts and arguments, and gave me much valuable advice where revisions are deemed necessary. I benefit greatly from his advice on the dissertation and the discussions with him.

I am grateful to Prof. Dr. Andreas Cahn for the support he granted to me in securing the opportunity for doctoral research. I also gained much from his broad and in-depth knowledge of corporate and financial law during my LL.M. study, which is beneficial to my research on insurance supervision.

I would like to express grateful thanks to Dr. Rolf Friedewald. As a long-time friend and mentor of mine, he provides me with much life and work advice based on his visions and experience. I benefit much from the inspiring talks and interaction with him.

I would express my gratitude to my parents for their unceasing emotional and financial support. I thank my wife, Xinchen Li, for her love and care. I thank all my family for their encouragement and help. I thank all my friends for the information, suggestions and assistance I obtain from them in both study and life.

Frankfurt am Main, May 2018 *Wenyu Qian*

Brief Contents

Contents

Abbreviations

ABI	Association of British Insurers
AIDA	Association Internationale de Droit des Assurances
BaFin	Bundesanstalt für Finanzdienstleistungsaufsicht (Germany)
BIS	Bank for International Settlements
BoE	Bank of England
C-ROSS	China Risk Oriented Solvency System
CBIRC	China Banking and Insurance Regulatory Commission
CBRC	China Banking Regulatory Commission
CDS	Credit Default Swap
CIRC	China Insurance Regulatory Commission
CPC	Communist Party of China
CPPCC	Chinese People's Political Consultative Conference
DG	Directorates-General
ECB	European Central Bank
EIOPA	European Insurance and Occupational Pensions Authority
ESFS	European System of Financial Supervision
FSB	Financial Stability Board
GDV	Gesamtverband der Deutschen Versicherungswirtschaft e.V.
IAB	Impact Assessment Board (EU)
IAIS	International Association of Insurance Supervisors
IMF	International Monetary Fund
ITS	Implementing Technical Standard
KPI	Key Performance Indicator
MCR	Minimum Capital Requirement (Solvency II, EU)
MCS	Minimum Capital Standard (C-ROSS, China)
NAIC	National Association of Insurance Commissioners (US)
NCAs	National Competent Authorities (EU)
NPCC	National People's Congress of China
OFR	U.S. Office of Financial Research
OECD	Organization for Economic Co-operation and Development
PBC	People's Bank of China

PRA	Prudential Regulation Authority (UK)
PRC	People's Republic of China
RTS	Regulatory Technical Standard
SCR	Solvency Capital Requirement (Solvency II, EU)
SOE	State-owned Enterprise
TEU	Treaty on European Union
TFEU	Treaty on the Functioning of the European Union

Introduction

The insurance sector has never received so much publicity in China as today. It should be ascribed to Chinese insurers' enormous investment in domestic stock market and their moves in foreign capital and real estate markets over the past several years. There is an increasing public awareness of the financial strength of insurance companies since they are found to be behind many of the largest transactions and projects nationwide. It is a rising trend in China that insurance products, particularly with-profits endowment policies and annuities, are used by households as an investment vehicle.[4]

A. Problems Facing China's Insurance Sector

In parallel with the momentum of China's insurance sector, the problems associated with insurers' growth and moves emerge and a few of them become contentious topics of discussion. A decline or fluctuation in solvency position, inter alia, is a crucial problem, which Chinese insurance undertakings of different sizes incur. It is usually caused by a surge in new policies underwritten. A rapid increase in new policies brings about a higher level of underwriting risk which requires to be covered by extra capital resources. The raised capital requirements resulting from the heightened riskiness will give rise to a lower capital adequacy level, unless the insurance undertakings concerned are able to secure sufficient recognized as-

4 As shown in the publicly disclosed annual reports of numerous largest life insurers in China, the top five insurance products that generate the most premium income for the life insurers mainly consist of with-profits endowment insurance and annuities. *See e.g.* China Life, *2016 Annual Report* (Disclosure Document, 2017) 20 <www.e-chinalife.com/IRchannel/files/report_20170323_GB_1.pdf> accessed 6 October 2017; Ping An Life, *2016 Annual Report for Public Disclosure* (Disclosure Document, 2017) 101 <resources.pingan.com/app_upload/file/life/2016-nianduxinxipilubaogao.pdf> accessed 6 October 2017; China Pacific, *2016 Annual Report* (Disclosure Document, 2017) 25 <www.cpic.com.cn/upload/resources/file/2017/03/30/35331.pdf> accessed 6 October 2017; New China Life, *2016 Annual Report* (Disclosure Document, 2017) 22 <www.newchinalife.com/resource/11313/11329/11346/1695218/2406976/2407236/2407884/2412103/15051072101971364072785.pdf> accessed 6 October 2017.

sets or capital to back their growing insurance obligations in a timely manner. A notable proportion of Chinese undertakings find it hard to make their capital position keep pace with business growth and herein lies the reason for the regular occurrence of volatile or deteriorating solvency conditions. Besides the surge in new policies, market movements are evidently a force for the fluctuation in solvency position. Chinese insurers have considerable risk exposures in domestic bond and stock markets. The materialization of market risk in market downturns was proved to have noticeable and adverse impacts on their capital position.

Over a long period of time, Chinese insurers have developed a great reliance on ad hoc injection of debt or equity capital, in the form of subordinated debt securities or new shares respectively. The constant reliance on ad hoc capital injection is a by-product of the unstable solvency conditions industrywide. The solvency pattern and the resultant reliance are characteristic of an immature insurance market.

Another issue, which gains prominence with the growth and expansion of the China's insurance sector, is insurer investment. Over the past few years, Chinese insurance companies invested heavily in a range of industries domestically and overseas, making them likely to be the biggest asset acquirers in China. They made aggressive moves in China's stock markets to seek the status of controlling shareholder in numerous target companies with enormous market capitalization. In parallel, considerable amounts of funds were spent by them on overseas real estate and financial assets. This draws a sharp contrast to how Chinese insures as a whole behaved in the past since they were always the most conservative and most low-profile institutional investor. The drastic change drew extensive media coverage and triggered wide debates between various interest groups. The debates centered around the appropriateness of insurers' risk-taking, the legitimacy of hostile takeovers by insurers and the impacts of ownership changes on the real economy. The wave of aggressive investments was contained to some extent after China Insurance Regulatory Commission (hereinafter referred to as "CIRC") made regulatory responses by adopting counteractive policies and measures. The supervisory authority held the opinion that the aggression of investment strategy was out of tune with the way in which an insurer is supposed to run its business, and concluded that the controlling shareholders of some insurance companies abused their position to turn the companies into vehicles for financing serving their needs for asset acquisition.[5]

B. Central Issues in Dissertation

It is clear that China's insurance sector has entered a new development stage featuring high growth and transition to maturity. The current insurer business structure and risk profile differ substantially from those in the previous decades, which are in line with China's economic transformation. Throughout the new development stage, gradual shifts in business structure and risk profile across the insurance sector are certain to be sustained. Unexpected and undesirable problems will arise in different aspects of insurance business and affect various stakeholders.

I. General Description

Given the factors above, it is vital to adapt China's insurance supervision to the essentially changed risk characteristics across the insurance sector. An overhaul of the major elements of China's insurance supervision shall be made to ensure the availability of appropriate supervisory tools, methods and procedures which would enable an effective oversight of the insurance market in transition and a sustained protection of policyholders and beneficiaries. And herein lies the subject of the dissertation. It is intended to examine how the supervision of insurance undertakings is conducted in China, identify the weaknesses of the supervisory mechanisms and propose feasible ways for improvements. The dissertation centers around the supervisory practices of the CIRC in key dimensions, including rule-making, objectives setting, supervisory review process, supervisory measures, supervisory transparency and public consultation.

The main supervised entities under discussion in this dissertation are individual primary insurers, who initially underwrite policies to accept liability. Most of the supervisory review tools and methods are applied to the type of entities. The supervision of reinsurers in China is not specifically discussed since it is similar or identical to the supervision of primary insur-

5 *See* Zhihong Li, 'CIRC to Send Inspection Panel to Life Insurance Companies – Percentage of Stock Investment with Obligation of Disclosure by Insurance Companies Lowering to 9%' *21st Century Business Herald* (Beijing, 7 December 2016).

ers in most respects. Group supervision is not an issue of concern in the dissertation, though the treatment of insurance groups is involved in the analysis of specified supervisory areas.

II. Focus Laid on Supervisory Practices Instead of Regulatory Requirements

The regulatory requirements imposed on Chinese insurers are partially involved in the dissertation and only referred to where an analysis of supervisory mechanisms necessitates the details of those requirements. The analytical emphasis is not placed on the insurance regulatory requirements. In financial sectors there is a marked tendency towards regulatory convergence at global level as countries are inclined to align their domestic regulations with internationally accepted standards. Rule-makers are motivated by the benefits of the alignment which is conducive to the formation of sophisticated and all-embracing regulations at a lower cost, particularly at a time when an increasing number of financial institutions operate and invest transnationally. Though differences in regulatory or technical details would arise from specific conditions of domestic financial markets and economy, there is remarkable degree of similarity and comparability between a large proportion of countries with regard to the structure, principles and scope of their financial legislation. The tendency towards global regulatory convergence holds equivalently for the insurance sector. The insurance legislation in mature economies is comprised of similar regulatory pillars, with homogeneous requirements prescribed within each pillar. Many of the developing economies are adapting or have adapted insurance regulatory rules to the latest internationally recognized standards.[6] Like other economies, China has made efforts to modernize its insurance regulatory system in recent years. As a major move in relation to insurance regulation, a new set of solvency-related rules was issued in 2015 by the CIRC and formally came into effect as of 1 January 2016.[7] The set of rules,

6 The internationally recognized standards refer to the Insurance Core Principles, the Common Framework and the Insurance Capital Standard developed by the IAIS (International Association of Insurance Supervisors) as well as the insurance regulation rules that are widely adopted in developed countries.

7 There are altogether 17 normative documents, which collectively constitute the main body of the China Risk Oriented Solvency System. The CIRC began to formulate these regulatory rules in 2012 and issued them in early 2015. Since then a transitional period - during which insurers were required to make solvency report-

referred to as the second generation of China's insurance solvency system, is aimed at setting quantitative and qualitative requirements on solvency conditions.[8] The Consistency with international standards was one of the major concerns that Chinese insurance regulators took into account when drafting the solvency-related rules. The regulations of developed countries and the standards of international organizations were therefore used for reference. Despite the narrower scope and less complexity of the CIRC's new rules, they bear conceptual and methodological resemblance to the regulations applicable in developed countries. The increasing regulatory convergence at global level leads to a lower possibility that insurers would be subjected to flawed regulatory requirements domestically, because the stringency of domestic regulatory requirements on diverse issues is progressively aligned with internationally accepted standards.

In contrast to the increasing convergence of insurance regulatory rules between jurisdictions, supervisory practices by national authorities do not exhibit a consistency or a clear tendency towards that. It seems much easier for a supervisory authority to require the supervised entities to conform to amended regulations than to adopt a modification of the mechanisms with which the authority functions. This could be ascribed to the fact that the manner in which insurance supervision is conducted in a specific jurisdiction is influenced by multiple forces – economic, political and cultural factors. The model and characteristics of governance, which are common to all types of administrative departments in a particular jurisdiction, would likewise be embedded in the functional mechanisms of the supervisory authorities in the jurisdiction. For this reason, the harmonization of insurance supervisory practices entails more complexities and difficulties than the convergence of regulatory requirements imposed on insurers. Despite all the barriers, it is necessary and beneficial to study how to improve the functioning mechanisms of the insurance supervisory authorities of developing countries in order for a further alignment with the more transparent and methodical practices by their counterparts in advanced countries. The working mechanisms of insurance supervisors are of significance to all stakeholders in the insurance sector. For insurance regulators and supervisors, widely-recognized regulation rules will be impossible without proper

---

ing under the provisions of the then regulatory rules and the prospective ones - was put in place so as to ascertain the results of the implementation of the newly-made rules. *See* CIRC, *Notification on Release of Supervisory Rules on Solvency Position of Insurance Undertakings (1 -17)* (Normative Document, No 22, 2015).

8 *Id.*

rule-making mechanisms in place. A full and effective implementation of regulation rules depends on continued supervisory monitoring, evaluation and intervention. For insurance undertakings, the intensity and frequency of supervisory activities has great impacts on their attitude towards supervision, which in turn influences their risk appetite, inclination for compliance, and course of action. For policyholders and beneficiaries, the level of confidence in the supervisory protection of their interests rests largely on the transparency and effectiveness of supervisory practices. Ordinary policyholders might be unable to form proper interpretation of specialized regulation rules. However, they could rely on the observation of supervisory actions and ensuing outcomes to make judgment about the efficacy of insurance supervision.

C. EU's Supervisory and Regulatory Mechanisms Used as Reference Point

In the dissertation, the comparison with the EU's insurance supervision is regarded as an analytical focus in parallel with the discussion of the relevant issues in China. The insurance supervisory mechanisms along with the rule-making approaches adopted in the EU are set as the reference points against which the corresponding elements of China are compared. The EU's insurance supervisory and regulatory practices being chosen as the benchmark is due to several reasons below.

I. Reasons for Selecting EU's Model as Benchmark

Firstly, the EU's insurance supervisory and regulatory practices have been fully reviewed and adapted to new market realities since the recent global financial crisis.[9] The adapted regime embraces sophisticated supervisory

9 The adaptation of the EU's insurance supervisory practices involved three major legislative and institutional changes, including the formulation of the Solvency II, the creation of the European System of Financial Supervision (ESFS) and the review of the Lamfalussy Process. As a matter of fact, only the creation of ESFS was done as a result of the 2007 financial crisis. The other two items were nevertheless not carried out for the same reason. The Solvency II project began with some earlier preparations and quantitative impact studies several years before the occurrence of the financial crisis. But the essential elements of the system were formulated and determined during the crisis. Likewise, the review of the Lamfalussy Process was not brought about by the financial crisis. The review was set to take place by the

mechanisms taking into account the actual risks, vulnerabilities and trends of the EU's and global insurance sectors. At the time when the 2007 financial crisis erupted, the Solvency II framework directive was in the phase of drafting.[10] The implementing details of the directive were sequentially formulated over a span of multiple years before the entry into force of the Solvency II system in 2016. The newly developed system introduces for the EU national supervisors the tools and approaches tailored to the current supervisory context subjecting the national competent authorities (hereinafter referred to as "NCAs") to a higher standard of functioning. Alongside a change of the insurance supervisory basis, an institutional reform in regard to the oversight of financial services took place in the aftermath of the financial crisis.[11] Several supervisory institutions were established at the EU level to underpin the micro-prudential supervision of financial institutions in banking, insurance and securities sectors as well as the macro-prudential supervision of the EU's financial system as a whole. As a consequence, the legal status of the specialized supervisory authorities,[12] which advise on union-level legal acts and focus on consistent application of rules, was enhanced. The Joint Committee of the foregoing specialized authorities serves as a mechanism for the cross-sectoral supervisory coordination that aims for a consistent approach to the oversight of financial conglomerates and the mitigation of systemic risk. A newly established union-level entity, known as the European Systemic Risk Board, is charged with monitoring, assessing, preventing and mitigating systemic risk in the EU financial system. The specialized supervisory authorities at the EU level are obligated to provide information for the macro-prudential supervisory body and ensure proper follow-ups to its warnings and recommenda-

---

end of 2007 in accordance with the requirements in the Directive 2005/1/EC. Although the financial crisis was not the cause for these two items, the problems exposed in the financial crisis were adequately taken into account in delivering the items.

10 Insurance Europe, *Solvency II: Understanding the Process* (Paper, February 2007) 8.

11 The institutional reform, as a response to the recent global financial crisis, was implemented under the proposals laid down in the report by the de Larosière Group who was mandated by the European Commission to advise on strengthened supervisory arrangements covering all financial sectors. *See* the High-Level Group on Financial Supervision in the EU Chaired by Jacques de Larosière, *Report* (Brussels, 25 February 2009).

12 They are referred to as the European Supervisory Authorities which consist of three institutions – European Banking Authority, European Insurance and Occupational Pensions Authority and European Securities and Markets Authority.

tions.[13] Meanwhile, the regulatory process for financial services in the EU, which is referred to as the Lamfalussy process,[14] was scrutinized and upgraded during the financial crisis.[15] The scrutiny of the Lamfalussy process in 2007 was intended to seek necessary improvements to the original regulatory approach devised in 2001.[16] As indicated in the review report by the then Commission of the European Communities,[17] changes and actions are proposed with respect to each level of the Lamfalussy process, in particular the third level thereof, with a view to facilitating supervisory convergence among EU member states and to addressing the increasing interconnectedness of financial institutions which emerged as a serious menace to financial stability.[18] In line with the improved regulatory process, impact assessments were extended to cover more types of legal acts, with rules supplemented to provide a more solid legal basis for cross-border supervision. The rule-making was rendered more transparent by enhanced disclosure of the results of public consultations.

Secondly, the EU's supervisory and regulatory mechanisms demonstrate broad applicability. There are economic, political and cultural disparities between the EU member states. The scale, complexity and risk profile between the insurance sectors in the member states differ greatly. Likewise, the focus of insurance supervision and concerns of consumers in a member state are dissimilar to those in another. Given the factors above, a pan-European supervisory regime must consist of elements that are able to work effectively in diverse supervisory contexts. As a matter of fact, applicability is indeed a dimension for which the European regulators have

---

13 Regulation EU No 1092/2010 of the European Parliament and of the Council of 24 November 2010 on European Union Macro-prudential Oversight of the Financial System and Establishing a European Systemic Risk Board [2010] OJ L 331/1, §§ 15, 16, 17.

14 The Lamfalussy Process will be discussed in Chapter 2 Part C, along with an analysis of its applicability to China's financial legislation.

15 Commission of the European Communities, *Review of the Lamfalussy Process Strengthening Supervisory Convergence* (Communication, COM(2007) 727 final, 2007) 2, 3.

16 *Id.*

17 Following the Treaty of Lisbon entering into force in 2009, the functional structure of the European Union was changed. With the reorganization, the term 'European Communities' was no longer present in the treaties. The European Union became the legal successor to the European Community. For this reason, the European Commission replaced the Commission of the European Communities.

18 *See supra note* 15, at 3, 13.

great regard in rule-making since a significant aim of the EU financial regulation is to achieve supervisory convergence among all member states. As far as the union-level acts in the insurance sector are concerned, they provide for supervisory mechanisms that show compatibility with and responsiveness to a variety of market specificities. The uniqueness of the EU insurance supervisory regime - that it is implemented in so many different nations – leads to its applicability greater than that of any other corresponding regime in the world. For China or another jurisdiction where the overall situations are entirely distinct from developed economies, the adaptability of a supervisory regime chosen as the benchmark is critical to the formation of apt regulation and supervision for its domestic insurance sector. The greater applicability of the EU's insurance supervisory regime means that its rules and approaches could be better adapted to local market situations and more easily integrated into the supervisory system of a specific jurisdiction.

Thirdly, the EU's financial regulatory process involves multiple actors, with interaction and balance between them.[19] It would provide implications for China's financial regulation. The existence of multiple regulatory actors at the union level stems from the need to balance the interests of member states and harmonize their regulatory and supervisory practices. Given the number of countries affected by the acts, the EU's financial regulatory process entails a higher level of prudence and complexity than that of most jurisdictions. Its sophistication is mainly represented by the division, delegation and balancing of powers between the actors at four regulatory levels. Of the techniques used to assign and exercise regulatory powers, the delegation of the rule-making power and the mechanisms for checks and balances are of great importance to the comparison of financial regulatory process between the EU and China, since these are the major aspects where the weaknesses of the China's regulatory process reside. In the

19 The regulatory actors in the EU regulatory process for financial services include the European Parliament and the Council which jointly adopt basic acts, the European Commission which is empowered to adopt delegated and implementing acts, the comitology committees which assist the Commission in adopting its acts and the European supervisory authorities which advise the Commission on legislative acts and implementing measures. Each of the regulatory actors is composed of representatives from all EU member states, which allows each member state to have a say in the making of the binding financial regulations. In the field of insurance, the responsible comitology committee and the European supervisory authority are respectively the European Insurance and Occupational Pensions Committee and the European Insurance and Occupational Pensions Authority.

EU, there are explicit rules on the exercise and revocation of delegation.[20] The scope and content of the non-legislative acts of which the adoption is delegated is exactly delimited in the legislative act providing for the delegation. In addition, checks and balances are in place to avoid the concentration of regulatory powers in the hand of one single regulatory actor. None of the legally binding acts applicable throughout the EU's insurance sector are drafted, reviewed, approved and issued by a certain regulatory actor alone. This draws a sharp contrast to the rule-making practice in China's insurance sector, which will be discussed in detail in the subsequent chapters.[21]

II. Particularity of Facts about EU's Insurance Supervision

It should be noted that although the comparisons of insurance supervisory standards and practices between the EU and China are drawn throughout the whole dissertation, the facts about the EU's standards and practices which underlie the comparisons are not set out in detail. In drawing each comparison, the dissertation gives basic introduction of the EU's supervisory mechanisms relevant to the context of a comparison, but the level of detail would not be so high as that of the information about China's corresponding elements. The distinct treatment shall be ascribed to the fact that the involvement of EU's elements in the dissertation is deemed to be a means to facilitate the analysis of the central subject matter of the dissertation - China's insurance supervision. Despite that, the facts presented about the EU's supervisory mechanisms have a necessary level of detail required for the understanding of the comparisons drawn.

III. Criteria for Adoption

Additionally, the relative merits of the EU's supervisory mechanisms, as a result of the comparisons in the dissertation, are not necessarily adopted as the solutions to the weaknesses of China's insurance supervision. Although

---

20 Consolidated Version of the Treaty on the Functioning of the European Union [2012] OJ C 326/47 (TFEU), § 290, 291; *See also infra note* 348, §§ 11, 12.

21 *See* Chapter 2 Part B.

many of the EU's relative merits are adopted partially or fully,[22] some are deemed infeasible for China and hence rejected. Suitability and cost-effectiveness are the main criteria for the decision on adoption. The former indicates the degree to which the beneficial supervisory mechanisms in the EU fit in with the general supervisory arrangements and market conditions in China, while the latter measures the extent to which a supervisory change would be effective in relation to its cost that could arise in various ways. A low level of either suitability or cost-effectiveness would lead to the rejection of a mechanism of relative merits.

D. Organization of Dissertation

The dissertation gives an analysis of the major aspects of China's insurance supervision in five chapters, mainly concerned with rule-making, supervisory objectives, supervisory review tools and methods, and supervisory transparency. Except Chapter 1, each chapter is comprised of sections serving homogeneous purposes. That is to say, the component sections of a chapter could always be divided into several categories according to analytical purpose, which include introducing China's supervisory practices, identifying the weaknesses, comparing with the counterparts of the EU, and proposing improvements based on comparison results. The analytical order of the sections in a chapter is not fixed, but varied to suit the need for coherence.

Chapter 1 gives an introduction of China's regulatory and supervisory hierarchy, with the primary focus on the actors in the hierarchy and their respective regulatory powers. The predominant role which the CIRC plays in insurance regulation and supervision is underlined.

Chapter 2 specifically identifies the major deficiencies of China's insurance legislation, the flaws in the exercise of rule-making powers by the CIRC in particular. A feasibility study into the possibility of applying the Lamfalussy approach to China's insurance legislation is conducted before an exploration of the viable alternatives for resolving the deficiencies.

Chapter 3 provides an insight into China's three insurance supervisory objectives of equal importance. Among them, the objective 'promoting the

22 Partial adoption means a supervisory mechanism of relative merits in the EU is adapted to some extent when being integrated into China's insurance supervisory arrangements, which is aimed at making it compatible with the existing mechanisms.

development of insurance sector' is focused on. The reasons for setting this particular objective are discussed, and deliberations are presented as to whether it shall be kept within the scope of supervisory responsibilities. In addition, the necessity for making policyholder protection above other supervisory objectives is also explicated. In the last part of this chapter, the dissertation carefully examines the systemic importance of Chinese insurers, calling for due supervisory considerations given to financial stability.

Chapter 4 makes a comparative analysis of the tools, methods and stages involved in the insurance supervisory review process between the EU and China. The emphasis of the analysis of China's insurance supervision is placed on the off-site appraisals employed in the supervisory assessment stage and on the supervisory measures imposed in the supervisory intervention stage. Based on the findings of the comparison, the dissertation specifies the necessary elements supplementary to the existing supervisory assessment arrangements in China and explicates the way to ameliorate the CIRC's supervisory intervention mechanisms.

Chapter 5 scrutinizes the overall aspects of the CIRC's supervisory transparency. The means utilized by the authority to disseminate information are fully revealed, which offers an insight into the actual level of supervisory transparency in regard to, inter alia, legislation, internal organization and procedures, supervisory activities and statistical disclosure. The shortcomings of the existing transparency mechanisms of the CIRC are discussed in detail. The approaches to enhancing its supervisory transparency are accompanied by comparisons with the arrangements of supervisory transparency in the EU, in particular the methods employed by the EIOPA.

Chapter 1. An Overview of China's Insurance Regulatory Regime

The insurance regulation system of China is characterized by a vertical structure. The legal system and the distribution of regulatory powers demonstrate such a feature. In the hierarchical institutional system, an institution lying on a higher authoritative level is entitled to greater regulatory powers, and could delegate powers partly or fully to an entity at a lower level. Institutions at each level are empowered to make regulatory rules.[23] The status of the legal acts, similarly, rank according to the level of the institution issuing the acts. The rules issued by an institution of higher regulatory position have superiority over those issued by an institution of lower position. The rules with lower legal status shall not contravene the principles or provisions laid down in those with higher status. The legal acts, according to the superiority in regulatory status, are shown below: (1) legislative acts issued by the NPCC; (2) administrative regulations issued by the State Council; (3) provincial regulations issued by provincial governments; (4) department rules issued by ministries or other departments with equivalent status, and provincial rules issued by provincial governments; (5) ordinances issued by local governments.[24] The institutions and their corresponding legal acts pertinent to the insurance sector are set out below, from the institution at the highest level in the regulatory system to the bottom.

23 The Legislation Act of China 2000, §§ 7, 56, 71; the Administrative Rules on the Supervisory Responsibilities of CIRC Agencies 2004, § 4 (2).

24 The Legislation Act of China 2000, §§ 78-80, 82. Statutorily, department rules are employed to implement the legislative acts of the NPCC and the administrative regulations of the State Council. Provincial rules are made for: (1) implementing legislative acts, administrative regulations and provincial regulations; (2) addressing specific administrative issues in a province. Nevertheless, in fact, either department rules or provincial rules go beyond the scope of implementation. This will be discussed in subsequent sections.

A. *Insurance Legislation of NPCC*

At the top of the regulatory system lies the legislature, the National People's Congress of China (hereinafter referred to as "NPCC"). It is conferred on the legislation power and defined as the institution with the highest authority in China.[25] The members of the NPCC comprise representatives from different provinces in the country.[26] The NPCC performs tasks mainly in four areas: enacting fundamental legal acts,[27] deciding on the heads of the government, reviewing and approving national budgets, and determining the establishment of provinces.[28]

In the field of insurance, the NPCC exerts regulatory authority at the highest level through the Insurance Act of China which serves as the legal basis for insurance regulation.[29] The NPCC could make amendments to the Insurance Act according to regulatory needs or changes in circumstances.[30] The Insurance Act lays down stipulations in several dimensions, including insurance incorporation, winding-up, business operation, contract, intermediaries, supervision and legal liability for non-compliances.

It functions more like a framework than a systematic insurance code. Except for the chapter of insurance contract and the chapter of incorporation, the Insurance Act is mainly comprised of simple principles, instead of clearly-defined requirements or conditions. In many areas, only the expected results and effects are briefly stated, even without any principles laid down. It leaves large room for the rule-making by a specified insurance supervisory institution, i.e. the CIRC.

Besides the Insurance Act, other acts enacted by the NPCC supplement the general insurance regulation framework. The Contract Act of China constitutes a complement to the sections on insurance contract provided in the Insurance Act,[31] while the Maritime Act of China sets out particular provisions on marine insurance contract.[32] Criminal Liabilities for certain

25 The Constitution of China 1982, §§ 57, 58.

26 *Id.* at § 59 I.

27 The scope of fundamental legal acts is provided in the Legislation Act of China 2000, § 8. Ten areas are identified as being within this scope. Fundamental economic and financial regime is listed among the ten areas, which constitutes the legal basis for the enactment of the Insurance Act by the NPCC.

28 *Supra* note 25, at §§ 62, 63.

29 The Insurance Act of China 1995.

30 The Legislation Act of China 2000, § 7.

31 The Contract Act of China 1999.

32 The Maritime Act of China 1993, ch 12.

defrauding activities are stipulated in the Criminal Act of China.[33] Moreover, The Company Act of China is applicable,[34] except for the areas where different requirements are prescribed in the Insurance Act.

In sum, the regulation of the NPCC, which constitutes the top level of China's insurance regulation system, is conducted by setting a basic frame, mainly through the Insurance Act, complemented by relevant or special provisions in other legislative acts.

B. *Regulatory Role of State Council*

The State Council is at the second level of the insurance regulation system. As the executive arm of the NPCC, it is headed by the premier and takes charge of national affairs administration.[35] All ministries and different types of departments are affiliated to the State Council.[36] The CIRC is also an affiliated entity among these departments. The State Council governs all national affairs at the highest administrative level, directing all government departments and local authorities.[37] It is accountable to the NPCC.[38] The standing committee of the NPCC supervises its work.[39]

The State Council engages in insurance regulation activities in four aspects. Firstly, it issues administrative regulations on insurance.[40] However, they are rather limited in quantity,[41] since the issuance of administrative regulations usually takes place where the formulation and implementation of a legal act would involve two or more ministries or departments affiliated to the State Council.[42] Most legal rules applicable to the insurance sector are formulated at a lower regulatory level, i.e. by the CIRC, which will be subsequently discussed.

---

33 The Criminal Act of China 1997, § 198.

34 The Company Act of China 2005.

35 *Supra* note 25 at §§ 85, 88 I.

36 The Regulation on Administration of the Establishment and Staffing of the Administrative Agencies of the State Council 1997, § 6.

37 *See supra note* 25 at § 89.

38 *Id.* at § 92.

39 *Id.* at § 67 (6).

40 Id. at § 89 (1).

41 These administrative regulations tackle issues mainly in three areas: agricultural insurance, compulsory motor vehicle liability insurance, and foreign insurance undertakings.

42 The Legislation Act of China 2000, at § 81.

The second type of activities the State Council conducts with regard to insurance regulation is to issue mandates to the CIRC.[43] It carries out the work in various forms, such as giving opinions and making specific instructions. The CIRC will unconditionally follow the mandates from the State Council, performing tasks accordingly.

The third item is reviewing proposals for new developments or reforms in the insurance sector. Before a significant policy initiative or scheme is put into force either nationwide or regionally, it shall be filed to the State Council for evaluation and approval.[44] Normally, the proposals related to the insurance sector are filed by the CIRC, either alone or along with other institutions. The proposals put forward in recent years include, for instance, expansion of the scope for insurer investment,[45] establishment of insurance exchanges in Shanghai and Shenzhen,[46] a pilot project of tax-deferred endowment insurance in Shanghai.[47]

Fourthly, the State Council coordinates and directs the cooperation between the CIRC and other supervisory institutions. Inevitably, certain activities of an insurance undertaking would be subject to the oversight by institutions in another sector, exceeding the supervisory scope of the CIRC. Under such a scenario, the supervisory requirements of the CIRC and the relevant institutions will be simultaneously imposed on the insurance undertaking. A typical example is the insurers investing on stock market, which is under the supervision of the CIRC and China Securities Regulatory Commission. In order to tighten control of the activities of this type, the CIRC needs to be informed of the up-to-date information about

---

43 *Supra note* 25, at § 90 II.

44 The specific circumstances where the State Council shall exercise the powers of review and approval, are provided dispersedly in regulations.

45 *See e.g.*, Xiaoping Lu, 'Detailed Rules regarding Investments of Insurers on Private Companies to Come Out This Month' *Shanghai Securities News* (Shanghai, 13 October 2009) (mentioning that the State Council permitted insurance companies to invest in non-public companies and the interim provisions would be soon issued.).

46 Yu Sun, 'Scheme to Establish Shanghai Insurance Exchange Submitted to State Council' *Securities Times of China* (Beijing, 17 February 2011) 1; Yurong Pan, 'Plan for Shenzhen Insurance Exchange filed to State Council possibly in future' *Securities Times of China* (Beijing, 3 February 2012) 5.

47 *See* XiaoHong Ouyang and Jingyu Ye, 'Tax-Deferred Endowment Insurance Looms: Pilot Scheme Launched in Shanghai This Year' *The Economic Observer* (Beijing, 4 May 2012) (noting the opinion of the State Council on introducing tax-deferred endowment insurance in Shanghai, and the fact that a vice premier stressed the importance of this issue at a meeting on the reform and development of the insurance sector.).

insurance undertakings' moves in other sectors. Therefore, there exists information exchange mechanism between the CIRC and other supervisory institutions.[48] Besides, they make joint efforts in other ways.[49] What should be noted is that it is difficult to form supervisory cooperation, since consensus is hard to be achieved on a number of issues, such as details of rules and division of responsibilities. The State Council plays an important role in facilitating the cooperation between the CIRC and other institutions, mainly because they are all affiliated entities subjected to mandates from the State Council.[50] Especially where a negotiation reaches an impasse, the State Council would intervene in and take measures to push it.

C. Supervisory Functions and Rules of CIRC

I. Introduction of the Institution

The CIRC, the institution on the third level of China's insurance regulatory system, is empowered to conduct insurance supervision in China. On condition that CIRC does not deviate from the principles laid down in the Insurance Act enacted by the NPCC, it could exercise considerable discretion in rule-making, authorization, investigation and other areas in order to achieve supervisory objectives.

---

48 *Supra note* 29, at § 158 I.

49 The latest significant progress in this area, is achieved in August 2013. A regular Ministerial Joint Meeting mechanism is adopted to enhance the financial supervision coordination between the central bank, supervisory authorities for banking, securities and insurance, and the foreign Exchange authority. *See* the State Council, *Reply on the Approval of the Establishment of Regular Ministerial Joint Meeting Mechanism for Financial Supervision Coordination* (Council Notification No 91, 2013). There exist quite a few rules jointly made. For example, *see* CIRC and CBRC, the Supervisory Guidelines on Commercial Banks Conducting Insurance Agent Services (Normative Document, No 10, 2011); the Pilot Rules on Insurance Institutions Investing and Establishing Fund Management Company 2013.

50 The central bank and all other financial supervisory agencies hold equivalent position as a ministry, affiliated to the State Council. The State Council is empowered to repeal the rules made by them. Supra note 25, at § 89 (13).

1. Overview of Supervisory Responsibilities

In case the State Council issues a mandate or assigns a specific task, the CIRC is required to act in conformity with that.[51] Due to the fact that the CIRC is affiliated to the State Council, the State Council could take actions to intervene in its supervision, where necessary.[52] Normally, the CIRC performs supervisory responsibilities without the intervention by the State Council, largely because of the technical nature of its supervisory work.

The NPCC and the State Council, as upper-level institutions in the regulation system, reserve the power to exert authority over the CIRC. In most scenarios, the CIRC could exercise autonomy in supervision.

Table 1: CIRC's Supervisory Responsibilities

Formulation	– policies, strategic direction of insurance sector; – department rules, normative documents
Authorization and Supervisory Approval	– incorporation of insurance undertakings, insurance asset management companies, insurance groups and insurance intermediaries; – establishment of affiliations by abovementioned insurance institutions domestically or overseas; – any material changes of insurance undertakings, e.g. merger, separation, dissolution;[53] – eligibility of executives – insurance clause and premium rate of newly developed life insurance products, compulsory insurance or those concerning public interests
Supervision	– solvency, market conduct and investment of insurance undertakings; – government-policy-related insurance, compulsory insurance;

51 *Supra note* 25, at § 89 (3).

52 *See e.g. id.* at § 89 (13) (prescribing that the State Council is empowered to amend or revoke the instructions or department rules issued by a ministry or a commission, which it considers inappropriate.).

53 *Supra note* 29, at § 84. According to the article, at least seven scenarios are subject to the review and approval by the CIRC: (1) change of name; (2) change of register capital; (3) Change of place of business; (4) closure of branches; (5) separation or merger; (6) modification of articles of association; (7) change of shareholders with more than 5% of total shareholders' equity.

	– insurance protection fund; – overseas entities established by Chinese insurance undertakings
Investigation and Discipline	– non-compliance and illegal conduct of insurance undertakings and practitioners; – non-insurance institutions operating insurance business
Analysis	– market conditions, development trend; – data about insurance sector

Source: the Insurance Act of China 1995; the Administrative Rules on Insurance Undertakings 2009.

Over forty regional bureaus are set up by the CIRC for the purpose of implementing close supervision of the market conduct of insurance undertakings.[54] Regional bureaus are empowered to formulate implementing rules which are applicable locally.[55] Moreover, they are delegated to make authorizations in certain areas.[56] The CIRC rely on the regional bureaus to monitor the market, identify new risks and ascertain non-compliant insurers.

2. International Relations

In terms of international relations, the entities with which the CIRC regularly interacts could be broadly categorized into three groups. First of all, it is the supervisory authorities in the special administrative regions of China, namely Hong Kong and Macau. Due to the special status of the two regions, they have high degree of autonomy and are not subject to the laws or regulations that are applicable in Mainland China.[57] The matters concerning the two special administrative regions are classified into the same

54 'Overview of Local Agencies' (CIRC) <www.circ.gov.cn/web/site0/tab5196/> accessed 23 April 2014. For the legal basis of the supervisory agencies, *see supra note* 29, at § 9 II.

55 The Administrative Rules on the Supervisory Responsibilities of CIRC Agencies 2004, § 4 (2).

56 *Id.* at § 4 (5), (6), (7).

57 Hong Kong and Macau, formerly the British and Portuguese colonies, were respectively returned to Chinese sovereignty in 1997 and 1999. The concept of special administrative region is based on the principle of 'one country, two systems' proposed by former Chinese leader Deng Xiaoping. The principle underlies the privileged status of the two cities that adopt different political, economic and legal regimes from the rest of China. Both of the special administrative regions are

category as and treated in a similar way to those concerning foreign countries. It is why the interactions with the two regions are within the responsibilities of the international department at all types of organizations in China. The insurance undertakings and intermediaries running business in the two regions are supervised respectively by Hong Kong Insurance Authority and the insurance supervision department of the Monetary Authority of Macau under the local ordinances.[58] The CIRC is unable to exercise authority over the insurance sectors of the two regions. The international department of the CIRC is therefore assigned the task of maintaining close cooperation with its counterparts in Hong Kong and Macau.

The second group of entities is the supervisory authorities outside of China. Mainly, the CIRC enters into cooperative relationship with the authorities in the EU, North America and Asia-Pacific region. The cooperating entities are not restricted to insurance supervisors, but could extend to include supervisors in other financial sectors depending on the aim of a cooperative arrangement.[59]

As to how the CIRC forms cooperative relationship with its counterparts within or outside of China, there are broadly two ways: memorandums of understanding and cooperative agreements. A memorandum of understanding is usually signed to provide basis for mutual supervisory as-

---

allowed to exercise autonomy in all aspects, except for defense and diplomatic relations. Given the high degree of freedom of legislation and justice, the two cities have their own legal system independent of the Mainland China. *See* the Basic Law of the Hong Kong Special Administrative Region of the People's Republic of China 1990 §§ 12, 13, 14, 16, 17, 19; the Basic Law of the Macau Special Administrative Region of the People's Republic of China 1993 §§ 12, 13, 14, 16, 17, 19.

58 The Hong Kong Insurance Authority is a new institution independent of the government, established in 2015. Its predecessor was the Office of the Commissioner of Insurance, which was a department of the government. The principal legislation forming the insurance regulatory basis in Hong Kong is the Insurance Ordinance (Cap. 41). The primary insurance legislation applicable to Macau's insurance sector is the Macau Insurance Companies Ordinance (Decree-Law no. 27/97/M of 30 June).

59 For instance, the CIRC signed regulatory cooperation agreements with securities regulators of eight Canadian provinces in 2010, for the purpose of "establishing a channel for regulatory cooperation in connection with Chinese insurance firms' overseas investments involving registered Canadian firms and recognized markets". *See* 'Eight Canadian Securities Regulators Sign Regulatory Cooperation Agreement with China's Insurance Regulator' *Canadian Securities Administrators* (Montréal, 10 November 2010) <www.securities-administrators.ca/aboutcsa.aspx?id=930> accessed 10 August 2017.

sistance, exchange of information and dialogue mechanisms.[60] Unlike the memorandums of understanding which are similar to each other in substance, the topics of the cooperative agreements between the CIRC and a foreign authority vary, ranging from anti-fraud measures to equivalence decisions.[61]

Apart from the supervisory authorities of foreign countries, the CIRC has interaction with insurance or non-insurance organizations around the world,[62] which constitute the third group of entities building a working relationship with the CIRC. Currently, the CIRC holds membership in some insurance organizations, including the International Association of Insurance Supervisors (hereinafter referred to as "IAIS") and the International Organization of Pension Supervisors. The representatives of the CIRC might participate in the day-to-day operation of the organizations, assist them in specific areas of activity as well as attend the conferences and programs the international organizations hold. In parallel, the CIRC organizes various forms of events including forums, seminars, conferences, etc. The international organizations along with supervisory authorities worldwide participate in these events. It should be highlighted as one major achievement by the CIRC in international networking that the CIRC led

---

60 *See e.g.* 'EIOPA and the China Insurance Regulatory Commission Sign a Memorandum of Understanding' *EIOPA* (Frankfurt am Main, 10 August 2017) <eiopa.europa.eu/Pages/News/EIOPA-and-the-China-Insurance-Regulatory-Commission-sign-a-Memorandum-of-Understanding.aspx> accessed 10 August 2017; 'NAIC Signs MoU Extension with China – Agreement Enhances Regulatory Cooperation' *NAIC* (Washington D.C., 28 March 2013) <www.naic.org/Releases/2013_docs/naic_signs_mou_extension_with_china.htm> accessed 10 August 2017; Australian Prudential Regulation Authority, Memorandum of Understanding between the China Insurance Regulatory Commission of the P.R.C. and the Australian Prudential Regulation Authority of the Commonwealth of Australia Regarding Insurance Regulatory Cooperation (Memorandum, 2015) <www.apra.gov.au/AboutAPRA/Documents/MoU-CIRC-of-China.pdf> accessed 10 August 2017.

61 *See e.g.* 'Signing of Co-operation Agreement between the Monetary Authority of Macau, China Insurance Regulatory Commission and the Office of the Commissioner of Insurance' *Government Information Bureau of Macau* (Macau, 18 December 2014) <www.gcs.gov.mo/showNews.php?DataUcn=84600&PageLang=E> accessed 14 August 2017; 'Equivalence Assessment Framework Agreement on Solvency Regulatory Regime signed by Office of the Commissioner of Insurance and China Insurance Regulatory Commission' *Hong Kong Insurance Authority* (Hong Kong, 16 May 2017) <www.ia.org.hk/en/supervision/int_dom_cooperation/files/pr_20170516.pdf> accessed 14 August 2017.

62 *See infra note* 329 at 36 (introducing generally the CIRC's dialogues and cooperation at international level).

the establishment of a supranational dialogue and cooperation platform, i.e. the Asian Forum of Insurance Regulators.[63]

II. Types of CIRC's Legal Acts

Rule-making is perceived as having a cornerstone status among the supervisory tasks carried out by the CIRC. The legal acts issued by the CIRC could be categorized as department rules and normative documents.

1. Department Rules

The name of department rules originates from the fact that the issuers of this type of rules are departments affiliated to the State Council, including ministries and other institutions of an equivalent status to ministries.[64] The CIRC is one of these departments. Actually, there exist two other institutions of identical nature as the CIRC, respectively, China Banking Regulatory Commission and China Securities Regulatory Commission. Here, in this context, department rules refer to the legal acts issued by the CIRC.

Department rules are directly applicable rules binding on all insurance undertakings and other entities concerned. The internal departments of the CIRC are in charge of the drafting of department rules within their respective areas of competence.[65] The legal department of the CIRC reviews the draft rules and submits the approved draft to chair meeting for final review.[66] Review or consent from a third party, including the State Council, is not required.[67] The CIRC only needs to submit the formally issued department rules to the State Council for record-keeping.[68]

63 The CIRC advocated the establishment of the forum in 2006. It is intended to be a regional platform where insurance regulators of different Asian countries can exchange opinions, enhance mutual understanding and strengthen cross-border coordination. As a major forum event, the annual conference is alternatively held by member supervisory authorities. For more information regarding the forum, see its website <www.afirweb.org>.

64 *Supra note* 30, at § 71.

65 The Rules on the Rule-making Procedures of CIRC Department Rules 2006, § 13.

66 *Id.* at §§ 23, 30.

67 *Supra note* 29, at § 135; *id.* at §§ 23-30.

68 The Regulation on Record-Keeping of Legal Acts 2001, § 3 (2).

Broadly speaking, department rules are aimed at providing implementing details for the Insurance Act of China and administrative regulations. In the Insurance Act and administrative regulations, there exist many areas where the CIRC is required to make detailed provisions. In accordance with the mandates the CIRC issues delegated acts in the form of department rules.

Where delegated acts are required, the Insurance Act of China sets out very few principles and does not specify what the CIRC shall stipulate in a particular supervisory area. The CIRC has a high degree of freedom in determining the stringency and scope of the provisions in the delegated acts.

The majority of department rules are formulated for the abovementioned purpose, however, there also exist a number of department rules covering areas where delegated acts are not explicitly required, or areas which are not even involved in the Insurance Act. This seems a breach of the delegation of powers, but in fact, the CIRC is empowered to exercise rule-making. Article 135 of the Insurance Act prescribes that the CIRC shall formulate and publish department rules for insurance regulation and supervision in accordance with legislative acts and administrative regulations. The provision indicates that the CIRC is actually conferred on the power to make department rules in any supervisory area, as long as those rules could contribute to the achievement of insurance supervisory objectives and do not contradict with the existing principles laid down in the upper-level legal acts.

2. Normative Documents

The second set of rules issued by the CIRC is normative documents, which are supervisory rules addressed to all insurance undertakings and other entities concerned. They are inferior to department rules in legal status. Essentially, they could be classified into three categories by nature: stipulatory, explanatory and guiding normative documents.[69]

Stipulatory normative documents approximate department rules in form and function to some degree. They are mainly formulated to provide further details for department rules or prescribe requirements on issues overlooked in department rules. The major purpose is to ensure that the

---

69 Bifeng Ye (ed), *Administrative Law and Administrative Litigation Law* (3rd edn, China Renmin University Press 2011) ch 6.

legal acts made by the CIRC could cover all types of activities by insurance undertakings in all possible circumstances.

Explanatory normative documents are formulated to clarify the definitions, procedures, provisions and other important elements in department rules or stipulatory normative documents. This type of normative documents imposes no requirements. The third type, guiding normative documents, provides unbinding directions to insurers. They are intended to initiate standards and advice on the improvement of governance functions and service quality of insurance undertakings.

Stipulatory normative documents are deemed to be an important supervisory means of the CIRC. The quantity of these documents is larger than department rules. In practice, the supervisors at the CIRC prefer to adopt stipulatory normative documents to prescribe requirements, because of the great leeway brought by them. Relative to department rules, the rule-making procedures of stipulatory normative documents are less complicated.[70] Unlike the process of making department rules, it doesn't require a demanding proposal expounding on all factors underlying the draft rules. Besides, the review and approval procedures are simpler. Where the supervisors are aware of an emerging issue that remains unregulated, a stipulatory normative document, instead of amendments to existing department rules, is likely to be issued. The CIRC is enabled to eliminate the absence of regulations in any area by adding new normative documents to the rule system.

D. Chapter Conclusions

The insurance regulation system of China is comprised of three levels. The institutions at the first and second level are statutorily more authoritative than the supervisory authority at the third level. However, the delegation from the two institutions with superior regulatory status makes the CIRC de facto active regulator and supervisor for China's insurance sector. Although the NPCC and the State Council reserve the power to exert control and rectify inappropriate supervisory practices, the CIRC could normally exercise autonomy in regulation and supervision.

70 *Compare* CIRC, *Administrative Rules on the Formulation of CIRC Normative Documents* (Normative Document, No 101, 2013) §§ 10-20 *with Supra note* 65, at §§ 7-30.

In regard of insurance legislation, the Insurance Act of China, as the legal basis for insurance regulation, is the framework law at the highest level. Following it, the administrative regulations by the State Council provide provisions on significant issues requiring joint supervisory efforts of several administrative departments. Nevertheless, there exist a rather limited number of administrative regulations applicable to insurance sector. Corresponding to the position of the CIRC, the department rules issued by the CIRC are legally inferior to and intended to implement the Insurance Act and administrative regulations. The department rules consist of the essential principles and requirements in major supervisory areas. Besides department rules, the CIRC issues the other type of legal acts, normative documents, which supplement the department rules by providing further implementing details. With a regulatory status inferior to department rules, normative documents are supposed to deal with supervisory issues of less importance relative to those in the department rules. However, in practice, normative documents are deemed to be the most important supervisory tool for the authority to impose restrictions on and exercise control of all supervisory issues. The frequency with which they are issued is much higher than that of the issuance of department rules. Regardless of the importance of a supervisory issue, normative documents are preferred by the authority to department rules mainly because of the less complicated rule-making process. Both of department rules and normative documents could be used as a form of legal act to stipulate supervisory requirements in the areas where the Insurance Act of China explicitly mandates the CIRC to provide implementing rules, the areas where such mandates are not explicitly available in the Act, and those areas that are not even involved in the Act. The full delegation of regulatory powers to the CIRC explains the significance of the two types of legal acts issued by the supervisory authority. It causes concern for the procedural legitimacy of the rule-making by the authority as well, which will be discussed in the subsequent chapter.

Chapter 2. Addressing Weaknesses of China's Insurance Legislation

In the previous chapter, China's insurance regulatory system is introduced in detail with the analysis of the major regulatory institutions and the different types of legal acts. This chapter is focused on the identification of the weaknesses inherent in China's insurance regulation, the comparison with the EU and the devising of counteractive mechanisms against the weaknesses identified. Before the discussion on the foregoing aspects, the EU's insurance legislation would be presented as the background information to facilitate the understanding of the subsequent issues that are involved in the comparison of the regulatory situations between the two jurisdictions.

A. Basic Facts about EU's Insurance Legislation

As similar to China's multi-level regulatory structure, the EU's insurance regulatory system could be divided into several tiers. But, the situation is relatively more complicated since the regulation of the EU's insurance sector involves rule-making and implementation at both the union and national level. Correspondingly, more actors participate in the regulatory process. The EU's insurance legislation and regulatory actors would be introduced in a nutshell in the following paragraphs.

The Solvency II Directive,[71] as the legal basis for the formulation of implementing details, is a fundamental legislative act at the top level of the EU's insurance regulatory system. It is jointly enacted by the European Parliament and the Council of the EU based on the formal proposal from the European Commission. Due to its framework nature, the EU member states are obligated to transpose the principles and requirements into their national laws. The framework directive seeks to achieve harmonization in regulation and convergence in supervisory practices across the EU member

71 Directive 2009/138/EC of the European Parliament and of the Council of 25 November 2009 on the Taking-up and Pursuit of the Business of Insurance and Reinsurance (Solvency II) (Recast) [2014] OJ L 335/1.

states,[72] employing principles-based approach to grant the NCAs leeway in the conduct of supervision and to allow for the idiosyncratic conditions of individual insurers.[73] The principles-based approach is used without prejudice to the principle of materiality as enshrined in the Article 290(1) TFEU,[74] insofar as all the essential elements relating to insurance supervision are stipulated in the Solvency II Directive instead of the delegated acts. In addition to the principle of materiality, the principle of proportionality as laid down in the Article 5(4) TEU is as well a crucial element of the Solvency II Directive,[75] insofar as a proportionate application of the directive by allowing for the risk profile and the size of insurance business is expressly underlined.[76]

At the second level lies the delegated regulation of implementing nature, which is adopted by the European Commission based on the fully consulted advice by the Committee of European Insurance and Occupational Pensions Supervisors (the predecessor of the European Insurance and Occupational Pensions Authority). The subject matter dealt with in the delegated regulation concerns the issues specified in the upper-level directive. As opposed to the principles-based approach by the framework directive, the delegated regulation employs a rules-based approach in order for the stipulations to be detailed.[77] The regulation is directly binding on all the member states and should thus be implemented without transposition.

In parallel with the delegated regulation there exist implementing and regulatory technical standards which are adopted by the European Commission based on the fully consulted drafts developed by the European In-

---

72 Meinrad Dreher, *Treatises on Solvency II* (Springer 2015) 8-12.

73 *See infra note* 137, at 931.

74 TFEU, § 290. *See infra note* 137, at 926 (analyzing that it will be inconsistent with the materiality principle to merely lay down a supervisory objective in the recitals of the framework directive). Additionally, it should be noted that the principle of materiality, as an overarching principle for regulation, is applied to all areas involved in the Solvency II regime. As pointed out by Dreher, "Similarly, the principle of materiality ensures that supervisory activities and regulatory requirements are dictated only by material circumstances. For example, immaterial information does not fall under the regulatory duties to report. Immaterial risks do not figure into the evaluation of the individual risk status of an insurance undertaking." *See supra note* 72, at 29.

75 Consolidated Version of the Treaty on European Union [2012] OJ C 326/13 (TEU), § 5.

76 *See infra note* 137, at 932-934.

77 *See supra note* 72, at 12-13.

surance and Occupational Pensions Authority (hereinafter referred to as "EIOPA"). In comparison with the delegated regulation, the technical standards are intended to address the issues of more technical nature in a more precise way within the scope delimited by the Solvency II Directive. The attribute common to the two types of legal acts is the binding nature. In other words, technical standards are likewise directly applicable across the EU member states.

Subordinate to the binding delegated acts mentioned above, the Solvency II guidelines are a form of regulatory instruments developed and issued by the EIOPA which is empowered to adopt them on the basis of the Solvency II Directive and the delegated acts. The guidelines are employed to ensure the harmonized and effective supervisory practices across the EU. The NCAs are expected to comply with the guidelines, despite the fact that the right to opt out is granted. In the event that a national authority decides not to be subjected to the guidelines, the reasons for non-compliance should be provided to the EIOPA.

B. Structural Deficiencies in China's Insurance Legislation and Comparison with EU

I. The Framework Act: Insufficiency of Principles

The intention of legislating the Insurance Act of China is to erect a comprehensive framework underlying insurance regulation and providing well-defined principles in overall aspects. However, this legislative purpose fails to be fulfilled, mainly out of the insufficiency of principles and requirements.

Table 2: Areas Overlooked or Delegated by the Insurance Act of China

Overlooked Areas	Delegated Areas
– Transparency	– Solvency capital requirements
– Group supervision	– Technical provisions
– Transfer of portfolio	– Public disclosure
– Accounting	– Dissolution
– Risk management	– Scope of business
– Internal control and audit	– Reinsurance
– Acturial	– Insurance guaranty fund
– Outsourced functions	– Investments
– Third country equivalence	– Insurance asset management companies
– Qualifying holdings	

– Valuation of assets and liabilities – Own funds	– Insurance clause and premium rate – Licensing for insurance intermediaries

The insufficiency means that the Insurance Act sets out no or very few principles in many important areas. These areas are either overlooked, or simply delegated to CIRC without imposing principles to which the delegated acts shall conform.

In the former scenario, the important areas that should have been addressed, are not involved or properly taken into account in the legislative act. For complicated issues, there should have been varied principles applied according to the nature or type of the subject matter, rather than general and undifferentiated principles. By overlooking certain important areas, the legislators effectively signify that these issues are deemed unimportant by them. The CIRC, upon receiving the signal, is likely to treat these issues in a similarly neglectful manner. This has been demonstrated by the fact that a large portion of important areas overlooked by the Insurance Act remains untouched or is inadequately addressed by the CIRC, such as governance system and group supervision.

In the latter scenario, where delegated acts are required, the non-existence of concrete principles results in the autonomy of the CIRC in setting requirements. The value of a framework law lies in the essential elements defined for shaping the entire regulatory and supervisory system. Unavailability of essential principles in delegated areas makes the Insurance Act deviate from its functional orientation. Comparatively, an advantage of the EU legislation practice is that the institution making delegated acts are excluded from the competence to stipulate essential elements in an area, which shall be prescribed and affirmed by higher legislative bodies through more rigid procedures.[78] It avoids the circumstance where delegated acts define thresholds and boundaries in such a way as to be inconsistent with the intention of the legislature.

II. Unavailability of External Check and Control

In the insurance sector of China, the regulation system exhibits a centralized pattern that powers and tasks are concentrated in a single institution, i.e. the CIRC. Simultaneously, a prominent problem pertinent to the cen-

78 TFEU, § 290.

tralized pattern arises that external check and control mechanism is not in place. Among the extensive powers of the CIRC, the rule-making function arouses the greatest concern in this regard. The reasons are twofold. Firstly, the vast majority of the legal acts applicable in the insurance sector are composed of the rules issued by the CIRC. That is to say, the CIRC plays a dominant role in insurance legislation. The rules have substantial impacts on the interests, rights and obligations of various stakeholders, such as policyholders, insurers and insurance intermediaries. Secondly, the way in which the CIRC exercises regulatory and supervisory powers is in conformity with self-formulated rules. The appropriateness and consistency of its own rules that govern the conduct of regulation and supervision is central to the effectiveness of its work.

Despite the importance of the rules made by the CIRC, the entirety of them are drafted, reviewed and approved by the CIRC alone. There exist no check procedures involving the participation of a third party, either preceding or following those rules entering into force. Although the CIRC solicits public opinions before making rules,[79] it could opt to take external opinions into consideration or to simply ignore them, given its exclusive competence in determining the substance of the rules. The actual process doesn't suffice to ensure that the propositions of the interested parties are duly considered. The review of draft rules is conducted by the internal legal department of the CIRC.[80] The non-independent position impairs its capability to make check and control in an impartial manner.

Adverse effects associated to the deficiency of an effective check mechanism have emerged. Many rules, shortly after being put into force, have to be materially amended or supplemented due to inappropriate stringency, failure to take into account important factors or neglect of market conditions.[81] Inconsistent changes in requirements and assessment methods lead to the instability of the supervisory system and the increase in compliance cost.

A comparison with the EU in insurance legislation further demonstrates the necessity of establishing an external check and control mechanism in China's system. In the EU, binding legislative acts, before entry into force,

---

79 *Supra note* 65, at §§ 19-21.

80 *Id.* at §§ 23-30.

81 Amendments to rules are provided in normative documents. *See e.g.*, CIRC, *Notification of the Adjustments to the Provisional Rules on Insurance Asset Management Companies* (Normative Document, No 19, 2011); CIRC, *Notification of Certain Issues relating to the Investments of Insurance Undertakings in Equity and Real Estates* (Normative Document, No 59, 2012).

require the approval from the European Parliament and the EU Council.[82] The ordinary legislative procedure, which is set as the default legislative process in most circumstances,[83] enables different regulatory actors to exert influence on the content of proposed legal acts and underpins a balance of regulatory concerns. In China's insurance sector, regulatory institutions could draft, review and issue legal acts on their own without review or approval from other entities as long as they find the necessity for a new rule. Do the benefits derived from rule-making efficiency exceed the costs brought about by excluding external checks from the legislative process? The answer is negative. If external checks are introduced, the appropriateness and consistency of supervision could be elevated to a higher level. Actually, there are many problems existing in China's insurance sector, which are ascribed to the deficiencies of supervisory rules to a great extent. Those deficiencies expose policyholders to reduced protection and disincentivize insurers to commit adequate resources to governance system.

As to the delegated acts, although the European Commission is authorized to adopt implementing measures, additional approval from external institutions is required. The Commission is required to submit the adopted acts to the Parliament and the Council for review. The two reviewing institutions have the power to raise objections within two months after receiving the acts. Only after the review by the two institutions could the delegated acts entering into force. The external approval procedure is utilized to identify whether the delegated acts formulated is aligned with the principles set in the framework directive. This institutional arrangement is not available in China's legal system. Delegated acts made by the CIRC are not subject to any external approval. Department rules are filed to the State Council only for record-keeping and the State Council does not un-

82 TFEU, § 289. Over the history, initially, the Council played a decisive role in the adoption of legislation while the participation of the European Parliament is only limited to providing unbinding consultation. Gradually, new treaties continually extended the power of the European Parliament in legislation. Eventually, it gained the status of co-legislator with the Council. For the changes of the legislative role of the European Parliament, *see* Karen Davies, *Understanding European Union Law* (5th edn, Routledge 2013). The change in the allocation of the legislative power in EU reveals a common characteristic of the development trend in legislation around the world - increased checks and balances. In the context of the China's insurance supervision, the rules made by the CIRC and other activities conducted by it shall be subject to check and control. Otherwise, pure autonomy in supervision could give rise to abuse of powers and enlargement of the room for rent-seeking.

83 The detailed description of the procedure is provided in TFEU, § 294.

dertake the responsibility of reviewing these adopted acts. Normative documents are not even required to be filed with any external institutions. Upper-level institutions do not exert control on the delegated acts. However, considering the much greater discretion of the CIRC in determining delegated acts relative to its European counterpart, the CIRC's rule-making should have been subject to more rigorous external review.

Besides the delegated acts, the implementing technical standards (hereinafter referred to as the "ITS") serve another example for revealing the fact that European legislators attach importance to external review. On the side of the EU, the EIOPA is responsible for formulating the ITSs that are set to be part of the implementing measures.[84] The standards made by the EIOPA shall be submitted to the European Commission for evaluation and consent.[85] Supposing that the legislative culture of China were adopted in the EU, the EIOPA would be delegated the combined power of drafting, reviewing and issuing ITSs which should subsequently be integrated into the implementing measures without the approval of the European commission. It is not put into reality in the EU because the importance of external checks and control is valued. Concentrating powers in an institution that discharges its responsibilities without surveillance and intervention, increases the possibility of rent-seeking, inappropriate functioning or even offences.

III. Shortcomings of Normative Documents

The Legal acts issued by the CIRC take up core position in the regulatory architecture of China. They provide provisions in overall aspects of insurance supervision. Even the issues outside the scope of the Insurance Act are covered. From the perspective of supervised entities, the two kinds of CIRC acts, i.e. department rules and normative documents, differentiate insignificantly with each other. As compared with normative documents, department rules are made to prescribe requirements on more important issues. Correspondingly, a more rigorous rule-making process is applied to

84 Regulation (EU) No 1094/2010 of The European Parliament and of The Council of 24 November 2010 establishing a European Supervisory Authority (European Insurance and Occupational Pensions Authority), amending Decision No 716/2009/EC and repealing Commission Decision 2009/79/EC OJ L331/48 (the Regulation Establishing EIOPA), § 15; EIOPA, *Cover Note for the Consultation on Implementing Technical Standards for Solvency II* (CP-14/011, 2014) para 2.6.

85 *Id.* (the Regulation Establishing EIOPA).

department rules. For this reason, the CIRC is inclined to make or revise regulations by adopting normative documents that enable it to take measures and make reactions promptly, rather than by formulating or amending department rules. In practice, the importance of issues handled in normative documents is not inferior to those addressed in department rules. A large portion of normative documents is intended to fill the gaps in the system of regulations, creating or modifying rules.

With regard to normative documents, there exists no exactly comparable counterpart in the EU's financial legislation regime. At the union level, the scope of binding legal acts is prescribed in legislative acts. It is prohibited to lay down stipulations outside the scope. In addition, no institution has the competence to independently formulate and issue rules at all times, as is the case with the CIRC.

Salient shortcomings of normative documents are discussed below. Firstly, an impact assessment is not required to implement before the introduction of a new rule. In the rules of procedure for making normative documents, the requirements on the public consultation for proposed rules are explicitly provided,[86] while the impact assessment is overlooked. The CIRC is not obliged to make detailed quantitative or qualitative assessment of the potential impacts of draft rules.

The impact assessment constitutes a reliable means to inspect the appropriateness of the requirements proposed in draft legal acts. The absence of this important procedure has substantial adverse effects on the quality and consistency of rules. By contrast, the analysis of potential effects of prospective rules is valued by rule-makers in the EU. Multiple instruments and methods are utilized to evaluate possible impacts. Evaluation outcome will be adjusted according to the feedback obtained in public consultations.

Secondly, the process of making normative documents lacks due stringency. Department rules are required to be filed to the State Council, but a similar requirement is not set for normative documents. Instead, normative documents could be issued right after the internal review by the CIRC. The stringency of rule-making process is not proportionate to the nature and impacts of the documents. The CIRC is able to prescribe any requirement in any area through this type of legal act. Many areas that are unmentioned in the Insurance Act, fall into the scope of normative documents, for instance, group supervision, accounting, qualifying holding,

86 CIRC, *Administrative Rules on the Formulation of CIRC Normative Documents* (Normative Document, No 101, 2013).

transfer of portfolios, etc. Such important areas, if put into legislation in EU, will be treated at the highest legislative level with a more prudent and democratic approach. Other institutions will in no case be granted the power to develop core principles in those fundamental areas.

The CIRC applies inadequately prudent procedures to the rule-making in important areas where more stringent procedures should have been adopted to ensure sound control. It is wrongly incentivized to develop high reliance on the oversimplified means of regulation to prescribe rules for both trivial and significant issues. The lack of impact assessment and prudent rule-making process causes the frequent occurrence of revocation or revision of normative documents in many areas.

Thirdly, normative documents are not made in a systematic manner. Normally, the rules regarding a particular issue are not consolidated in a single normative document. There exist a number of documents in a supervisory area and each of them imposes requirements specifically for a certain circumstance. The CIRC continually issues new documents so as to fill the gaps in the regulations. Nevertheless, they are neither integrated into the existing department rules, nor assembled to form an organized unity. It exacerbates the disorder of the regulation system and raises the difficulty in legal compliance. Take the area of investments as an example for illustration, a department rule was initially formulated to set full-scale requirements in this area.[87] Subsequently, a number of normative documents were made to supplement the department rule. Each of the following issues is dealt with in a separate normative document: principles on asset allocation, the internal control and compliance management for investment, ratios for funds appropriation, establishment of insurance risk owner, enhancement of investment management capability, etc.[88] Some of these normative documents amend the existing requirements in the department rule, while others stipulate provisions on the issues that have not

87 *See* Provisional Rules on the Utilization and Management of Insurance Funds 2010.

88 For these normative documents, *see* CIRC, *Provisional Rules on Insurance Assets Allocation* (Normative Document, No 61, 2012); CIRC, *Supervisory Rules on the Grading of the Internal Control and Legal Compliance of Insurance Funds Utilization* (Normative Document, No 54, 2014); CIRC, *Notification on Enhancement of the Supervision on Ratios of Insurance Funds Utilization* (Normative Document, No 13, 2014); CIRC, *Notification on Issues Pertinent to Investment Risk Owner of Insurance Institutions* (Normative Document, No 28, 2013); CIRC, *Notification on Issues Pertinent to the Improvement of Investment Management Capability of Insurance Institutions* (Normative Document, No 10, 2013).

been therein included. In fact, the principles set in the normative documents overlap partially with those in the department rule. The department rule should have been amended to accommodate changes, so that the parallel existence of multiple legal acts on the same subject matter could be avoided.

Relatively, EU insurance regulation system is better organized, which forms functional connections between upper-level and lower-level legal acts. In China's regulation system, upper-level acts do not strictly delimit the regulatory boundaries of lower-level acts. The only prerequisite for rule-making is that a contradiction with the explicit requirements provided in upper-level acts should be avoided. In comparison, the lower-level acts in the EU's regulation system are not allowed to prescribe rules on a certain issue unless otherwise required in an upper-level legal act. It leads to clear linkages between the levels of the EU insurance regulation system in that an upper-level act is supplemented by a specified amount of lower-level acts with a predetermined scope.

C. Resolving Structural Deficiencies: What Route to Follow?

I. Impracticality of Adopting Lamfalussy Process

After the analysis of the major deficiencies of China's insurance regulation system, a conclusion is drawn that the flawed framework act is responsible for the problems, given the absence of concrete principles in many areas and the lack of clues about the scope of the delegated acts. Comparatively, the EU Solvency II system which is built with the Lamfalussy Process demonstrates strengths in the aspect where the drawbacks of China's insurance regulation system lie. The Lamfalussy Process, four-level legislative approach, was devised to adapt the rule-making in the EU for better responding to the needs and changes of financial markets, enhancing the clarity of the union law and consistency in transposition.[89] The first level of the Lamfalussy Process requires that a framework legislation shall be in

89 For the materials about the Lamfalussy process, *see e.g.*, the Committee of Wise Men chaired by Alexandre Lamfalussy, *Final Report on the Regulation of the European Securities Markets* (European Commission Report, Final, 2001) ch 2; Takis Tridimas, 'EU Financial Regulation: Federalization, Crisis Management, and Law Reform' in Paul Craig and Gráinne de Búrca (eds), The Evolution of EU Law (2nd edn, Oxford University Press 2011) 785-788; Alexander Schaub, 'The Lamfalussy Process Four Years on' (2005) 13 (2) Journal of Financial Regulation and

place, which should contain "broad but sufficiently precise framework norms" and "clearly specify the nature and the extent of the technical implementing measures that should be taken at the second level".[90] At the second level, implementing measures supplementing the framework legislation shall be delivered, confined to the extent and scope which the level-1 framework sets for the delegated acts.[91] The third and fourth levels of the Lamfalussy process mainly focus on the facilitation and enforcement regarding the convergence of supervisory practices of the national supervisory authorities of different EU member states.[92] The first and second levels of the Lamfalussy process are relatively more relevant in this context, based on the fact that the insurance supervision across China is consistently conducted by the single supervisory authority, i.e. the CIRC.

Assuming that the legislative approach of the level-1 and level-2 in the "Lamfalussy Process" (hereafter referred to as Lamfalussy approach for simplicity) is adopted in China, the CIRC would be only mandated to make rules on the specified issues within the precise scope of delegated acts as predefined in the legislative act. In such a circumstance, the CIRC is divested of the autonomy in determining the content and amount of the delegated acts. With an increased clarity of the connection between the framework law and delegated acts, the disorder of the CIRC's system of rules would be well mitigated. Simultaneously, in conformity with the Lamfalussy approach, essential elements for insurance regulation are laid down in the legislative act, and the CIRC would no longer stipulate these core principles. This would make the actual internal review mechanism of the CIRC justifiable and sufficient to handle this kind of delegated acts which merely concern non-essential elements according to the precise mandates provided in the Insurance Act of China.

Compliance 110; Joana Mendes, *Participation in EU Rule-Making: a Rights-Based Approach* (first published 2011, Oxford University Press 2011) 273-301; François Haas, 'Current State of Play' in Jörg Decressin, Hamid Faruqee and Wim Fonteyne (eds), *Integrating Europe's Financial Markets* (International Monetary Fund, 2007) 58-60.

90 *Id.* (Final Report by the Committee of Wise Men), at 19, 23. *See also* Alexandre Lamfalussy, 'The Release of the Committee's Final Report on the Regulation of the European Securities Markets' (opening comments to the Press, 15 February 2001) <ec.europa.eu/internal_market/securities/docs/Lamfalussy/wisemen/lamfalussycomments_en.pdf> accessed 31 July 2014 (noting that the split between the first and second level legal acts shall be conducted on a case by case basis).

91 *See Id.* (Final Report by the Committee of Wise Men), at 28-36.

92 *Id.* at 37-40.

1. The Flip Side of Adopting Lamfalussy Approach

The bright side of the Lamfalussy approach has been thoroughly discussed in the previous section. Replicating the EU Insurance legislation model in China seems a straightforward structural option for resolving the existing deficiencies. However, after studying the cost of adopting the option, its practicality is seriously doubted. The key elements of the first-level of the Lamfalussy Process include the establishment of concrete principles in every regulatory area as well as the identification of the specifics of delegated issues. The introduction of the two elements would bring about a more detailed framework act and a clear-cut scope of the delegated acts, which could translate into a strict restriction imposed on the CIRC's regulatory power. The cost of introducing them is analyzed below from several perspectives.

Firstly, supplementing the Insurance Act by input of principles would result in the whole insurance regulation system being almost remade in light of the fact that all legal acts would be significantly changed either in form or substance. In the Insurance Act of China, the shortage of concrete principles occurs in most areas with the exception of insurance contract and incorporation. It would involve a great deal of procedural work in the significant revision of the provisions in all areas covered in the framework act and those areas outside the coverage. Not only new principles but also precise definition of the scope of delegated acts should be formulated. The radical transformation of the framework act in form and substance will entail profound impacts on all the legal acts on insurance.[93] Essential principles laid down by the CIRC would be removed from all department rules and normative documents. A large proportion of the legal acts issued by the CIRC need to be revised to varying extent in order to be in line with

---

93 In the subsequent analysis, the impacts on the legal acts issued by the CIRC would be presented. What need to be pointed out is that the administrative regulations of the State Council would also inevitably be affected by the overarching changes in the framework legislation. Core principles provided in existing administrative regulations should be stipulated in the legislative act. Hence, they have to be removed from the administrative regulations and replaced by the new principles available in the legislative act. The implementing details based on the removed principles would, at the same time, be adapted to the new principles.
There exit only several administrative regulations on insurance. The State Council does not assume a major role in making implementing details. Almost all of the implementing rules is comprised of the legal acts issued by the CIRC, which constitute the counterpart of the Level-2 implementing measures of the European Commission.

the overarching changes in the legislative act. Simultaneously, the local regulations made by the regional bureaus of the CIRC are subjected to similar modification. For rule-makers at different level of the insurance regulation system, much time would be devoted to structural and relational adjustments.

Secondly, unless this model could be accepted by the NPCC as the new direction for the reform of legislation in wider sectors in China, it is extremely difficult to make the regulatory approach in the insurance sector an exception. Currently, the structure of the legislative act and the delegation of rule-making in the insurance sector are similar to the way that is applied in other sectors. When the structural option is considered, a prominent issue would arise as to whether it is justifiable to allow the insurance sector to have a different regulatory model from other sectors. Apparently, if the Lamfalussy approach is adopted in the insurance sector, the regulatory model should be extended to at least cover other financial sectors where similar problems about the regulation system exist. The difficulty in achieving the consensus among policymakers on a fundamental change of the regulatory models in extensive sectors hinders the adoption of the Lamfalussy approach in the insurance sector.

Thirdly, the CIRC's ability to amend rules in a timely manner would be weakened. Under the Lamfalussy approach, in case rules are absent in a certain area, amendments should be initially made in the Insurance Act and then come the changes of the implementing rules at the level of the CIRC. Without an amendment to the framework law and corresponding provisions of the delegated acts, the CIRC would not have the competence to deliver supplements or alter existing rules for the purpose of tackling emerging or overlooked issues. If the Lamfalussy approach is put into practice, the Insurance Act of China should always be ready for embracing modification in order to introduce new principles to those areas where necessary regulations are absent. However, in reality, Chinese legislators take a so prudent attitude towards the amendment to the framework act that it would not be amended unless there exist extensive or substantial flaws. An overhaul would then be carried out to identify weaknesses that have been exposed in the implementation.

Fourthly, the powers of the CIRC will be lessened and the institution would have to be reformed. The flexible rule-making competence on which the CIRC relies to counteract problems and risks will become unavailable. The role of the CIRC in insurance regulation would be redefined. The CIRC has to alter the way it supervises and restructure its functional arrangements. Meanwhile, the regional bureaus of the CIRC would encounter similar problems.

Lastly, on macro level, financial stability could be adversely impacted as a result of the dramatic changes in the insurance legislation.

2. Conclusions

In a nutshell, the restructuration of the regulatory model by adopting the Lamfalussy approach would result in radical transformation of the insurance regulation system. The adoption of the Lamfalussy approach in the insurance sector is conditional upon the viability of introducing the regulatory model to wider sectors, which further lessens the likelihood of the structural option.

Considering the immature legal environment, the instability of the transitional economy and prevalence of weak corporate governance in China, dramatic changes in the regulation regime could trigger many unintended negative consequences, which could outweigh the benefits brought by the restructuration. It is more practical to follow a path of gradual and mild changes.

For the reasons above, it is better to devise an alternative which could effectively mitigate the deficiencies of China's insurance regulation system with insignificant influence on its functioning.

II. Viable Reform Options

From the analysis of the problems associated with the introduction of the Lamfalussy approach, it becomes clear that a reorganization of the entire insurance legislation entails excessively high costs. A moderate reform shall be implemented without substantially lessening the regulatory powers conferred on the CIRC. In subsequent parts, three initiatives will be presented, which are intended to tackle the prominent weaknesses analyzed in the previous sections. They could resolve problems with fewer impacts and costs incurred, counterbalancing to a large extent the absence of clear-cut delimitation of delegation.

1. Introducing Institutional Veto Point

a) Proposal to Establishing External Reviewing Entity and Mechanism

In order for a control over the discretion of the CIRC in rule-making, a reform option could be pursued to establish an external review mechanism. With such a mechanism in place, the principles and implementing details formulated by the CIRC would be subject to external evaluation of their stringency and proportionality. The mechanism, to some extent, makes up for the absence of concrete principles in the framework act by ensuring delegated acts in line with the policy direction set by the NPCC. It could tackle the major deficiency of China's insurance regulation system at much lower cost for all stakeholders.

For the purpose of establishing an effective external review mechanism for the CIRC which plays a major role in insurance legislation, an institutional veto point shall be introduced for the interference in its rule-making process. The institutional veto point is an entity whose approval is required for a policy or rule change.[94] In a political system, veto players exercise control over proposed rules. The quality of regulations could be enhanced with the intervention of an external entity capable of blocking draft where it finds amendments necessary. Through block and conciliation, the interests of different stakeholders would be better balanced and the stringency of the draft regulations would be calibrated to a more proper level. Veto points contribute to policy stability, serving as credible commitments of a government.[95] Empirical studies show that the increase in veto points results in a political system being less susceptible to rent-seeking opportunities,[96] and a reduced incentive of political actors to grant benefits to interest groups at the expense of the public.[97]

---

94 *See* George Tsebelis, *Veto Players: How Political Institutions Work* (Princeton University Press 2002) 19.

95 *See* Dorothy M. Daley, Donald P. Haider-Markel and Andrew B. Whitford, 'Checks, Balances, and the Cost of Regulation : Evidence from the American States' (2007) 60 (4) Political Research Quarterly 696, 702.

96 Puspa Delima Amri and Brett Matthew Kocher, 'The Political Economy of Financial Sector Supervision and Banking Crises: A Cross-Country Analysis' (2012) 18 (1) European Law Journal 24, 38.

97 *See generally*, Witold J. Henisz and Bennet A. Zelner, 'Interest Groups, Veto Points, and Electricity Infrastructure Deployment' (2006) 60 (1) International Organization 263, 264 (analyzing how political actors transfer targeted economic benefits to specific interest groups with the cost borne by the whole society.);

Given the technicality of the supervisory rules and their importance to the financial stability, experts in financial supervision, instead of normal lawyers without expertise in the particular area, shall fulfill the responsibility of evaluating proposed rules. From the perspective of competence and independence, the legal department of the NPCC or that of the State Council is not an ideal alternative. The dissertation advises for the establishment of an independent committee specifically in charge of the check and control of the financial legislation.

In order to ensure efficiency, external review procedures could be divided into two tracks, prudential procedures for department rules and simple procedures for normative documents. The rationale behind the differentiated treatment of the two kinds of legal acts is that department rules, generally speaking, handle essential principles in supervised areas. Normative documents are generally inferior in importance to department rules, but the issuance frequency of normative documents is higher. That is why a streamlined procedure is proposed to be applied to the review of normative documents.

Under prudential procedures, draft rules shall be not only passed internally by the CIRC, but also approved by the independent committee mentioned above. If draft rules are rejected by the committee, meetings shall be held between the two entities to exchange views and discuss amendments. The CIRC shall make amendments based on the results of the meetings. The amended draft still requires the approval by the committee.

Under simple procedures, draft rules shall be submitted to the independent committee for evaluation prior to issuance. The committee shall comment on the draft and propose amendments if it deems necessary. The CIRC could decide whether to accept the position of the committee. If it rejects the opinions of the committee and declines to make amendments accordingly, it could still issue the new rules which subsequently take effect. However, in that case, the CIRC is obliged to disclose publicly why it declines to follow the advice of the independent committee.

The way to check and control under the simple procedures approximates how the EIOPA reacts to the national authorities that decline to comply with guidelines.[98] Although the independent committee does not impose its position, the public disclosure would serve as a soft constraint and exert pressure on the CIRC. The soft constraint prevents supervisory

---

Bruce Bueno de Mesquita and Hilton L. Root (eds), *Governing for Prosperity* (Yale University Press 2000).

98 The Regulation Establishing EIOPA, § 16.

efficiency from being impaired by a block by the veto player and retains the check mechanism effectively in place.

b) Relative Merits of the Option

The establishment of an external review mechanism would not entail such a high level of complexities and even impracticality as the transformation of the regulatory model. Above all, extensive changes to the existing structure of the legal acts are avoided. It has few impacts on the functioning of the supervisory authority. No legal acts are required to be modified as a result of the establishment of the independent committee. Besides, changes in the regulatory model are normally deemed to be an overarching reform which should involve all sectors, but the establishment of a reviewing mechanism could be perceived as a special arrangement for particular sectors. This increases the possibility of the option being adopted in the insurance sector and wider financial sectors. Further, the capability of the CIRC to promptly counteract problems or risks through rule-making would not be weakened. The dual review procedures tailored to different regulatory instruments ensure the efficiency of the rule-making activity, while imposing necessary monitoring and control on it. In addition, though the introduction of an institutional veto point involves the alteration of the CIRC's rule-making process, the alteration will not lessen the rule-making powers delegated to it. Hence, the CIRC would not be faced with material functional changes and the tactics it employs to counteract problems could be sustained.

2. Building Impact Assessment System

The second initiative is intended to incorporate the impact assessment in the CIRC's rule-making process. The impact assessment could contribute to more informed decisions on policy options and facilitate the coherence of supervisory rules. It has been noted that the qualitative, quantitative and monetary analysis of the costs and benefits of proposed rules and other alternatives is overlooked in the course of insurance legislation in China. The importance of such an analysis to various stakeholders and the economy is not sufficiently recognized. The CIRC would rather make amendments ex post to rectify inappropriate requirements than devote adequate resources to ex-ante impact assessments.

a) Reasons for Drawing on EU's Experience

The European Commission issues guidelines in this regard to promote and harmonize the impact assessment practices at the union level.[99] Insofar as the EU's insurance legislation is concerned, the standards set out in the guidelines are strictly adhered to. The EIOPA carries out impact study and maintains functional set-up in accordance with the guidelines. In terms of process and methodology, the impact assessment system defined by the guidelines presents an excellent example. Over the past years, this mechanism was applied to all sectors when legislative acts, delegated acts, or even non-legislative initiatives which concern future policy directions are proposed.[100] With adjustments based on supervisory practices, the impact assessment mechanism in the EU has evolved into a mature and effective evaluation tool used to weigh up policy options and consequences.

The EU impact assessment system could be introduced to China's insurance sector with some necessary adaptations. The system is proposed to be established within the CIRC and the institutional arrangements are comparable to those inside the European Commission, which are discussed in detail below.[101]

---

99 European Commission, *Impact Assessment Guidelines* (SEC (2009) 92, 2009).

100 *See* European Commission, *Impact Assessment Board Report for 2013* (Government Report, 2013) ch 1.2.

101 In the EU, the impact assessment system is established inside the European Commission. All Directorates-General (hereinafter referred to as "DGs") follow the code on impact assessment. In China, the institution corresponding to the European Commission is, actually, the State Council. However, the transposition could not be made in the State Council, because introducing the system to the State Council and all affiliated departments is a so significant agenda that it far exceeds the scope of the discussion about insurance supervision. That's why the system is proposed to be built within the CIRC.
A problem might be raised as to whether completing all the procedures of an impact assessment process inside the CIRC would negatively affect the quality of the assessment. Indeed, in the case of the EU, procedures are not entirely conducted inside an individual DG. The review of the assessment report is held outside the DG which produces the draft report. Theoretically, the ideal model for China's insurance regulation should be similar to the arrangement in the EU - the review is conducted by the State Council to which the CIRC is affiliated. But, such arrangement cannot be set in China. It would otherwise assume a central quality control function for impact assessment available in the State Council.
Generally speaking, the problem put forward above is not serious, because the assessment result would be submitted with other documents to the independent committee proposed in previous dissertation sections for examination and com-

b) Set-up of Impact Assessment System

The primary step is to establish a pertinent functional unit and mechanism inside the CIRC which plays a major role in insurance legislation. Firstly, as the internal departments of the CIRC are entitled to draw up binding legal acts, impact assessment support unit should be available in each of them so that the assessment staff is able to obtain guidance and assistance in a particular supervisory area. Besides, a central impact assessment commission in charge of quality control over all impact assessments conducted in all internal departments shall be established and accountable directly to the chairperson of the CIRC.[102] Further, each time an impact assessment is to be conducted, a group steering the whole process of the particular assessment need be formed. In order to make full use of the supervisory expertise available and generate a comprehensive assessment, members of the steering group shall consist of the impact assessment support unit in the lead internal department, the counterparts in the internal department of which the supervisory work is affected and the policy coordination function of the CIRC.[103] Lastly, an inter-department consultation shall be launched from the beginning of each impact assessment to foster coordination and solicit views from the policy research department and those internal departments with a legitimate interest in the regulatory initiative on the basis of their responsibilities or the nature of the initiative.[104]

For a thorough consultation with stakeholders and an accurate estimation of costs and benefits for various policy options, it requires a series of work involving joint efforts of different functions and a long period to complete all procedures. The main steps are illustrated in Figure 1.

---

ments. With the institutional veto point in place, the impact assessment result would be closely evaluated. For this reason, the external reviewing entity would undertake the role which the Impact Assessment Board (hereinafter referred to as "IAB") plays in the impact assessment system of the European Commission to a great extent.

102 The function of this entity is analogous to that of the IAB at the European Commission.

103 *See supra note* 99, at 8-9.

104 *See* L Schaik, M Kaeding, A Hudson and J Ferrer, *Policy Coherence for Development in the EU Council: Strategies for the Way Forward* (Centre for European Policy Studies 2006) (noting the special role the Legal Service plays in the process and introducing the 'fast track' inter-service procedure initiated by the lead DG).

Figure 1: Impact Assessment Procedures Based on EU Guidelines with Adaptations for Integration into CIRC's Rule-Making Process

Beginning Phase: Preparatory Work
– Making the plan, timetable and roadmap for an impact assessment – Engaging with the impact assessment support unit in the lead internal department – Establishing a steering group and having it participate in all phases

↓

Middle Phase: Consultation and Drafting
– Consulting stakeholders and the wider public, providing feedback and seeking external expertise – Conducting an impact assessment study – Analyzing the results and presenting findings in the formal report

↓

Final Phase: Review and Modification
– Sending the report and executive summary to the central impact assessment commission for review, and then making adjustments according to the opinions of the commission – Launching the inter-department consultation by filing the report, proposal and commission opinions to the internal departments concerned for review, and incorporating the recommendations received in the consultation into the report – Submitting the finalized report, executive summary, commission opinions, proposal and other documents required to the legal department which is responsible for overall review of the initiative

Source: European Commission, *Impact Assessment Guidelines* (SEC (2009) 92, 2009) ch 2; European Commission, *Part III: Annexes to Impact Assessment Guidelines* (explanatory policy paper, 2009) ch 2; Rules on the Rule-making Procedures of CIRC Department Rules 2006, §§ 13-30; CIRC, *Administrative Rules on the Formulation of CIRC Normative Documents* (Normative Document, No 101, 2013), §§ 10-20.

The impact assessment procedures could be smoothly integrated into the CIRC's rule-making process without any collision with existing procedures. The assessment report would provide evidence for policy appraisal and bring about a more objective review of an initiative. As regards the content of the report, six aspects need be addressed. Firstly, the problem should be clearly stated. Various dimensions of the problem shall be clarified, including but not limited to the nature, severity, risks, causes and sensitivities. Secondly, the report shall describe the aims of the initiative. It must be ensured that the aims set would not collide with other regulatory aims. In order to prevent the aims being obscurely generalized, the aims need be divided into levels, from general to operational, and long term to short term.[105] Thirdly, possible effective policy options in response to the problems should be presented. Fourthly, quantification, qualitative analysis and monetization should be applied to the evaluation of the impacts of each policy option.[106] All types of potential effects shall be included in the analysis, including direct or indirect consequences, administrative burdens, risks and uncertainties aroused, etc.[107] Fifthly, the report shall weigh up the costs and benefits of different policy options and make comparisons between these options with proper evaluation criteria or analysis methodology.[108] Through the comparison, the options need be ranked. Lastly, a scheme for future monitoring and evaluation of the effectiveness and implementation of the selected policy option should be provided in the report. Indicators which will be used to measure these issues need be devised.

There exist several principles essential to the assessment and the application of them in insurance legislation is laid down as follows. Above all, before an impact assessment is carried out, the proportionate level of the analysis must be properly determined. The proportionality decision relates to what level of resources and what scale of efforts shall be dedicated to the entire impact assessment.[109] It not only refers to the decision on the depth and scope of the analysis, but also involves the decisions on the efforts devoted to all other procedures. Unnecessary efforts which do not match the significance and sensitivities of the policy options should be avoided.[110] As far as China's insurance legislation is concerned, more resources and efforts are required for the formulation of department rules relative to the normative documents. Different normative documents vary considerably

---

105 *See supra note* 99, at 27.

106 *See id.* at 5.

107 *See* HM Government, *IA toolkit: How to Do an Impact Assessment* (Guidance Document, 2011) paras 85-93.

108 The main methods used in the comparison include cost-benefit analysis, cost-effectiveness analysis, and multi-criteria analysis, while the evaluation criteria for policy alternatives, generally speaking, refer to effectiveness, efficiency and coherence. *See supra note* 99, at 45-48; OECD, *Introductory Handbook for Undertaking Regulatory Impact Analysis (RIA)* (version 1.0, 2008) ch 4. Multi-criteria analysis is a useful tool to evaluate non-monetized items. *See generally*, UK Department for Communities and Local Government, *Multi-criteria analysis: a manual* (Guidance Document, 2009) ch 4 (introducing all techniques for multi-criteria analysis and 'the types of application in which they may be used').

109 *See supra note* 107, at 8.

110 *See supra note* 99, at 13.

with regard to significance. The scale, duration and distribution of the likely impacts of a normative document must be studied in advance to ensure a proper level of analysis defined for subsequent assessment. Besides, a stakeholder group shall be established to promote the efficacy of the consultation on impact assessments and other elements involved in a policy decision. Particularly, for developing an impact assessment, consultation is involved throughout the whole process of it.[111] The extent to which consultation participants represent all interested parties has a substantial effect on the achievement of the goals of a consultation. The EIOPA has an insurance and reinsurance stakeholder group with a balanced representation of diverse interested parties. The stakeholder group is maintained under well-defined rules on its composition, appointment, serving period, tasks and powers.[112] Such an arrangement of standing stakeholder group is unavailable in China. Normally, participants would be invited to consultation conducted by the CIRC on an ad hoc basis.[113] There exist no requirements prescribing the criteria or methodology for the selection and scale of consultation participants. Arbitrary decisions on the scale and candidacy of participants materially impair the quality of a consultation. The situation calls for the establishment of a stakeholder group, for the purpose of shaping a well-functioning consultation mechanism which would be conducive to informed impact assessments and policy decisions.

Further, it is important to develop a clear baseline scenario, which refers to the situation where the existing policy situation continues or no intervention was made.[114] When impacts of a policy option are assessed, only net changes, or put into another words, the increments relative to the baseline scenario should be presented.[115] A clear and accurate definition of the baseline scenario is central to the comparison between several policy options. Lastly, quantification and monetization shall be applied to the analysis of the costs and benefits of policy options.[116] In presenting the measurement of costs and benefits, quantitative analysis is preferred if the items under appraisal are quantifiable.[117] Robust analysis and data would lend credibility to the impact study.

---

111 *See id.* at 19-20.
112 The Regulation Establishing EIOPA, § 37.
113 Chapter 5 of the dissertation introduces and analyses the public consultation by the CIRC in great detail.
114 *See Supra note* 99, at 24; *supra note* 107, at 19.
115 *See id.* (HM Government guidance).
116 *See supra note* 99, at 31, 32.
117 *See supra note* 107, at 23; *see id.* at 32.

3. Consolidating Normative Documents

Essentially, the third proposal aims to resolve the disorder of normative documents by establishing a clear linkage between normative documents and the legal acts with superior regulatory status. It is grounded in the fundamental nature of the CIRC's normative documents that this type of legal acts is intended for the implementation of the Insurance Act of China, the administrative regulations issued by the State Council and the CIRC's department rules.[118]

The way in which the system of normative documents is organized is responsible for its ambiguity. The discreteness of the normative documents hinders the ascertainment of the overall requirements prescribed in a specific supervisory area. It is analyzed in the section B III as one of the prominent disadvantages of the normative documents. For the sake of the systematicness and effectiveness of the regulatory regime, it is crucial to form a linkage between an upper-level legal act and the normative documents aimed at providing implementing details in diverse aspects for the legal act.

Loosely speaking, the items functionally comparable to the normative documents in the EU's Solvency II regime are the level-2 and level-3 legal acts, namely the delegated regulation,[119] the technical standards and the guidelines.[120] As a matter of fact, the arrangement proposed here is similar to the organizational structure of the delegated regulation in which the delegated rules related to the various dimensions of the framework directive are sorted and incorporated.

As regards the system of technical standards and the guidelines, it resembles that of the normative documents since the standards and guidelines available are not integrated respectively into a single unity. Nevertheless, on account of the differences with the technical standards and guidelines, the system of the normative documents should not be organized in the same manner. The technical standards and guidelines provide further im-

---

118 *Supra note* 86, § 2.

119 Commission Delegated Regulation (EU) 2015/35 of 10 October 2014 supplementing Directive 2009/138/EC of the European Parliament and of the Council on the taking-up and pursuit of the business of Insurance and Reinsurance (Solvency II) [2015] OJ L12/1.

120 The Solvency II technical standards are issued by means of implementing regulation, separately published in different issues of the Official Journal of the European Union. The guidelines are published on the EIOPA's website <eiopa.europa.eu/publications/eiopa-guidelines> accessed 15 December 2015.

plementing details for the Solvency II framework directive or the delegated regulation thereof. It means that the standards and guidance are associated with two upper-level legal acts. But in the case of the normative documents, the range of the superior legal acts they supplement is wider, which in turn leads the normative documents to vastly outnumber the technical standards and guidelines for the Solvency II. The lack of consolidation of the normative documents poses hindrance to supervised entities in ascertaining the supervisory requirements applicable to specific circumstances.[121] Moreover, it causes the contradictions between some of the normative documents.

Interrelated normative documents should be merged to compose a single regulation serving as the consolidated implementing rules for a particular upper-level legal act. The merger presupposes an association whereby the normative documents involved complement, amend or revoke the elements contained in the same superior legal act. For the sake of the coherence of a consolidated implementing regulation, the merger will entail a coordination of interrelated normative documents in structure. Where new rules on a specific issue are made, they shall be incorporated into the corresponding implementing regulation that combines implementing details for the supervisory area to which that specific issue belongs. The informational impediment or conflicted rule-making stemming from the low systemicness of the normative documents can hence be counterbalanced by the consolidation to a large extent. As a result, discrete normative documents in the same supervisory area will be transformed into coherent component sections of a consolidated implementing regulation. Each legislative act, administrative regulation and department rule will thus be accompanied by a single implementing regulation.

D. *Chapter Conclusions*

The CIRC effectively exercises a rule-making power that exceeds the scope of mandate by the Insurance Act of China, i.e. the framework act in China's insurance legislation. According to the empowerment defined in this

121 Many of the normative documents prescribe conditions or requirements for special circumstances, as distinct from those applicable to general situations. The unsystematic way of making normative documents greatly reduces the transparency of China's insurance legislation, and therefore has a negative effect on the implementation of the normative documents.

act, the legal acts by the CIRC are supposed to provide implementing details. However, given the absence of concrete principles in the framework act in a range of supervisory areas, fundamental elements underlying implementing rules are actually prescribed in the department rules and normative documents issued by the CIRC. Based on the fact, framework principles, which should have been developed through rigorous legislative procedures at the parliamentary level, are largely in the hands of the CIRC. The other problem that exacerbates the situation is that the CIRC makes all the legal acts, regardless of the magnitude of impacts, without any external check. That is to say, the supervisory authority drafts, reviews and approves legal acts alone, even though part of the acts are not of implementing nature. The factors above thus give rise to concerns over the legitimacy and democracy of the CIRC's rule-making activities.

At the first thought of the direction of a reform, introducing the regulatory model of the Lamfalussy Process along with narrowing the scope for delegated acts stand out. Whereas, the upsides of the option are outweighed by the high costs incurred. A practical reform of the insurance regulation system of China should be initiated from the alteration of the CIRC's rule-making process. The emphasis is placed on the imposition of mechanisms for external intervention and quality assurance. The initiatives proposed would not weaken the regulatory power of the CIRC. The role that the CIRC assumes in the regulation regime could be maintained, but should no longer be proceeded without adequate surveillance and control.

Additionally, a main cause for the disorder of the normative documents is determined that the requirements related to the same supervisory area are separately available in discrete normative documents. Consolidation of interrelated normative documents is put forward as a feasible way to resolve the disorder.

Chapter 3. Reflections on China's Insurance Supervisory Objectives

A. Introduction

Supervisory objectives are laid down in the Insurance Act of China,[122] consisting of goals in three dimensions: protecting policyholders and beneficiaries, promoting the development of the insurance sector, and safeguarding social and economic order. The legislators attach equal importance to the objectives - they parallel each other in priority.

Protecting the legitimate interests of policyholders and beneficiaries is a widely accepted objective of insurance supervision in almost all jurisdictions. In China, the interpretation of this objective is consistent with the understanding shared among countries worldwide. As a party to an insurance contract, a policyholder is exposed to counterparty risk. Provision of benefits to policyholders could be disabled due to poor solvency position of insurers. Besides, insurers have a dominant position in insurance contracting, particularly when transacting with individual consumers.[123]

Another supervisory objective relates to the development of the insurance sector. Giving impetus for the sector growth is among the major tasks of Chinese supervisors. Making strategies and schemes for the development of the insurance sector is at the top of the CIRC's agenda along with supervisory tasks.[124] The CIRC and the State Council issue guiding opinions periodically to foster the sector growth and take measures to prompt changes in insurance business. A wide range of issues are involved therein, such as diversification of product lines, expansion of reinsurance market and directions for asset allocation.[125]

---

122 *Supra note* 29, at §§ 1, 134.

123 See Ying Xu, 'Analysis of Establishment of Insurance Supervisory Objectives in China' (2009) 8 Journal of Shanghai Insurance 10 (presenting the relatively weaker position of consumers due to the lack of specialized knowledge and the standardized terms of insurance contracts).

124 CIRC, 'Main Responsibilities' <www.circ.gov.cn/web/site0/tab5200/> accessed 11 September 2014.

125 *See e.g.* the State Council, *Opinions on Boosting the Development of Modern Insurance Service Industry* (Council Announcement No 29, 2014); CIRC, *Planning*

A third objective is to safeguard social and economic order and the public interests. This supervisory objective, which could be applicable to the supervision in any sector, is broad and obscure to some degree. It remains unclear as to how to construe the objective in the context of insurance supervision and how to measure the extent to which the objective is fulfilled.

B. Relationship between Government and Insurance Sector

The reason why promoting sector development is valued by Chinese insurance supervisors largely lies in the historical background and ownership structure of the insurance undertakings in China. In the first decade since the foundation of the People's Republic of China (hereinafter referred to as "PRC") in 1949, the insurance market was effectively monopolized by a wholly state-owned insurance undertaking whose earnings were seized for government treasury.[126] The government assumed the responsibility to guarantee the financial strength of the undertaking and make reimbursements as the last resort.[127] In the following two decades, insurance business, broadly speaking, was prohibited due to the political situation at the time.[128] The ban on insurance business was not lifted until the policy on reform and opening-up was adopted in 1978.[129] A hefty tax was then imposed on the foregoing insurer and the government promised to assume reimbursing responsibility in case of catastrophes excess of loss.[130] From

---

Outline for the development of China's insurance sector from 2011 to 2015 (CIRC Announcement No 47, 2011).

126 The monopolist in the insurance market was the People's Insurance Company of China. At the time, there exist other insurance undertakings. However, they were only authorized to conduct business in rather limited number of regions and their premium incomes are not comparable to the monopolist. Foreign insurance undertakings had very little market share and withdrew from the China market in 1952. *See* Xuejun Zhao, 'An Analysis of China's Insurance Market in the Historical Period Since Foundation of PRC' (2003) 2 China's Economic History Research Journal 74, 75, 79-81; Fabing Zhou, 'Insurance History after Foundation of PRC' (2013) China's Journal of Insurance Intermediary.

127 *See* Cheng Yuan, *A Study on the Insurance Supervisory Regime of China* (1st edn, Nanjing University Press 2011) 87 (noting that the government would settle claims as the last resort in the event of the illiquidity of the insurer.).

128 *See supra note* 126 (Zhao), at 83, 84.

129 In 1979, the State Council approved the operation of insurance business by endorsing and forwarding the Meeting Minutes of the Heads of the Branches of People's Bank of China. China's insurance market was revived in 1980.

130 *See supra note* 127, at 87, 88.

early 1990s, modern corporate and regulatory regime came into existence in China's insurance sector. Changes took place in many aspects, including shareholding structure, business model, government intervention and corporate governance. Foreign insurance undertakings were authorized to enter the market and domestic non-state-owned enterprises were allowed to invest in the insurance sector.

Currently, state-owned insurance undertakings dominate China's insurance market. These undertakings are held directly by the government, by state-owned enterprises (hereinafter referred to as "SOE"), or by state-owned banks. Their business size and market share far exceed non-state-owned ones.[131] A few large state-owned insurance groups are classified as SOEs of vice-ministerial level.[132] Correspondingly, the heads of these insurance groups have a high political status as a vice-minister and are nominated by the government.[133] An important source of candidates for the managerial positions in the largest insurance groups is senior officials from the government departments related to the financial sector.

Throughout history, insurance undertakings in China were closely connected with the government. The government, initially as the solo shareholder of the monopolistic insurer, evolved into the major shareholder of many large insurance groups. However, the essence remains that the insurance sector is largely in the hands of the government and constitutes a significant state-owned asset. An important objective that the government is in pursuit of, in supervising and managing state-owned assets, is to create more value or at least maintain the assets value, according to the clarification on the tasks of the State-owned Assets Supervision and Administration Commission of the State Council.[134] In China, the largest and the most influential SOEs are subject to the supervision by this commission, with the exception of the SOEs in the financial sector.[135] Financial SOEs

---

131 Ping An Insurance Group is an exception. It is one of the largest insurers in China and its biggest shareholder is a foreign investor. *See* Paul J Davies, 'China Approves HSBC's Ping An Stake Sale' *Financial Times* (Hong Kong, 1 February 2013).

132 Yan Li, 'Conjectures about the "Promotion" of the Big Four Insurance Undertakings' (2012) 14 China Economic Weekly 56.

133 *Id.*

134 The State-owned Assets Supervision and Administration Commission of the State Council, 'Main Responsibilities' (official website, 3 November 2008) <www.sasac.gov.cn/n2506699/ n7738060/n7738079/7738171.html> accessed 15 September 2014; *see also* Provisional Regulation on the Supervision and Administration of State-Owned Assets of Businesses 2003, §§ 1, 14 (3).

135 *See id.* (the Provisional Regulation), at § 2 II.

are subject to the supervision by specialized institutions. Along with the supervisory responsibility, the task of promoting value-creation is assigned to the specialized institutions. It accounts for why the CIRC is assigned the task to drive the growth and development of the insurance sector.

With the majority interests in many insurance undertakings, the government derives part of the treasury intake from the profits generated by them. Besides, the government is able to effectively mandate the allocation of the financial resources of the insurance undertakings to help achieve its policy aims, especially short-term targets of the incumbent government. For example, insurance undertakings, on government appeal, invest in the capital market to revive it or invest in infrastructure projects to contribute to urbanization, although the outlook for the investments might be blurred.[136] The growth of the insurance sector would amplify the benefits brought by the ownership in insurance undertakings and the influence over their business.

Abovementioned factors explain why the CIRC sets the task of fostering sector development high on the agenda, and why the Insurance Act attributes equal weight to protecting consumers' interests and promoting insurance sector development. The relationship between China's government and Chinese insurance undertakings impels the supervisors to make tradeoffs between the somewhat countervailing objectives when making policy decisions.

---

136 See *supra note* 125 (the State Council), at para 13, 14; Yan Zhao, interview with Xiaobo Xu, deputy director of the department of fiscal and financial affairs of the National Development and Reform Commission, and Zhiguo Xiong, director of the department of policy research of the CIRC, *'Fostering the Development of Modern Insurance Sector'* (the website of China's government, Beijing, 28 August 2014) <www.gov.cn/wenzheng/wz_zxft_ft42/node_18486.htm> accessed 15 September 2014. The CIRC also takes supporting measures in response to the demand of the government. *See e.g.* Baochen Zhu, 'CIRC Further Relaxes Rules on Insurance Investments: Effective from 1 May' *China Securities Daily* (Beijing, 19 April 2014). Meanwhile, some argue that high risks might be incurred due to the government's intervention in the asset allocation of insurance undertakings. *See* Peike Su, 'Funds of Insurance Companies Shall be Free from Government Intervention' *China Business Journal* (19 July 2014); 'Stock Market Shall Not Always Count on Insurance Institutional Investors' *Beijing Times* (Beijing, 11 July 2014).

C. Grounds for Prioritizing Supervisory Objectives

The insurance supervisory objectives in the EU differ from China largely. Unlike China's supervisory objectives existing in parallel with each other, the insurance supervisory objectives set in the EU are differentiated in priority. They are divided into two levels.[137] The primary objective is to protect policyholders and beneficiaries.[138] At the secondary level, without detriments to the primary objective, the EU insurance supervisors are required to take into account the effects of their decisions on financial stability and the cyclicality of their actions.[139]

The only realm where China's supervisory objectives overlap with the EU's is the protection of policyholders and beneficiaries. Sector development and growth is not within the spectrum of supervisory responsibilities in the EU, as opposed to the situation in China. Safeguarding social and economic order, which is referred to as one of the three insurance supervision objectives in China, is distinct from the notion of financial stability and cyclicality, which constitute a secondary supervisory concern in the EU. By specifying the aspects affected by supervisory decisions and actions, the EU regulators clearly identify the elements to be taken into consideration in the decision-making by the national authorities. This contrasts with the generalized concern 'social and economic order and the public interests' as the relevance of the overarching objective to insurance supervision is unspecified.

---

137 In a paper by Wandt and Sehrbrock, the explicit and implicit supervisory objectives provided in the Solvency II system are analyzed in detail. The explicit supervisory objectives include the policyholder protection as the main objective, with financial stability in combination with the prevention of pro-cyclical effects – as a whole - made as the secondary one. The creation and preservation of fair and stable markets might also be deemed to be an explicit secondary objective, but the credibility of the proposition is limited due to the mere reference to the objective in the non-binding recitals of the Solvency II Directive. Apart from the explicit supervisory objectives, several supervisory objectives are implicitly provided by way of specific regulatory techniques. The implicit supervisory objectives refer to the integration of major insurance directives, the enhancement of supervisory convergence, the facilitation of the amendment of technical rules and the expansion of the leeway in the application of the Solvency II system. *See* Manfred Wandt and David Sehrbrock, 'Legal Aspects of the Solvency II Framework Directive' in Caroline V Schoubroeck et al. (eds), *Over Grenzen: Liber Amicorum Herman Cousy* (Intersentia 2011), 923.

138 Solvency II Directive § 27.

139 *Id.* at § 28.

Should policyholder protection be defined as a prioritized supervisory objective superior to others in China? The dissertation supports the prioritization and gives analyses below. Firstly, policyholders are the group of stakeholders whose interests are directly harmed by an insurer failure. They would incur greater losses than other group of entities connected to the insolvent insurer. Policyholders are not supposed to obligatorily bear risks like shareholders who seek equity risk premium for compensation. However, policyholders have to assume the negative consequences of insolvency on their part. It is difficult for them to exert disciplinary effects on insurance undertakings.[140] Policyholders, especially retail policyholders, are unable to diversify insurance exposures across insurers.[141] In contrast, insurance undertakings would not be financially harmed to the same extent by the insolvency of a reinsurer to whom they cede liability, since they make diversification of reinsurance credit risk and are capable of adjusting the arrangements.[142] An insurer failure could also cause the decline in the market value of other insurers with a similar business model and risk exposures. But, the spillover effects on other insurers are less direct than the impacts on policyholders, and the magnitude of the spillover effects is contingent on firm-specific factors.[143] Policyholders are therefore the group of entities that most deserves supervisory protection. Policyholder protection shall be deemed to be the fundamental value of insurance supervision.

140 Simon Debbage and Stephen Dickinson, 'The Rationale for the Prudential Regulation and Supervision of Insurers' (2013) Bank of England Quaterly Bulletin 2013 Q3, 218, 219.

141 *Id.*

142 *See* Terri M. Vaughan, 'Financial Stability and Insurance Supervision: The Future of Prudential Supervision' (2004) 29 (2) The Geneva Papers on Risk and Insurance 258, 262-263 (presenting the analysis by the National Association of Insurance Commissioners (hereinafter referred to as "NAIC") that "ceding companies typically diversify their reinsurance credit risk"); George E. Rejda and Michael J. McNamara, *Principles of Risk Management and Insurance* (global edn, 12th edn, Pearson 2014) 128-131.

143 *See id.* at 262-264 (Introducing the definition of common shock contagion. It also presented the findings of Brewer and Jackson that both intra-industry and inter-industry contagion effects in the commercial banking sector and life insurance sector are largely ascribed to firm specific variables and "contagion in the life insurance sector was more likely to be explained by firm-specific characteristics than contagion in the commercial banking sector".); Elijah Brewer III and William E. Jackson III, 'Inter-industry Contagion and the Competitive Effects of Financial Distress Announcements: Evidence from Commercial Banks and Life Insurance Companies' (2002) Federal Reserve Bank of Chicago Working Paper 2002-23.

In addition to abovementioned factors, unethical business conduct further necessitates regulatory and supervisory emphasis placed on policyholder protection. "With the fast development, some illegal issues or noncompliances arise, especially, misleading sales, which have become the most salient problem in the life insurance marketplace," said Wenhui Chen, vice-chairman of the CIRC. "misleading sales have severe negative impacts on the reputation and image of the insurance sector and might undermine the basis for the sustainability of a fast sector growth."[144] Unfair or deceptive policy sales and claims settlement practices have been tough issues for a long time for both consumers and supervisors in China. A widespread complaint in China is that insurers or their agents misrepresent products by exaggerating benefits or concealing material disadvantages.[145] Chinese consumers require enhanced protection from the supervisory authority and the criticality of the task exceeds any other one.

Secondly, with three supervisory objectives in parallel, the supervisory authority has to distribute supervisory resources, such as human capital, funding and time, between the objectives in a balanced way. Instead of concentrating on an objective of primary importance, the authority splits its attention into several parts, which would distract the supervisors from

144 Wenhui Chen, 'keynote speech' (the Meeting on Comprehensively Tackling Misleading Insurance Sales, Beijing, 16 February 2012) <www.circ.gov.cn/web/site0/tab5212/info194486.htm> accessed 26 September 2014.

145 In the first half of 2012, the CIRC carried out a selective inspection to rectify misleading sales. A large number of agents, practitioners and executives were held liable for misleading selling conducts. There were 91,000 selling persons being checked in the special rectification program and 26,000 misleading selling cases were found. Besides, among the 3 million insurance policies inspected, about 12.5% of them are problematic due to flawed selling. The striking figures demonstrated the seriousness of misleading selling in China's insurance sector. In fact, the problem remains until today. According to the white paper on financial law cases issued by the Higher Court of Shanghai, the number of insurance dispute cases topped the statistics for financial litigations in 2013. What's more, in the first half of 2014, the number of consumer complaints received by the CIRC about insurance disputes, largely consisting of contractual disputes, rose by 28% compared with the previous year. Base on the facts above, consumer protection must be made a priority for the supervisor, otherwise public confidence in the insurance sector would be substantially impaired. *See* Dong Ding, 'CIRC: 26,000 Insurance Sales Persons Involved in Misleading Selling in First Half Year' *China News Sevice* (Beijing, 27 July 2012); 'Shanghai Higher Court Issues 2013 White Paper: Insurance Disputes Tops' *Laodong Daily* (Shanghai, 4 April 2014); CIRC, *Statistics for Insurance Consumer Complaints in First Half of 2014* (Normative Document of CIRC Consumer Protection Department, No 117, 2014).

the fundamental value of insurance supervision, i.e. policyholder protection. On one side, supervisory resources are limited.[146] On the other side, the authority needs to continually monitor, assess and exercise control of the market conduct and financial conditions of insurance undertakings. It is better to align limited supervisory resources with the priority of objectives in order to ensure that the fundamental value of insurance supervision is not undermined by inappropriate supervisory focusing and resources allocation.

Thirdly, attaching equal weight to all supervisory objectives is problematic where conflicts between the parallel objectives arise.[147] In the case of the CIRC, promoting insurance sector development is rendered equivalent in priority to protecting policyholders and beneficiaries, which implies a high level of regard for the collective interests of insurers. However, the interests of the two groups of stakeholders are inevitably contradictory on some aspects. In rule-making and oversight, the CIRC would have to make compromises to balance the two somewhat competing objectives. Without policyholder protection identified as a preferred objective, it is not mandatory for supervisors to give priority to the objective, particularly where it has to be achieved at the expense of the premium income or operational cost of insurers. In short, the desire to pursue incompatible objectives will induce deviation from the fundamental value of insurance supervision.

Based on the reasons above, it is necessary to prioritize the protection of policyholders and beneficiaries as the primary objective of China's insurance supervision so that supervisory resources and attention will be first and foremost dedicated to ensuring the achievement of this objective. In this way, its fulfillment would not be undermined by the concessions to other objectives.

D. Promoting Insurance Sector Development: A Necessary Objective or Not?

In the preceding section, it is indicated that policyholder protection shall be defined as the primary objective of insurance supervision. Other objec-

146 Jose Viñals, Jonathan Fiechter, et al., 'The Making of Good Supervision: Learning to Say "No"' (2010) IMF Staff Position Note SPN/10/08, 14.

147 *See* Larry D. Wall and Robert A. Eisenbeis, 'Financial Regulatory Structure and the Resolution of Conflicting Goals' (2000) 17 (1) Journal of Financial Services Research 223 (noting Horvitz's theory that Congress assigns multiple goals to financial regulators and they often have inconsistent implications for regulatory policies.).

tives, including promoting insurance sector development, shall be put inferior in priority to it. A further question comes: should promoting sector development be retained as a secondary supervisory objective or excluded from the scope of supervisory objectives? It depends on the extent to which promoting sector development relates to the rationale and the component elements of insurance supervision.

I. Rationale and Means of Insurance Supervision

The necessity of insurance regulation and supervision stems from the special nature of insurance products.[148] In purchasing normal goods, consumers have the capacity to compare quality and price tangibly, understand product specifications and eventually reach informed decisions.[149] However, insurance policies are not normal goods since they deliver a promise to make compensations under specified circumstances at an uncertain future time point. The long delay in functioning makes it difficult for consumers to determine quality at an earlier time.[150] More importantly, the digestion of complicated contractual terms and pricing information requires specialized knowledge in insurance,[151] which results in information asymmetry about insurance products between consumers and insurers,[152] and a disparity in bargaining power that parties to insurance con-

148 Wandt defined insurance as a complex legal product characterized by an exchange of promise to perform for money and based on technical terminology which is difficult for average consumers to well comprehend. *See infra note* 164.

149 In an address delivered by director of insurance with the Consumer Federation of America, the reasons for defining insurance as an essential public good rather than a normal good are presented. J. Robert Hunter, 'Why is Regulation of Insurance Necessary' (Statement before The Task Force on Long-term Solutions for Florida's Hurricane Insurance Market, 14 November 2005).

150 *See also infra note* 164 (noting that "the absence of any physical manifestation of the mere promise to perform hinders a visual inspection as it is possible under contracts for the exchange of goods.").

151 *Id.*

152 The informational asymmetrical problem in the context of insurance fits the definition for the so called "lemons" problem that sellers know much more about the quality or service than buyers. For the discussion about the information problems and market imperfections existing in financial markets including the insurance market, *see* W. Jean Kwon, 'Economic Rationale for Insurance Regulation' in *Insurance Regulation Reflections for a Post-Crisis World* (Report, the Geneva Association, January 2012).

tract are not negotiators of equal weight in the marketplace.[153] Meanwhile, the information asymmetry allows insurers to create their market powers by market segmentation, product differentiation and price discrimination.[154]

Given the complexity and significance of insurance, public intervention is necessary for protecting the interests of the weaker contractual party in the insurance marketplace. Both the market conduct and financial conditions of insurance undertakings are subject to the oversight by supervisors. Market conduct regulation typically encompasses the oversight of rate and form, product type, sales operations, claims settlement and other market-related practices.[155] Supervisory agencies check and assess the fairness of the treatment of consumers in transactions by examining market conducts to reduce the probability that consumers are charged an unreasonable price or excluded from due benefits owing to their disadvantaged contractual position. The solvency regulation shifts the regulatory focus to insurer financial adequacy in order to ensure that undertakings have sufficient technical provisions and capital resources to meet their obligations and prevent disruptions in the provision of effective insurance covers to policyholders. Supervisory efforts on insurer solvency are particularly critical to ensuring an adequate level of policyholder protection in the case of long-maturity insurance covers. For instance, life insurance undertakings which provide annuities for policyholders in the long run are more susceptible to adverse market developments and the policyholders concerned are less able to hedge risk exposures through alternative means.[156]

The two types of regulation entail oversight from different perspectives. However, the ultimate aim of them is consistent: supervisors keep overseeing and exerting control over the aspects closely related to consumer welfare. Firm behavior, products and capital adequacy require continual monitoring as consumers lack the capability to identify flaws in the respects where risks are most likely to materialize. Market integrity is mainly maintained by effective oversight and assessment of market conduct and

153 Spencer L. Kimball, 'The Purpose of Insurance Regulation: A Preliminary Inquiry in the Theory of Insurance Law' (1961) 45 Minnesota Law Review 471, 523.

154 *Supra note* 152, at 14.

155 *See* John Dembeck, 'Insurance Regulation in a Nut Shell' in *PLI's Course Handbook: Understanding Insurance Law* (Practising Law Institute, 2008) 5; *Infra note* 157 (NAIC); the Center for Insurance Policy and Research at NAIC, *State Insurance Regulation* (Publication, 2014) 5.

156 *Infra note* 158, at 5-6.

solvency conditions. In fact, the two complementary regulations comprise the major parts of the micro-prudential regulation which aims to promote the safety and soundness of individual financial institutions with the ultimate objective being protecting consumers.[157] For insurance sector, the intensity and frequency of micro-prudential supervision varies with firm-specific issues based on exogenous risk factors facing an insurer and with potential adverse effects an insurer poses to the integrity of the financial system.[158]

In discussing the components of insurance regulation and supervision, macro-prudential regulation has to be mentioned for its complementary role in financial regulation. Macro-prudential policies and tactics aim to focus on and limit the system-wide risks and distresses, avoiding losses to the real output of the wider economy.[159] In contrary to the bottom-up model of the micro-prudential supervision which addresses risks at the level of individual entities, macro-prudential regulation adopts a top-down approach by mitigating risks arising from interconnectedness, sector concentration, and pro-cyclicality.[160] In fact, macro-prudential issues are valued in EU insurance regulation as they are one of the two major supervisory objectives pursued. In the following subchapter, the dissertation will analyze the necessity of building up macro-prudential supervision for China's insurance sector and discuss the relevance of insurers to China's financial stability.

Based on the discussion of the underlying and component elements of insurance supervision, the dissertation could then proceed to examine to

---

157 *See* the Center for Insurance Policy and Research at NAIC, *Market Conduct regulation* (Brief Abstract of Key Issue, 8 May 2014) <www.naic.org/cipr_topics/topic_market_conduct_Regulation.htm> accessed 2 October 2014 (noting the complementarity between financial solvency regulation and market regulation); Claudio Borio, 'Towards a Macroprudential Framework for Financial Supervision and Regulation?' (2003) BIS working papers no 128, 2-3.

158 *See* the Prudential Regulation Authority (hereinafter referred to as "PRA") of the Bank of England, *The Prudential Regulation Authority's Approach to Insurance Supervision* (Introductory Report, June 2014) 5-7. PRA is the prudential regulator and supervisor for UK's insurance sector. Its supervisory approaches, to a great extent, exemplify the characteristics of micro prudence. What should be noted is that financial stability, as a major concern for macro-prudential supervision, is also included in the range of its tasks.

159 Jacek Osiński, Katharine Seal, and Lex Hoogduin, 'Macroprudential and Microprudential Policies: Toward Cohabitation' (2013) IMF Staff Discussion Note 13/05, 6-7.

160 *Supra note* 157 (Borio) at 2.

what extent promoting insurance sector development pertains to these elements. In order to resolve the question, we need to ascertain the resultant factors of the insurance sector development and make a further reflection on the interplay between these resultant factors and the underlying elements of insurance supervision, which will be conducive to the assessment of the legitimacy of setting sector development promotion as a primary insurance supervisory objective.

II. Irrelevance to Fundamental Purpose of Insurance Supervision

1. General Discussion

As a result of the development in the insurance sector, insurance, as a tool for risk management, will be more widely employed by individuals, households and organizations. Increased demand for insurance will give rise to enhanced risk transfer in the market.[161] If translated into economic indicators, it could be represented by a rise in both insurance penetration and density.[162] For policyholders, more varieties of products would be available to help avoid losses and facilitate transactions by securing property value.[163] From the perspective of insurers, premium income and assets size would increase.

---

161 *See* Peter Haiss and Kjell Sümegi, 'The Relationship between Insurance and Economic Growth in Europe: A Theoretical and Empirical Analysis' (2008) 35 Empirica 405, 408-409 (introducing the function of insurance in providing risk transfer and its positive impacts on economic efficiency). *See also* Damian Ward and Ralf Zurbruegg, 'Does Insurance Promote Economic Growth? Evidence from OECD Countries' (2000) 67(4) The Journal of Risk and Insurance 491 (presenting the benefits from risk transfer and indemnification, and discussing the positive externalities generated by them).

162 Insurance penetration is measured as the ratio of direct premiums to GDP, while insurance density is calculated as the ratio of premium to aggregate population. The two indicators reflect the development level of the insurance sector in a country. *See e.g.* Yu-Luen Ma and Nat Pope, 'Foreign Share, Insurance Density, and Penetration: An Analysis of the International Life Insurance Market' (2008) 11(2) Risk Management & Insurance Review 327. With regard to the statistics for the two indicators for major insurance markets around the world, *see* OECD, *Insurance Statistics 2013* (Annual Publication, 2014) Part I. <dx.doi.org/10.1787/ins_stats-2013-en> accessed 6 November 2014.

163 Marco Arena, 'Does Insurance Market Activity Promote Economic Growth? A Cross-country Study for Industrialized and Developing Countries' (2008) 75 (4) the Journal of Risk and Insurance 921, 923-928

Nevertheless, it should be made clear that the intrinsic nature of insurance products remains unchanged despite the benefits derived from insurance sector development. Above all, insurance products will constantly be a legal product characterized by an exchange of a promise of performance for money instead of an exchange of physical goods for money.[164] Besides, regardless of the stage of insurance sector development, the complexity of the legal product in question will not diminish given the inevitable involvement of a specific contractual arrangement stipulating the rights and obligations for insurers and policyholders with frequent use of legal language and technical terminology.[165] For an average policyholder, it is difficult to comprehend even the most common product differentiations arising from primary risk description, secondary risk exclusion and tertiary risk reinclusion.[166] Furthermore, the uncertainties surrounding the insured objects and the likelihood of losses will continue to exist whatever changes will take place in the insurance sector. Such uncertainties necessitate the sophistication of insurance policies that underpin the risk-bearing capacity of insurers. Insurers are likely to adapt their business operations to market conditions. Nevertheless, they are unable to provide insurance protection without delicately devised restrictions and premium rates.

Based on the reasons above, the conclusions could be drawn that market boom alone could hardly contribute to the mitigation of the information asymmetry in insurance transactions. The rise in insurance demand might lead to adjustments in the conduct of insurance business but would have few impacts on the mechanisms of insurance contracting and pricing. Consumers are therefore unable to rely on thriving market development to prevent being treated under unfair coverage terms.

2. Does Market Competition Help?

It might be argued that with the development in the insurance sector, market competition will be intensified and an intense competition could effectively ensure a high level of consumer welfare. In fact, the trend of market

---

164 Manfred Wandt, 'Transparency as a General Principle of Insurance Law' (joint seminar by the Turkish and German chapters of AIDA on Transparency in Insurance Law, Istanbul, May 2012) 11 <www.aida.org.uk/pdf/Transparency%20book.pdf> accessed 26 July 2018.

165 *See id.* (noting that insurance is a legal product in the form of paper and language, but its linguistic manifestation is not limited to common language.).

166 *Id.*

competition structure is hard to ascertain. Competition is not necessarily to be intensified with sector development. Germany's insurance market serves as a typical example of the obscure competitive tendency. The level of competition is represented to a large degree by market concentration level,[167] as monopolistic practices are more likely to occur where a small number of the leading market players account for the bulk of the market share in a sector than where even the largest players are of relatively small importance.[168] By using the concentration ratio CR_5 which measures the aggregate market share of the five largest entities in the sector, we observe the changing market concentration situation in Germany. In the life insurance sector, the CR_5 declined gradually from 37% in 1980, bottomed at 31% in 2000, and then rose to 38% in 2010.[169] In the same time period, the CR_5 for property and casualty insurance sector experienced a steady increase from 25% in 1980 to 33% in 2010, whereas, the CR_5 for private health insurance sector decreased continually from the peak (57%) in 1980 to 51% in 2010.[170] The fluctuations in the life insurance sector, coupled with contradictory evolvement in the other two sectors, reveal the changeable nature of market competitive trend.

In China's insurance market, over 90% of total market share was held by four largest insurance groups over a long time period in the past.[171] The competition turned abruptly more intensified in 2006, and then the concentration ratio declined continually.[172] The CR_4 for each industry seg-

167 Market concentration level is the extent to which a small number of firms account for the total share or production in a given industry.

168 Gideon Rosenbluth, 'Measures of Concentration' in Universities-National Bureau (ed), *Business Concentration and Price Policy* (Princeton University Press 1955).

169 Gesamtverband der Deutschen Versicherungswirtschaft e.V. (hereinafter referred to as "GDV"), *Statistical Yearbook of German Insurance 2013* (Annual Publication, 2013) 22.

170 *Id.*

171 *See* Zhanghui Xu, 'The Evolvement of Market Concentration in Insurance Sector and Resolution' (2006) 3 Journal of China Youth University of Political Studies 78, 80 (presenting the evolvement of the CR_4 from 1996 to 2003 on the basis of the market share of the largest four insurance companies in China); Lingling Gao, 'Analysis of China's Insurance Market Concentration' (2013) 1 China's Journal of Regional Financial Research 52, 53 (presenting the CR_4 and the CR_8 from 2002 to 2009, respectively based on the market share of the largest four and eight insurance companies).

172 *See id.* (Gao).

ment fell to below 70% in 2013,[173] indicating enhanced competition among insurers. However, it is uncertain how long the decline of concentration ratio will persist. Relative to China, Germany's insurance market has a longer history and is in a more advanced stage. Germany's pattern of competitive evolvement provides implications for the estimation of China's competitive tendency in the coming decade. Currently, in China's market, the several largest insurers that used to possess monopolistic market powers are facing greater challenges from competitors who attained relatively faster growth by virtue of niche market orientation, strategic flexibility or alliance with foreign partners. Despite abated growth and shrined market share, the largest insurers are superior to their rivals in size and financial capacity. As far as they are concerned, it is feasible to rely on scale economy effects and financial strengths to retrieve market share.[174] They are very likely to resort to acquisition to maintain their market position. The dissertation estimates that a phenomenal increase of consolidation will take place in China's insurance sector in the following decade. When a wave of consolidation comes, concentration ratio will rise immediately. By and large, market concentration is unlikely to continually drop to a very low position where even a large insurer possesses an insignificant market share. The largest insurers will make use of scale advantages to prevent from losing leading position to competitors. The concentration level, in the near future, is likely to rebound like the evolvement in Germany's life insurance market.

Even we assume an extreme circumstance where competition is highly intense to the extent that the largest insurer has only trivial market share, market competition still has material limitations in preserving consumers' interests. Market forces cannot exert binding effects on insurer solvency position. The rivalry between insurers do not center on capital adequacy, but on the aspects in relation to price, coverage scope, services, marketing, etc. Additionally, in an intensely competitive environment, insurers are especially vulnerable to aggressive rivalry strategies, such as substantially undercutting competitors, breaking risk limits or greatly raising compensa-

173 The CR_4 for life and health insurance sector reached 64%, with the same ratio for property and casualty insurance sector standing at 69.71%.

174 For the discussion on economies of scale in the insurance sector, *see supra note* 152 at 9 (noting that "in the market with scale economy effects, the larger the entity the more efficiently it can operate" and scale economy effects contribute to market power.).

tions for third-party sellers.[175] These risks, once materialized, could wipe a large portion off an insurer's capital shortly. Further, in long-term competitive interaction, market players could form implicit conventions which induce conformity for common gains and cost saving. These implicit conventions, in many scenarios, acquire effects akin to collusion, harming consumers' welfare.

3. Business Growth and Insurer Solvency Conditions

The development of insurance sector could be best characterized by a common growth and expansion in insurance business across undertakings in diverse segment markets. Business growth is evidently of the interests of all insurance undertakings on account of the fact that more premium income can be generated and more financial resources would be at their disposal. Nevertheless, it is inappropriate to identify business growth with financial soundness since the improvement in business indicators would not necessarily bring about a strengthened solvency position.

For an insurance undertaking, its solvency position is influenced to a great extent by the underwriting and investments it conducts. Both of them constitute the most essential activities by an insurer in the pursuance of insurance business. Insurers derive and increase financial resources mainly through the two types of activities, and the risks that an insurer incurs largely arise from them as well. The quality of underwriting has significant effects on the magnitude of perils covered, the value of insurance liabilities and the amount of loss claims. As for investment, it is a critical means for an insurer to hold adequate assets to back insurance liabilities as a going concern and ensure the ability to meet insurance obligations without disruption. For an insurer, investment is the source of market risk to which it is exposed and also an important factor giving rise to counterparty risk.

To maintain a solid solvency position, an insurer is expected to have proper resources, methods and process in place for sound decision-making and implementation with regard to underwriting and investment. It is likewise important to employ appropriate tools to mitigate the various types of risks inherent in the activities. None of the elements required for

175 *See supra note* 149 at 3 (analyzing that reverse competition drives up the price to consumers as the high cost of compensation made to third-party sellers would be assumed by consumers)

ensuring the quality of underwriting and investment has anything to do with insurance business growth. The growth of insurance business is certain to cause increase in the values of premium income, technical provision and capital requirement for an insurer.[176] It means that, alongside the increased revenue, mounting pressure would be exerted on the liabilities and capital position of the insurer. It completely depends on the capabilities and preparedness of individual insurers to deal with the mixed results. The business growth thus poses a challenge to an insurer – whether it is able to make sufficient recognized assets available to counterbalance the increase in liabilities to the extent that the resultant capital position would be commensurate with its actual risk profile. It is clear that business growth brings about both favorable and adverse conditions for an insurer in financial terms. Its effects on individual insurers are merely limited to the financial aspect, and the remaining aspects of insurance business are not impacted. The business growth together with the ensuing elements cannot directly result in any improvement to an insurer's ability to conduct underwriting and investment. Because it is up to the insurer to decide how many resources are allocated to a particular type of activities and what mechanisms are employed in the conduct of that activity, unless otherwise specified in a regulation. For this reason, business growth is not of relevance to the determinants of solvency position.

The past solvency pattern of China's insurance sector proves the irrelevance of business growth to insurer solvency conditions. Despite the continued and rapid increase in aggregate premium income and asset size of the whole sector in the last two decades,[177] a notable portion of Chinese insurance undertakings, including some of the undertakings with largest market share, underwent solvency crisis over a lengthy period – their capital position was persistently at a level below or narrowly above the regula-

---

176 In spite of the fact that there are distinctions in the calculation method for technical provisions between jurisdictions, it is certain that insurers will have to set aside more assets to make provisions for the increasing loss exposures arising from the growing number of insurance policies. Likewise, the capital requirements imposed on an insurer will be heightened as a consequence of the growth in insurance business, because a higher level of underwriting risk and risks of other types are incurred, which will result in the escalation of capital requirements that are closely associated with the insurer's risk profile.

177 Ying Zhang, 'Successful Transition of Insurance Sector: Strengthening the Role of Risk Coverage and Achieving Rapid Developments' *International Financial News (China)* (16 October 2017) (noting that the aggregate premium income of China's insurance sector sustained approximately a 20% annual rate over the past twenty years).

tory threshold for years.[178] In many cases, a sharp decline in capital position would recur after a substantial improvement in the capital adequacy ratio as a result of capital increase. In recent years, the solvency conditions of most Chinese insurance undertakings turn better – a majority of the undertakings possess a capital position that is continually above the regulatory threshold. Notwithstanding the fact, their capital adequacy ratios demonstrate a high level of volatility. Essentially, the decline, deterioration or fluctuation of the solvency conditions can be ascribed partly to the financial market downturn at the time but more importantly to firm-specific factors, such as risk appetite, risk-taking methods and risk-management capability.

4. Beneficial Mainly on Macroeconomic Level

The insurance sector development brings benefits to the economy. More insurer investments will flow into various fields and more employment will be created, boosting the output of the real economy.[179] In addition, the government also benefits from insurance sector development. As a major stakeholder in the sector, China's government could have more financial resources in place to deploy, aiding the achievement of certain policy aims. But, what should be noted is that these resultant benefits have nothing to do with policyholders' interests. The impetus is merely given to eco-

---

178 Before 2010, a number of insurance undertakings, including life and non-life insurers of different business sizes, showed weaknesses in solvency conditions, which lasted for a few years. Although there was a lack of the aggregate statistical data published by the CIRC about the developments of the average capital adequacy position of the insurance sector over that period of time, it is still possible to find plenty of press coverage of the persistent financial distress that several larger insurance undertakings experienced, the counteractive measures taken by those insurers as well as the regulatory and supervisory responses by the CIRC at the time. For example, New China Life and China Insurance (formerly referred to as China United) are respectively among the five largest life and non-life insurance undertakings in China in over a decade. There was a great quantity of media reports on their failing to meet the regulatory capital requirements in several consecutive years. *See e.g.* Yongjie Sun, 'New China Life Plunged into a Solvency Black Hole: Raising 15 Billion Debt Only 50 Days after a Shrunk IPO' *The Time Weekly (China)* (9 February 2012); Xiaoyu Sun, 'Warning Signal for China United Appears Again' *Investment & Finance* (22 June 2011).

179 Patrick M. Liedtke, 'What's Insurance to a Modern Economy?' (2007) 32 the Geneva Papers 211, 215-216; HM Treasury, *The UK Insurance Growth Action Plan* (Policy Paper, 2013) ch 1 and 4.

nomic developments. There exists no causal relationship between the positive effects generated on macroeconomic level and the financial soundness of individual insurers.

5. Conclusions

With the analysis above, a conclusion is drawn that the insurance sector development is conducive neither to the mitigation of consumers' weak position in insurance contracting, nor to the reduction of the information asymmetry stemming from complicated insurance policies. The authority's actions aimed at advancing this objective are not of supervisory nature, but part of the broader strategies for developing the economy. The actions taken for the fulfillment of the objective do not involve supervisory activities targeting individual entities with regard to market conduct, governance system or solvency conditions. Instead, they are devised and implemented to benefit the whole insurance sector and foster collective business growth.

A prosperous insurance sector could provide impetus for the economic development of China, a large economy in transition. It's natural that China's government attaches importance to the growth of the sector and put it on top of the agenda of the pertinent government department. Nevertheless, assigning the task of promoting insurance sector development to the CIRC is inappropriate by nature. Through the discussion, it becomes clear that setting sector development promotion as an objective can hardly be justified by the elements underlying insurance supervision. The task of promotion involves almost no typical supervisory activity and could cause conflicts in the CIRC's rule-making activities. The irrelevance of the task to the fundamental value of insurance supervision and the potential conflicts arising from it, in combination, render it unnecessary to keep the promotion of sector growth even as a secondary supervisory objective. In other words, it should be excluded from the supervisor's scope of tasks given that the CIRC is not a suitable institution to pursue the objective. Actually, there exists an institution apt for the task, namely the National Development and Reform Commission affiliated to the State Council. The task of promoting insurance sector development could be assigned to the commission since it is exactly consistent with the functional orientation of this commission.[180] Besides, administrative institutions which do not play any

180 National Development and Reform Commission of China, 'Main Functions of the NDRC' <en.ndrc.gov.cn/mfndrc/> accessed 6 January 2015.

regulatory or supervisory role in financial sectors could provide assistance to the commission in this regard.

Promoting insurance sector development falls out of the scope of supervisory objectives under the Solvency II. It is absolutely necessary for the CIRC to follow the practice and adjust the arrangement of supervisory objectives. The elimination of the promotion task will lead the CIRC to be more focused on policyholder protection and less inclined to make concessions for the collective interests of insurers.

E. *Financial Stability: A Necessary Dimension to China's Insurance Supervision*

National supervisory authorities within the EU, in making decisions and actions, are required to take into account the potential impacts of their supervision on financial stability and the procyclical effects.[181] But, the Solvency II also stresses the secondary status of this perspective relative to policyholder protection.[182]

The emphasis placed on the relevance of insurance supervision to financial stability should be attributed to the increasing awareness of the systemic importance of insurers. The evolvement of the financial markets intensifies insurers' interconnectedness with other financial institutions, adding variety to the avenues for investments and transactions. It likewise results in a wider scope of business activities emerging in the insurance sector insofar that insurers engage in more non-traditional and non-insurance activities.[183] Insurers' procyclical herd behavior during the recent financial crisis which aggravated the market downturn,[184] plus the failure of the

181 Solvency II Directive, § 28.

182 *Id.*

183 Traditional insurance business is characterized by several key elements: insurable interest, uncertain and long-term contractual obligations, as well as traditional investment and funding functions. In contrast, non-insurance or non-traditional (NINT) insurance business refers to the activities that deviate from or miss entirely some of the abovementioned features. NINT activities substantially change the risk profile of insurers and increase their systemic relevance. *See* IAIS, *Insurance and Financial Stability* (Paper, 11/2011) 14-17.

184 Impavido and Tower Indicated that insurers' investment decisions could have material impacts on capital market. They analyzed that the sales of equity and other class of instruments have become more widespread in recent financial crisis than the equity market fall between 2001-03. Collective selling contributed to a downward spiral in the market when insurers attempted to liquidate port-

AIG,[185] make the insurance sector identified as a notable source of systemic risk. At the global level, international communities and authorities have developed policy measures and committed to preventing the materialization of the systemic risk triggered by insurer failures. The Financial Stability Board (hereinafter referred to as "FSB"), on request of the G20 Summit, published a list of global systemically important insurers among which there is a Chinese insurer.[186]

Back to the discussion about China's insurance market, it is important, in the first place, to figure out whether a correlation between insurer distresses and financial instability exists, based on the actual model of insurance business in China. The following analysis is intended to establish the existence of the evidence corroborating the relevance of insurers to China's financial stability. In case no compelling evidence emerges, supervisory considerations in this regard are unnecessary. Conversely, if such evidence is established, a further discussion need be proceeded with as for the extent to which supervisory efforts shall be made to ensure financial stability.

I. Reflections on Size and Financial Stability

In China, banking institutions make up the major part of the entire financial system. The total assets of insurers account for 6% of the total assets held by all financial institutions, while banks reach roughly 92% for this

---

folios to bolster their solvency position and balance sheets. *See* Gregorio Impavido and Ian Tower, 'How the Financial Crisis Affects Pensions and Insurance and Why the Impacts Matter' (2009) IMF Working Paper WP/09/151, 43.

185 For the analysis in regard to the AIG failure case, *see e.g.* Etti Baranoff, 'An Analysis of the AIG Case: Understanding Systemic Risk and Its Relation to Insurance' (2012) 31 Journal of Insurance Regulation 243; *supra note* 183 at Appendix A3 and A7.

186 FSB, *2014 Update of List of Global Systemically Important Insurers (G-SIIs)* (Publication, 6 November 2014) <www.financialstabilityboard.org/wp-content/uploads/r_141106a.pdf> accessed 7 January 2015.

measure.[187] The ratio of insurers' total assets to banks' stands at 6.5%,[188] far below the level in the euro area where the same ratio reaches 26% and the level in the U.S. (55%).[189] This reflects the larger role that the insurance sector plays in mature economies.

We could further make a few comparisons between the two financial sectors in China. The total profits of the banking sector are more than 8 times those of the insurance sector.[190] The 'value added' of the banking sector represents more than 5% of the national GDP, while the same ratio for the insurance sector equals approximately 1%.[191] It indicates a much higher net output from banks to the economy.

---

187 The data on the assets of different financial sectors is published by the PBC, China's central bank. As shown in the statistics by China's central bank, the asset of the central bank is included as a part of the aggregated assets of the entire financial sector. The asset of all financial institutions is therefore calculated as the difference between the two foregoing items. *See* the Financial Stability Analysis Group of the PBC, *China Financial Stability Report 2017* (Publications, July 2017) appendix Table 6.

188 *See id.*

189 The percentages are calculated based on the proportional relationship in regard of total assets between all insurance and banking institutions in the two regions. For detailed figures, *see* the European Central Bank (hereinafter referred to as "ECB"), *Aggregated balance sheet of euro area insurance corporations* (report, December 2017) 1; ECB, *Aggregated balance sheet of euro area credit institutions* (report, January 2018) 1; Federal Insurance Office of U.S. Department of the Treasury, *Annual Report on the Insurance* Industry (report, September 2017) 13; U.S. Federal Reserve, *Assets and Liabilities of Commercial Banks in the United States (Weekly)* (Statistical Release, H.8, June 2017) 3.

190 *See* EY, *2016-2017 White Paper on Risk Management in Insurance Sector* (Publication, July 2017) 3; KPMG, *2017 Survey Report on China's Banking Sector* (Publication, July 2017) 5.

191 According to the definition laid down by the World Bank, value added is "the net output of a sector after adding up all outputs and subtracting intermediate inputs. It is calculated without making deductions for depreciation of fabricated assets or depletion and degradation of natural resources." *See* the World Bank, *Industry, value added (% of GDP)* (Data, World Development Indicators, 2014) <data.worldbank.org/indicator/NV.IND.TOTL.ZS/countries?display=map> accessed 9 January 2015. As for the value added (% of GDP) of China's insurance or banking sector, the up-to-date figures are not published by any government department. The dissertation deduces the figures based on the study of the proportional relationship between the historical value added (% of GDP) of various financial sectors as presented in a paper by Zhao et al. and the value added (% of GDP) of the whole financial sector as published by China's National Bureau of Statistics. *See* JianChao Zhao, Chunping Zhao and Zhenjiang Peng, 'The Measurement of the Contribution of Financial Industry to Economic

The comparisons provide a general landscape of the relative size of China's insurance sector. Size reveals the scale of balance sheet items. However, it cannot be viewed as the only determinant for systemic relevance. A financial institution which has very few linkages with other parts in the financial system and merely engages in business with non-financial institutions, whatever size it possesses, is unlikely to cause financial contagion.

The Bank for International Settlements (hereinafter referred to as "BIS") defined financial instability as the condition that results in substantial losses or failures at financial institutions in response to normal-sized shocks and causes 'serious dislocations to the real economy'.[192] The IAIS summarized the views of the IMF, the FSB and the BIS on systemic risk, defining it as the risky events, being caused by 'an impairment of all or parts of the financial system', leading to 'disruption to the flow of financial services' and likely triggering 'negative consequences for the real economy'.[193]

Assuming that the insurance sector could be a source of disturbance leading to financial instability, we are able to deduce from the definitions the key stages in the development of a systemic event that originates from the insurance sector. It begins with an external shock. Subsequently, one or a few insurers with vulnerabilities in this regard are negatively affected by the shock and become severely distressed. Then, the insurer distress evolves into material disruptions in the wider financial system. Eventually, disruptions in the financial system result in losses to the sectors in the real economy.

The intricacy of the process lies in how the rest of the financial system is impacted by crises at one or a small number of insurance undertakings. Whether insurers have systemic importance largely depends on if there exist certain ways in which the financial distress can spread from the insurance sector to other financial sectors.

Growth with the Comparison between China and the U.S.' (2014) 4 Chinese Journal of Financial Regulation Research 77-78; 'Value Added (% of GDP) per Sector' (*National Bureau of Statistics of China*, 2017) <data.stats.gov.cn/easyquery.htm?cn=C01&zb=A0201&sj=2016> accessed 22 February 2018.

192 Claudio Borio and Mathias Drehmann, 'Towards an Operational Framework for Financial Stability: "Fuzzy" Measurement and Its Consequences' (2009) BIS Working Paper No. 284, 4.

193 IAIS, *Systemic Risk and the Insurance Sector* (Note, 25 October 2009).

II. Systemic Importance of Insurers in China

1. An Assessment of Systemic Relevance and Interconnectedness

The dissertation reviews the disclosed reports and financial statements of the five largest insurance groups in China, which in combination represent 55% market share in China's life and health insurance market and 74% market share in the property and casualty insurance market.[194] The aspects pertinent to the systemic relevance of the five largest insurance groups are examined in detail. These insurers are chosen as the study samples due to their much larger balance-sheet size relative to their peers, which implies a higher degree of connections with other types of financial institutions. The business lines and exposures of medium- and small-sized insurers are a subset of the largest insurers'. In case the largest insurance groups are found to show a low level of systemic relevance, a conclusion could be drawn that the financial soundness of insurers would not have notable effects on China's financial stability. The following analysis will serve to reveal where the systemic relevance of Chinese insurers resides and to what extent they could affect other entities in the financial system.

Table 3: Systemic Relevance of Large Insurance Groups in China (figures as of 31 December 2016, unless otherwise specified)

Dimension	Background of Dimension	Actual Conditions
Ownership Structure	– The examination of the dimension is aimed at ascertaining the stakes held by financial institutions in the largest Chinese insurance groups. A high level of shareholding will associate financial institutions	– The controlling stakes in these insurance groups are not held by financial institutions. Banks, asset management companies and other types of financial institutions only have insignificant shares of the insurance groups.

194 As of 31 Dec 2016, the five largest insurance groups in China, ranked in order of premium income, are China Life, Ping An, Anbang, PICC and China Pacific. The data for all insurance subsidiaries of the Chinese insurance groups and solo insurance undertakings is available at the CIRC website, *see* '2016 Fact Sheet for Primary Premium Income of Life and Health Insurance Companies' (*CIRC*, 22 February 2017) <www.circ.gov.cn/web/site0/tab5203/info4060025.htm> accessed 16 February 2018; '2016 Fact Sheet for Primary Premium Income of Property and Casualty Insurance Companies' (*CIRC*, 22 February 2017) <www.circ.gov.cn/web/site0/tab5202/info4060014.htm> accessed 16 February 2018.

	closely with the insurance companies they invest in.	– Three out of the five groups are largely owned by the government, with the finance ministry, state-run investment firms, or industrial SOEs as the controlling shareholders.
Shareholding in Non-Insurance Financial Institutions	– A controlling or even a non-controlling interest in non-insurance financial institutions complicates the systemic importance of an insurer and might amplify its connectedness to the rest of the financial system. – here exists interdependence, to varying degrees, between a parent undertaking and its subsidiary or associate financial institutions.	– China Life owns 43.7% stake in a mid-sized bank and 35% stake in a futures firm.[195] – Ping An holds majority stakes in a range of financial institutions in the sectors of banking, securities, trust, investment funds, financial lease, financial assets exchange, etc. – PICC owns 14% stake in a big-sized bank, 20% stake in a mid-sized bank and 33% stake in a trust firm.[196] – China Pacific does not have shareholding in non-insurance financial institutions. – Anbang owns 17.8% stake in a big-sized bank, 11.63% stake in another big-sized bank, 35% stake in a small-sized bank, 100% stake in a small-sized foreign bank and 66.8% stake in a financial lease firm.[197]
Repo (Repurchase Agreement)	– Repo is a major approach for Chinese insurers to obtain short-term funding. In a repo transaction, insurers pledge financial se-	– The outstanding repo positions held by the largest Chinese insurance groups are shown below.

195 In this context, banks with over RMB 5 trillion (EUR 685 billion) assets are defined as big-sized banks. Those with assets worth more than RMB 1 trillion (EUR 137 billion) and less than RMB 5 trillion (EUR 685 billion) are categorized as mid-sized banks. Banks with assets below RMB 1 trillion (EUR 137 billion) are designated as small-sized ones. The categorization is based on a comparative analysis of the asset scale of all listed Chinese banks.

196 *Id.*

197 *Id.*

	curities for liquidity from other parties, and buy back the securities at a little higher price in a future date. – The size of repo serves as a measure of the extent of insurer borrowing from other financial institutions on China's interbank bond market and stock exchanges where short-term lendings between financial institutions take place.	China Life: RMB 89 billion (EUR 12.2 billion) Ping An: RMB 89.2 billion (EUR 12.2 billion) PICC: RMB 33.1 billion (EUR 4.5 billion) China Pacific: RMB 39.1 billion (EUR 5.4 billion) Anbang: RMB 4.3 billion (EUR 0.59 billion)
Reinsurance Arrangement	– The aspect is concerned with the degree of reinsurance concentration.	– The five largest insurance groups all have diversification of reinsurance arrangements. However, they have not detailed how the ceded insurance policies are divided between specific reinsurers. – China Re Group is consistently the largest reinsurer with about one-third market share in China's reinsurance market.
Derivative Transaction	– It is mainly intended to ascertain the degree of credit default swap (hereinafter referred to as "CDS") protection or CDS-like derivatives sold by insurers since the financial derivatives connect insures closely with other financial market players. The buyer of the CDS will incur considerable losses where the protection seller runs into distress and fails to make reimbursements. – Secondly, other types of derivative trading by insurers should be examined	– Currently, these insurance groups do not engage in CDS transactions. They provide no protection to those demanding covers for hypothetical losses on reference entities without insurable interests. Interconnectedness arising from CDS transactions does not exist in China's insurance sector. – The derivative positions held by these insurance groups are insignificant as compared to other asset items on their balance sheets. Most derivatives are traded for hedging purpose. The overall riskiness is low in this regard.

	to determine the extent of risk exposures and the impacts on other financial institutions.	
Credit and Guaranty Insurance	– In China's insurance market, credit and guaranty insurance, as an instrument to cover counterparty risk and facilitate transactions, mainly includes surety bond, fidelity bond and trade credit insurance.	– One primary insurance product in this category is the loan guaranty insurance. Under the coverage of a loan guaranty insurance policy, the lending institution (the insured) is covered against the loss of principal and interest where the borrower (i.e. the policyholder) defaults on the loan. A loan guaranty insurance cover raises a borrower's credibility and hence underpins an unsecured loan. – Life insurers do not sell this type of products. The non-life subsidiary undertakings of the five largest insurance groups all operate the business. Among them, Ping An Property & Casualty is most reliant on the credit and guaranty insurance line which is ranked second among all of its business lines in order of premium income. For Anbang Property & Casualty, credit and guaranty insurance line ranks as one of the most important sources of premium income as well.
Debt and Equity Securities Holding	– It determines whether a fire sale by insurers in market downturns will substantially exacerbate market conditions and detriment market resilience. – The balance-sheet items at issue include financial assets at fair value through	– The whole insurance sector holds 6.75% of the total debt securities outstanding (by value) in China's financial system. China Life and Ping An are the biggest debt investors among the leading Chinese insurance groups. The former holds 1.77% of the total value of outstand-

	profit or loss, available-for-sale financial assets, held-to-maturity investments and long-term interests in associates and joint ventures.	ing debt market positions, while the latter has 1.43%. – The whole insurance sector holds 3.5% of all equity securities (by value) in China, including stocks and investment fund shares. Anbang and China Life hold larger portfolios than any other Chinese insurance group. The size of their portfolios both amount to above 0.5% of the total market capitalization of China's stock exchanges.
Exposure to Real Estate Sector	– This dimension examines the insurance groups' exposure to the real estate sector. The sector is of significance to China's financial stability and the soundness of its real economy. Banks have huge credit exposures to real estate companies. Financial institutions in general hold massive property portfolios. – For Chinese insurers, the exposures to the real estate sector are mainly formed in two ways. The exposures are established either directly through an investment in commercial real estate or indirectly through an investment in the financial instruments related to real estate. The scale of the indirect exposures is much larger than that of the direct ones. By the investment in real estate and the relevant financial instruments, Chinese insurers act as buyers	– Broadly, insurers are among the biggest institutional investors in China's real estate market. Insurers' exposures to real estate sector become increasingly larger over the years. With regard to the investment in real estate, the commercial property portfolios of the five biggest insurance groups range from RMB 8 to 50 billion (EUR 1.1 to 6.9 billion). By comparison, the size of the investments in real-estate-related financial instruments is greater. The median amount of the debt investment plans held by the five groups, which extend credit to infrastructure and real estate projects, and the median amount of the wealth management products held by them, which include a notable portion of products concerned with equity or debt investment in real estate sector, both exceed RMB 60 billion (EUR 8.2 billion). Two of the insurance groups hold respectively RMB 12.7

	of properties and lenders for property development. – Currently, property bubble has accumulated to a high level in China. House sales slow down with downward pressure on house prices around the country. The burst of property bubble will have severe impacts on the institutional investors with a large exposure to the sector.	billion (EUR 1.7 billion) and RMB 26.9 billion (EUR 3.7 billion) worth of shares of listed real estate companies. – Among all insurance groups, Ping An has the largest exposure to real estate sector.
Related Party Transaction	– The review of this dimension is intended to ascertain the extent to which an insurance group could impacts on its non-insurance financial related parties through transactions of all types. – If the non-insurance financial entities related to an insurance group are found to have material business concentration or large counterparty risk exposures due to the transactions with the insurance group and the failure of such entities is likely to trigger the materialization of systemic risk, the insurance group should be deemed systemically relevant.	– The transactions between the largest insurance groups and their related entities in banking, securities, trust and other financial sectors are reviewed. The finding is that the transactions with all types of related financial entities show few signs of systemic relevance. – In the study of related party transactions, the emphasis is placed on the transactions between the insurance groups and the banking entities in which the insurance groups own minority or majority interests. The largest transactions between these insurance groups and their related banking entities basically consist of deposits, loans and debt investment. Although the three classes of transactions are larger in size than other ones between the insurance parent groups and their related banking entities, they only account for a fraction of the same classes of transactions that the banking entities conduct with all counterparties. The percent-

		age of loans to the related insurance group and the percentage of debt instruments issued by the related insurance group are both well below 1% for each of the related banking entities. The percentage of deposits by the related insurance group ranges from below 1% to near 3%, with the exception of Anbang's deposits in its subsidiary bank which is a small-sized bank.

Source: group-level data collected from 2016 financial statements of China Life, Ping An, Anbang, PICC, China Pacific and China Re; industry-level data collected from 2016 monthly or yearly statistical releases by the PBC, the CIRC, Shanghai Clearing House, China Central Depository & Clearing Co. Ltd. and China Securities Depository and Clearing Corporation Limited.

2. Main Findings

From the analysis above, we have established the evidence corroborating the systemic importance of insurers to China's financial stability, which is discussed below.

a) Shareholding in Financial Institutions

As shown in Table 3, four of the five largest insurance groups hold stakes in non-insurance financial institutions. Some of the shareholdings constitute controlling interests in the invested entities, while a larger part of them are non-controlling interests.[198] The invested entities include a variety of financial institutions, with banks as a focus of the investments.

198 Controlling interest mostly means the ownership of more than 50% voting shares of a company, serving to ensure an effective control of the company. But holding of less than 50% voting shares could also qualifies as a controlling interest in case that the remaining shares are highly dispersed among many investors. *See* Lexicon, 'Definition of Controlling Stake / Interest' (*the Financial Times*) <lexicon.ft.com/Term?term=controlling-stake%2Finterest> accessed 9 March 2018.

The results of the study are consistent with the developments in China's insurance sector over the past several years. A larger portion of the insurance companies aim to evolve into financial conglomerates and achieve synergies by acquisition of the stakes in business entities in different financial sectors. Due to the reason, many Chinese insurers hold minority or majority stakes in domestic financial institutions, and some of the insurers own interests in multiple institutions.

In the circumstance of controlling interests, the invested financial institution becomes a subsidiary of the insurer.[199] The financial subsidiary is expected to operate in a way that best serves the interest of the controlling shareholder, following the group-level strategies. Transactions of various types and financial assistance are certain to occur between the insurer and its financial subsidiary. The insurer, as the parent company, could have overarching impacts on the subsidiary. In the circumstance of non-controlling interests, the insurer cannot exert such a level of control over the invested entity as the case with a subsidiary. However, the associate entity could still be financially impacted, providing the exposure to the counterparty risk arising from the conduct of business with the insurer accumulates.

Suffice it to say that systemic risk will materialize in the event of the insolvency of an insurer, which holds stakes in several sizeable financial institutions with business or financial dependence on it.

b) short-term credit exposures

The short-term credit exposures to the large insurance groups are considerable enough to be systemically sensitive, given the size of outstanding repo positions they hold. With the funding channel connecting insurers and the rest of the financial system, the solvency position of insurers becomes a serious concern for their counterparty institutions. A delay in redemption resulting from insurer capital inadequacy is certain to aggravate maturity mismatch of the lenders. In a market distress, it could plunge the lenders into a liquidity gap.

199 Subsidiary company is defined as 'a company of which more than half is owned by another company'. *See* Lexicon, 'Definition of Subsidiary Company' (*the Financial Times*) <lexicon.ft.com/Term?term=subsidiary-company> accessed 9 March 2018.

c) Fire Sale

Extensive fire sales among insurers would pose material menaces to financial stability. Under normal market conditions, insurers hold the portfolios and expect to gain from interest payments or capital appreciation. However, in exceptional times where the market volatiles or drops dramatically, insurers are likely to seek to liquidate positions promptly at a low market price in order for compliance with capital requirements.

As shown in Table 3, Chinese insurers allocate significant investments to debt and real estate markets. Concurrent fire sales of assets by some big insurers during a financial crisis could substantially amplify market fluctuations and worsen market conditions. Considering the large positions held by insurers in China's debt market, a wave of sell-offs by insurers is able to disseminate financial distresses across the market, magnifying the losses of institutional investors. Moreover, fire sales could have more severe impacts on the real estate market than on the debt market. The poorer liquidity of the real estate market renders the divestiture of investment properties within a short period much harder. In an illiquid market, a prompt liquidation is usually accompanied by a substantial compromise on trading price. Owing to this, widespread fire sales might result in a greater magnitude of market price decline in the real estate market. After a shock, it will take far more time for the real estate market to be restored to the previous state. The intrinsic value of debt securities largely depends on market interest rate and default probability. Providing the two factors are immaterially changed, the debt market will rally shortly after the information of insurers' withdrawing funds is digested. However, the situation is entirely different for the real estate market. In China's real estate market, insurers act not only as a major group of buyers but also as an important group of financiers for the sector. In the circumstance where the insurance sector is reluctant to extend credit, liquidity shortage could be incurred by numerous real estate companies and by large-scale property projects nationwide. If some of the big insurers concurrently divest property assets in response to pro-cyclical regulatory requirements or a common shock, a widespread panic would emerge and other investors are likely to follow the sell-offs on receiving the signal. To sum up, any factor resulting in a common incentive for insurers to make fire sales could bring about market havoc, and even unbearable losses for other market participants.

d) Credit and Guaranty Insurance

Credit and guaranty insurance entails high risks from the standpoint of banks and insurance undertakings. This type of products offered by insurers is basically identical with a guaranty. The beneficiary under the insurance cover possesses an equivalent status to an obligee in a guaranty relationship, entitled to the indemnification from the insurer (guarantor) on policyholder (debtor) default. In China, loan guaranty insurance products are central to the business line of credit and guaranty insurance at property and casualty insurance undertakings. A policyholder taking out the particular type of cover is entitled to loans from a cooperative bank of the insurer without providing collateral. Both individuals and small businesses can apply for the insurance cover. In view of the characteristics of the coverage purchasers, the insurance undertaking actually incurs a high risk of adverse selection. The potential consumers are the entities having difficulty in accessing bank loans mainly because of the inability to post commensurate collateral. The cash flows of small businesses are usually unstable and their risk profiles are difficult to assess compared to larger companies. In a lending underpinned by loan guaranty insurance, the policyholder is obliged to make regular repayments of principal and interests, alongside the payments of high insurance premiums. The high premium rate is charged in return for the compensation of the default risk assumed by insurers. The policyholders are willing to bear the high cost of guaranty insurance since they have to rely on it to enhance their credibility and obtain the access to loans. Inevitably, the financial position of the policyholder would be strained by the periodic cash outflows to a great degree, which consequentially increases the likelihood of default. A second problem with the insurance product lies in the linkage stemming from the cooperative agreement between insurers and banks which causes exposure concentration on the bank's side. In practice, an insurer contracts exclusively with one bank for the business cooperation in a city or a province. The bank, bound by the contract, grants loans to all the policyholders under the coverage provided by the cooperative insurer. As mentioned above, the creditability and financial capacity of the borrowers are not comparable to normal clients in lending transactions, which could give rise to a much higher rate of default. From the standpoint of the bank, the availability of reimbursement by the cooperative insurer has notable effects on the sustainability of the special lending channel. In the circumstances where overdue reimbursements accumulate due to a financial distress of the insurer, banks are likely to have liquidity problems.

At current stage, loan guaranty insurance is an emerging segment market and only several big insurers provide the product. Expectedly, more small- and medium-sized insurers would become new market entrants, competing with the big insurers for the market share. The business partners of the small- and medium-sized insurers are likely to be the banks of similar market position, instead of the biggest banks. In this case, both parties to the cooperative agreement would have lower loss-absorbing capacity and therefore are more susceptible to adverse factors. In market competition, small- and medium-sized insurers might have to build up their edges with more favorable terms than larger insurers in key dimensions such as premium rate and underwriting standards. Nevertheless, these elements will cause high degree of risks for the smaller insurers and their cooperative banks. Consequentially, with the expansion of the loan guaranty insurance market, systemic risk could be increasingly heightened. Without adequate supervisory surveillance or intervention, market-wide losses and financial contagion are likely to arise.

The loan guaranty insurance products analyzed in the preceding paragraph refer to those without government participation. There exist policy-related loan guaranty insurance programs coordinated by the government, which gain increasing popularity around China. It is oriented to enhancing the credit availability of small businesses given the fact that a marked proportion of the entities has a difficulty in obtaining bank loans. In a typical setting of such a program, a provincial or municipal authority would request several banks and insurers to have coordinated participation in the program. For the losses arising from the default in loan repayment, banks and insurers would normally share losses at the ratio of three to seven. The government will make some compensation to the insurers for the excess of reimbursements over 150% of the premiums collected. Insurers are required to charge premium rate below 3%. The government-led programs mainly serve the financing needs of small tech companies, big farms and small start-ups in the government-favored sectors. For the government, the desired default rate is below 5%. In fact, under the given loss-sharing ratio, only when the default rate is kept below 3.8% could insurers avoid incurring losses from this type of government-led programs.[200] Such a low default rate is however unreasonable to expect given the pertinent facts about

200 The default rate is calculated based on the assumption that the aggregate premiums collected just match the claims of the banks. Other conditions are determined according to the typical setting of a government-led program, with the bank loan rate equal to 7.3%. Given the assumption and conditions, the result

the traditional secured bank loan market. Currently, the average default rate for traditional bank loans to small companies capable of providing collateral far exceeds 2%.[201] These small companies that are able to independently secure bank loans are mostly superior to the target companies of government-led programs in terms of asset scale, profitability and stability. Besides, sector diversification makes traditional bank loans less risky in relation to the unsecured loans granted to the companies with sector concentration. The majority of government-led programs have preference for tech start-ups in order for the potential benefits brought by these companies for the transformation and upgrade of the local economy.[202] In addition to tech start-ups, agricultural businesses are also a major target of these programs.[203] The target preferences entail high risks for insurers. As far as tech start-ups are concerned, there exist high degree of uncertainties surrounding the practicability and market acceptance of their innovations. As regards farming businesses, insurers are exposed to the risk of geographical concentration since all the farms covered by a specific guaranty insurance program are in the same region where the program operates. The likelihood of borrower default in government-led programs will be underestimated if the default rate in the case of secured bank loans is used as the benchmark for insurance rate-making. Currently, loan guaranty insurance plans that are independently operated by insurers require an annual premi-

---

'3.8%' approximates the break-even point, with a difference between them representing the insurer's operating cost.

201 *See* Liuran Wuhong, 'Step up Efforts to Meet Regulatory Requirements on Loans to Small Business' (2014) 31 Caixin Century Weekly.

202 Pinyu Yue, 'PBC, CIRC and Other Authorities Issue Policies to Support Tech Companies with Provision of Loan Guaranty Insurance' *Beijing Business Today* (Beijing, 16 January 2014).

203 The programs initiated by several provincial governments demonstrate the feature, for instance, Yunnan province, Zhejiang Province and the city of Chongqing. *See* 'Yunnan Province to Launch Pilot Project of Small Loan Guaranty Insurance in 2014' (*Yunnan Express*, 15 January 2014) <www.yn.gov.cn/yn_ynyw/201401/t20140115_13158.html> accessed 12 January 2015; Deliang Yue, 'Zhengjiang to Expand Provision of Small Loan Guaranty Insurance: Facilitating Credit Borrowing for Small Business' (*Xinhuanet*, 14 September 2014) <news.xinhuanet.com/fortune/2014-09/14/c_1112472523.htm> accessed 12 January 2015; Chi Zhang, 'Chongqing to Launch Pilot Project of Small Loan Guaranty Insurance: Maximum Three Million' (*Xinhuanet*, 2 June 2012) <news.xinhuanet.com/fortune/2012-06/02/c_112099800.htm> accessed 12 January 2015.

um rate from 6% to 24%, conditional on the risk profile of applicants.[204] In comparison, government-led insurance programs are much underpriced. The low proportion of losses retained by participating banks and the insufficient government indemnification for excessive losses, in combination, could hardly compensate the high risks shifted to participating insurers. The losses from government-led insurance programs are likely to enlarge across the insurance sector with more municipal and provincial authorities initiating such programs, which could contribute to the accumulation of systemic risk.

e) Reinsurance Concentration

Reinsurance concentration is a potential systemic risk concern. Normally, a Chinese insurer maintains reinsurance arrangements with several reinsurance providers, but ceded loss exposures are not split between these reinsurers in a balanced way. Market data shows the largest portion of the policies ceded by primary insurers goes to a single reinsurer, China Reinsurance Group (referred to below as China Re), which has approximately a third of China's reinsurance market share.[205]

Compared to internationally active reinsurers that pool idiosyncratic risks at global level, China Re lacks the benefits of geographical diversification. Almost all of its loss exposures originate from China. So far, geographical concentration has not imposed significant negative effects on it since the overall insurance penetration across the country lies at a very low level.[206] But, with the increasing insurance awareness and demand, its vul-

---

204 The premium rate for this product varies among insurers. Averagely, the policyholders assume the premium cost equal to 10 – 20% of the loan amount. Ping An P&C provides the product at a monthly rate of 1.8%. *See* Wenyan Xu, 'Multiple Insurers Enter Personal Loan Guaranty Insurance Market' *Ningbo Evening News* (Ningbo, 26 February 2013) (introducing the market conditions of personal loan guaranty insurance in Ningbo city); Gaifang Gao, 'Yidai Enters into O2O Market: Ping An Accelerating Strategic Deployment' *China Securities Journal* (2 December 2014).

205 *See infra note* 329, at 47; China Reinsurance Group, *Annual Report 2014* (Publication, 2015) 1; 'China Re Releasing 2016 Business Results: Stable Business Conditions and Market Position' (*Xinhuanet,* 31 March 2017) <www.xinhuanet.com/money/2017-03/31/c_1120734513.htm> accessed 26 February 2018.

206 The average insurance penetration rate nationwide is 4.16% as of the end of 2016. *See* Monetary Policy Analysis Group of the PBC, 2017 *Financial Performance of Regions in China* (Report, 2017) 47 <www.pbc.gov.cn/zhengcehuobisi/1

nerability to catastrophe losses would continually increase and the potential risks it poses to intra-industry stability will grow dramatically. Each year, various severe natural disasters occur in different parts of the big nation, which causes businesses and households to incur huge direct economic losses. However, due to the low insurance density of China,[207] indemnities from insurers are negligible relative to loss amounts. The average ratio of insurance indemnities to loss amounts falls below 1%, while the same ratio amounts to 30% to 40% in mature economies.[208] The low ratio explains why (re)insurers have fairly limited loss exposures even in the event of a severe catastrophe resulting in huge losses over a large region. Nevertheless, it is worth noting that the importance of catastrophe insurance is increasingly recognized by the government, businesses and households after the occurrence of numerous severe disasters in recent years. For example, in many regions where severe natural disasters occur with high likelihood, municipal governments begin to purchase catastrophe insurance from primary insurers for the whole local population so that public expenditures on rescue and indemnities would be reimbursed to a great extent.[209] Surely, more acquisition by local authorities of catastrophe insurance coverage means considerable business opportunities for China's insurance sector. However, a high level of adverse selection is difficult to be averted. Consequentially, for China Re, more loss exposures with high geographical concentration would be ceded from primary insurers. If China Re's market position is not weakened, the scenario the reinsurer is likely to encounter in the future is that the occurrence of a severe natural disaster to which many accepted cessions are exposed materially impairs its solvency position.

In terms of the intra-industry interconnections, the banking sector is characterized by horizontal connections between banking institutions due

---

25207/125227/125960/126049/3356630/3356459/index.html> accessed 4 May 2018.

207 Currently, China's insurance density stands at 325 USD per capita as of the end of 2016. *See id.*

208 Yang Xu, 'Junbo Xiang: The Reimbursements for Catastrophe Losses Less Than 1% of Actual Loss Amounts' (*Xinhuanet*, 11 March 2014) <news.xinhuanet.com/politics/2014-03/11/c_119708822.htm> accessed 12 January 2015.

209 *See e.g.* Yangteng Yang, 'Shenzhen Begins to Implement Catastrophe Insurance Program' *Economic Daily* (Shenzhen, 10 July 2014); Yuanyuan Fang, 'Ningbo Government to Purchase Catastrophe insurance Coverage at the Cost of 38 Million for Residents: Starting from 11th ' (*People's Daily Online*, 10 November 2014) <nb.people.com.cn/n/2014/1110/c365604-22864147.html> accessed 12 January 2015.

to the inter-bank lending, while vertical connections between reinsurers and primary insurers on the basis of reinsurance arrangements are observed in the insurance sector.[210] Horizontal connections between primary insurers are weak. In an insurance market where reinsurance market share is distributed evenly, the distress or failure of a reinsurer will not cause industry-wide instability. However, in the case of China's insurance sector, given the marked reinsurance market concentration, the dominant reinsurer establishes wide vertical connections with most primary insurers and its financial soundness has material effects on the stability of the entire insurance sector. If China Re falls into crisis, its reimbursing capacity will be sharply weakened and might be unable to promptly deliver on the reinsurance recoverables of the ceding insurers. A primary insurer constantly holds the liability to perform contractual obligation to the claimants, irrespective of whether the insurance policy has been ceded. Where premiums have been ceded to the reinsurer, the collected premiums are unavailable to the insurer to back technical provisions. Given the structure of reinsurance arrangements, failure to receive reinsurance recoverables is likely to give rise to the financial distress of the ceding insurer. For this reason, the financial crisis at China Re will have immediate negative impacts on a large proportion of primary insurers in China, leading to industry-wide instability.

III. Conclusions

The analysis above reviews the major channels through which the financial distress of insurers spreads to the rest of China's financial system. Except for reinsurance concentration, all the dimensions relate to the associations between insurers and other financial institutions, banks in particular. These dimensions entail high systemic risk. Contagion to other parts of the financial system is most likely to arise through these channels due to distressed conditions of insurers. As for reinsurance market concentration, although it seems a risk factor that might merely trigger instability within the insurance sector, the intra-industry instability with high severity has the potential to cause contagion through existing connections with the rest

210 See IAIS, Reinsurance and Financial Stability (Report, July 2012) 8-11 (defining the interconnections between cedants, reinsurers and retrocessionnaires as a horizontal structure which contains no feedback mechanisms and 'stifles the potential proliferation of shocks across the whole insurance sector'.).

of the financial system. In reviewing the systemic relevance of China's insurance sector, it is found that there do exist individual insurers of high systemic importance. Ping An and China Life are identified as the most systemically important insurers for their salience in the measurements as shown in Table 3.

Supervisory efforts committed to ensuring financial stability is in the interests of insurance consumers. Components of the financial system are so interconnected that distress at one part of the system could give rise to losses at the wider parts, which could in turn reversely affect the original part. The financial contagion as a result of the interconnections could amplify the losses at extensive entities and complicate the resolution of a systemic crisis. Insurance consumers are certain to be subjected to higher risk of losses in case that an already distressed insurer faces a deterioration in financial conditions because of the spillover effects of other financial institutions in crisis.

The systemic importance of insurers to China's financial stability has been corroborated. Regard for financial stability should be enshrined in the Insurance Act of China as a supervisory focus secondary to policyholder protection, as is the supervisory practice adopted in the EU. By including financial stability as a component element in the supervisory objectives, it is granted the significant status in insurance supervision which it deserves. It is vital that the CIRC prudently evaluate the potential impacts of their decisions and actions on the stability of the entire financial system. Without adequate considerations in this respect, regulators and supervisors might impose requirements that unintentionally magnify systemic risk. In many circumstances, supervisory requirements create incentive for insurers to take procyclical actions to minimize cost or maximize payoff in response to market movements. A typical example is that insurers could be induced to liquidate positions at the time of declining asset prices to avoid the non-compliance with solvency requirements or the imposition of tougher capital requirements, which results in a further decline in asset price. Besides paying regard to the potential negative byproducts of its supervisory decisions and actions, the CIRC should also take measures aimed at ensuring financial stability on its own initiative, contributing to sustained financial integrity from the perspective of insurance supervision. It could exercise authority to make and enforce rules that specifically serve the needs of financial stability, since the mitigation of systemic risk requires the coordinated efforts of supervisory authorities in all financial sectors.

Preservation of financial stability is expected to be adopted as a secondary objective of China's insurance supervision, replacing the obscure objective 'safeguarding social and economic order and the public interests'. Confining the supervisory objectives to the context of financial system is of more practicality to insurance supervision than generalizing about them.

F. Chapter Conclusions

In terms of setting supervisory objectives, Chinese insurance supervisors could adopt changes in alignment with the EU Solvency II system. The supervisory priority should be given to the protection of policyholders and beneficiaries to ensure that supervisory focus and resources are concentrated on it. Other objectives should not be made equal to policyholder protection in priority, otherwise they can be legitimately achieved at the expense of policyholders' interests on the grounds of the need for balance between parallel supervisory objectives.

The CIRC's promoting insurance sector development is not of supervisory nature, since the necessity of the task is incoherent with the rationale for insurance supervision. There exists little causal relationship between the growth of insurance sector and the enhancement of policyholder protection. The development of Insurance sector can lead to neither changes in the insurance contracting and pricing mechanism, nor steadiness of insurer solvency position. Given that the task of sector development promotion causes conflicts of interests at the CIRC in making decisions, it should therefore be carried out by a non-supervisory institution.

Chinese supervisors need show due regard for financial stability, in particular the potential impacts caused by supervisory rules and decisions, since the insurance sector is found to have systemic importance to China's overall financial stability. Preservation of financial stability could be included as a supervisory objective secondary to policyholder protection. Apart from the due regard for the procyclicality and systemic impacts of its policies and actions, the CIRC is also expected to contribute to financial stability on its own initiative through rule-making and other supervisory activities.

Chapter 4. Scrutinizing CIRC's Supervisory Review Process

A. Components of China's Supervisory Review Process and Comparison with the Counterparts in EU

As provided for in the guidelines on supervisory review process,[211] the NCAs in the EU are advised to carry out supervision by accomplishing agendas in three stages, sequentially, risk assessment framework, detailed review and supervisory measures. At each stage, various analytical tools and methods are used to evaluate and form conclusions about each insurance undertaking's risk profile and deficiencies.

Comparatively, the structure of the CIRC's supervisory review process is simpler. The process comprises two stages: supervisory assessment and supervisory measures. At the stage of supervisory assessment, the means whereby the CIRC conducts review are categorized as on-site inspections and off-site appraisals.[212] This supervisory arrangement is akin to the approaches employed in the detailed review stage of the Solvency II supervisory review process.[213] However, they are distinct from each other in nature. For the EU supervisors, detailed review is conducted at a later stage of the entire review process and premised on the risk assessment outcome obtained at the prior stage. The two types of tools are used to focus on specific risk areas which are identified at the risk assessment framework stage. In China, on-site and off-site supervisory activities are conducted at the supervisory assessment stage, which constitutes the only stage involving evaluation and classification throughout the supervisory review process. Supervisory measures are premised on the outcomes of the on-site and off-site activities carried out at the supervisory assessment stage.

211 EIOPA, *Guidelines on Supervisory Review Process* (EIOPA-BoS-14/179 EN); *see also* Solvency II Directive, § 36.

212 The Administrative Rules on Insurance Undertakings 2009, § 59.

213 *See supra note* 211 (Guidelines), at §§ 25-32; *see also* Solvency II Directive, § 36.

I. The Anatomy of the Supervisory Assessment Stage

For this reason, the supervisory assessment stage in the CIRC's supervisory review process differs entirely from the detailed review stage embedded in the Solvency II despite the resemblances in regard of means. Functionally, the former is similar to the risk assessment framework stage as provided in the Solvency II Guidelines.

At the stage of supervisory assessment, analyses and appraisals are made on the basis of the input from several sources: (i) the supervisory reporting made by insurance undertakings; (ii) the information requested by the CIRC from insurance undertakings; (iii) the disclosed information of insurance undertakings; (iv) the opinions from external entities commissioned by the CIRC to make inspections or evaluations; (v) the information from rating agencies; (vi) other information the CIRC considers relevant. Among them, type (i) is comprised of a wide range of reports required by the supervisory authority, including periodical reports related to various areas, reports under pre-defined circumstances, insurer own assessments, stress test results, etc. Type (iv) refers to the scenario where a third-party institution is authorized by the CIRC to assess specified areas of certain insurance undertakings using its expertise. Rating agencies have the legal obligation to submit relevant documents as required by the CIRC and notify the supervisory authority of the non-compliances they identify.[214] Generally speaking, there are no obvious distinctions between China and EU in regard to the input to supervisory review process, with the exception that the information shared within the supervisory college is taken as an additional source in the EU.

The CIRC exercises on-site inspections to ascertain the extent of the compliance, authenticity and effectiveness of the mechanisms functioning inside an insurance undertaking. Regular or ad-hoc on-site inspections made at the discretion of the CIRC encompass evaluation of insurance undertakings in various risk areas. In opposition, on-site supervisory activities are not supposed to be carried out at the corresponding stage in the Solvency II regime, i.e. the risk assessment framework stage.

From the perspective of Chinese supervisors, off-site appraisals compose the major part of the evaluations conducted at the supervisory assessment

214 CIRC, *The Supervisory Rules on the Solvency Position of Insurance Undertakings No 15: Credit Rating of Insurance Undertakings* (Normative Document, No 22, 2015), §§ 19, 20.

stage. The off-site appraisals consist of the ongoing evaluation, integrated risk rating and theme-focused evaluations.

Firstly, ongoing evaluation is defined as the continuing assessment of insurance undertakings in the ordinary course of supervision. After receiving reports and collecting data, analysis is made to examine the individual conditions of an insurance undertaking in regard to the particular aspects that the reports or data concern. Evaluations are conducted based on criteria or methods selected by the supervisory authority. If risks or non-compliances are identified, follow-up actions or supervisory measures would be taken. The ongoing evaluation approximates the high-level assessment which is one of the essential components of the Solvency II risk assessment framework.

Secondly, the integrated risk rating is intended to reflect the solvency risk profile of an insurer on a quarterly basis. Statutorily, the CIRC categorizes the risks inherent in solvency position into two kinds: quantifiable risks and difficult-to-quantify risks.[215] The quantifiable risks include insurance risk, market risk and credit risk, while the difficult-to-quantify risks refer to operational risk, strategic risk, reputational risk and liquidity risk.[216] The integrated risk rating addresses the two kinds of risks with different approaches and purposes. With regard to the quantifiable risks, solvency ratios are used to evaluate insurer capacity to withstand the adverse impacts if risks materialize,[217] whereas the likelihood and severity of the risk exposures are not measured. As for the difficult-to-quantify risks, a combination of quantitative and qualitative indicators are employed to measure the degree to which an insurer is exposed to these risks, but an evaluation of insurer risk-bearing capacity for the risk areas would not be performed. As a result, each insurance undertaking would be assigned scores based on the performance and conditions in abovementioned as-

215 CIRC, *The Supervisory Rules on the Solvency Position of Insurance Undertakings No 10: Integrated Risk Rating* (Normative Document, No 22, 2015), § 4(2).

216 *See id.*

217 To measure the loss-absorbing capacity, two solvency ratios are devised, including core solvency ratio and aggregated solvency ratio. The former is defined as the ratio of core capital available to minimum capital required, while the latter is the ratio of the sum of core capital available and supplementary capital available to minimum capital required. A higher level in the ratios means a lower probability of financial distress incurred due to adverse changes or events. The escalation in ratio level will therefore lead to a better outcome for the integrated risk rating. *See* CIRC, *The General Framework of China's Second-Generation Solvency Supervisory System* (Normative Document, No 42, 2013) Sec 4 (1).

pects. The undertakings that are determined as having similar solvency risk profile are classified into the same risk-rating grade and would be subject to supervisory actions or measures of which the intensity is proportionate to the grade. The definition for each grade is shown in Table 4.

Table 4: Explanations for Integrated Risk Rating Grades

Grade	Grade Definition
A	Compliant with solvency coverage requirements, and insignificant degree of operational risk, strategic risk, reputational risk and liquidity risk
B	Compliant with solvency coverage requirements, and low degree of operational risk, strategic risk, reputational risk and liquidity risk
C	– Not compliant with solvency coverage requirements; or – Compliant with solvency coverage requirements, but with high degree of operational risk, strategic risk, reputational risk or liquidity risk
D	– Not compliant with solvency coverage requirements; or – Compliant with solvency coverage requirements, but with very high degree of operational risk, strategic risk, reputational risk or liquidity risk

Source: CIRC, The *Supervisory Rules on the Solvency Position of Insurance Undertakings No 10: Integrated Risk Rating* (Normative Document, No 22, 2015)

The functional status of the integrated risk rating of the China Risk Oriented Solvency System (hereinafter referred to as "C-ROSS") is analogous to the Solvency II undertaking risk classification.[218] The two approaches serve similar purposes: determining risk profile of insurers, in particular, the risks associated with financial and solvency conditions. They also overlap in the evaluation method given that both attach importance to the analysis of the processes, structures and functions within an insurance undertaking. Notwithstanding the common elements, there exists a major difference between them, which resides in the evaluation focus. Throughout the process of the C-ROSS integrated risk rating, supervisory efforts are largely committed to identifying those difficult-to-quantify risk factors. Whereas, the focus of the Solvency II undertaking risk classification rests on the determination of the extent to which an insurance undertaking is able to withstand negative effects triggered by the materialization of risks. The

218 For the details of undertaking risk classification, *see supra note* 211 (Guidelines), at § 17; *see also* Solvency II Directive, § 36.

difference leads to the disparity in the indication of evaluation results. The conclusion of the former is made on riskiness, while the latter's is laid on the level of resistance to adverse conditions. Although risk-bearing capacity is also factored in China's analytical approach, the level and scope of such analysis is relatively limited. The EU's approach, as compared to its Chinese counterpart, could better reveal an insurance undertaking's capability to assess, monitor, manage and report the risks it faces.

Thirdly, the CIRC applies theme-focused evaluations to several areas where Chinese insurance undertakings are conventionally considered to show substantial weaknesses. In the judgment of the CIRC, particular concerns shall be given to these areas and an escalation in oversight intensity is necessary. In the Solvency II supervisory review process, the same kind of evaluation is regarded as part of the detailed analysis.[219] The EU insurance supervisors reach the decision on the specific issues treated with theme-focused analyses based on the findings of the risk assessment framework. The themes of the analyses vary depending on the deficiencies identified. In contrast, the issues dealt with through the theme-focused evaluation remain unchanged in China because they are confined to a narrow scope of risk areas where regulations have explicitly provided for the application of the evaluation technique. For this reason, the theme-focused evaluation conducted by Chinese supervisors fails to respond dynamically to the changing pattern of risk areas across the insurance sector.

At the moment, four areas are subject to the theme-focused evaluation, as presented below. (i) Solvency risk management:[220] The purpose is to evaluate on a yearly basis the insurance undertaking's capacity to assess and manage various types of risks that have relevance to solvency position.[221] It is necessary to clarify that the evaluation does not overlap with the integrated risk rating since the evaluation mainly concerns the ability of an insurance undertaking to analyze its own risk profile and to control risks. The quality of risk-management system constitutes the analytical focus.

---

219 *See Supra note* 213.

220 *See* CIRC, *The Supervisory Rules on the Solvency Position of Insurance Undertakings No 11: Requirements and Assessments of Solvency Risk Management* (Normative Document, No 22, 2015).

221 The evaluation is also intended to help determine the level of capital that each insurance undertaking should hold against a specific risk. The evaluation outcome actually serves as an input to the formula for the determination of the capital held for the risk that a failure in the identification and the control of quantifiable or difficult-to-quantify risks might arise due to the deficiencies of governance system. *See id.* at §§ 1, 3(3), 100.

However, the evaluation outcome suffices to determine neither the insurer capability to absorb losses on risks materializing nor the magnitude of potential loss exposures. The theme-focused evaluation is hence complementary to the integrated risk rating. In the evaluation, metrics and criteria are used to assess the basis, environment, objectives and tools that insurers maintain in place for risk management. Accordingly, grading is utilized to reflect the extent of compliance with the supervisory requirements in relevant areas. The aggregated score an insurer is assigned indicates its ability to assess and manage the risks intrinsic to solvency position, and supervisory actions would be taken to foster correction. (ii) System of governance:[222] The quarterly evaluation in this supervisory area is targeted at the conditions of the governance system of an insurance undertaking. The outcome is derived on the basis of the scores in two parts: insurer own evaluation and supervisory evaluation. The former involves the assessment of the existing structure and the functioning of the governance system, while the latter ascertains the actual degree of conformity to all of the applicable binding rules and the non-binding guidance. On the grounds of the evaluation outcome, insurers are classified and can incur supervisory measures tailored to their classifications. The outcome might be taken into account in reaching supervisory decisions on the authorizations for certain business activities. (iii) Investment:[223] The CIRC adopts a semi-annual evaluation of the internal control quality and the compliance conditions in the area of investments. A same baseline score is prescribed for each insurance undertaking. Scores would be added or subtracted from the baseline for beneficial practices or non-compliances identified. The addition or subtraction varies depending on the significance of such practices or non-compliances. (iv) Market conduct: For the purpose of facilitating market discipline, several important aspects of insurance business practices are evaluated on a semi-annual or annual basis, including sales practices,[224] business conditions,[225] service quality,[226] etc. Each of the evaluation is conducted using a

---

222 CIRC, *Provisional Rules on the Evaluation of Corporate Governance of the Insurance Institutions with Legal-Person Status* (Normative Document, No 112, 2015).

223 CIRC, *Supervisory Rules on the Scoring of Internal Control and Compliance of Insurance Funds Allocation* (Normative Document, No 54, 2014).

224 CIRC, *The Evaluation Methods for the Overhaul of the Misleading Sales in the Personal Insurance Sector* (Normative Document on Trial, No 105, 2012).

225 CIRC, *The Set-up of Metrics for Evaluating the Business Conditions of Insurance Undertakings* (Normative Document on Trial, No 80, 2015).

226 CIRC, *The Supervisory Rules on the Evaluation of the Business Services of Insurance Undertakings* (Normative Document on Trial, No 75, 2015).

set of metrics or ratios as required in the relevant normative document. Insurance undertakings will be either classified into levels or graded on the basis of the conditions in relevant aspects. Unlike other theme-focused evaluations, they will not lead the undertaking to incur supervisory measures. The evaluation results will be disclosed in order for more informed selections and analyses by consumers and market entities.

II. Further Distinctions

In preceding sections, the three methods used by the CIRC to conduct off-site appraisals are introduced and compared with the methods adopted in the Solvency II risk assessment framework. Besides the differences mentioned, there exist two more issues. Firstly, the EU supervisors are required to implement an assessment of not only the risks insurance undertakings are exposed to but also the risks posed by them to other stakeholders. Alongside the risk classification, it is included in the risk assessment framework an impact classification determining the potential impacts of an insurance undertaking on its policyholders, beneficiaries and the market.[227] The main aim of the classification is to ascertain the magnitude of the impacts inflicted by an insurer failure. By virtue of the outcome for the impact classification, the EU supervisors are able to be informed of each undertaking's importance to the market and the stakeholders' sensitivities to the various activities of an undertaking, so that they could align supervisory policies with the impacts of an undertaking. What should be noted is that such an analytical perspective is absent in the CIRC's supervisory review process. Secondly, classification is applied in both China's and the EU's assessment process, but the classification outcomes are used for distinct purposes. According to the rules issued by the CIRC, the classification or grade is used to make decision on supervisory measures, while it is used as an input to the supervisory plan in the Solvency II risk assessment framework. The supervisory assessment activities carried out by the CIRC conclude with classification outcomes. In opposition, according to the Solvency II requirements, a classification lays the foundation for detailed assessment activities in the subsequent review stage.

227 *Supra note* 211 (Guidelines), at § 15; *see also* Solvency II Directive, § 36.

III. The Stage of Supervisory Measures

1. Types of Supervisory Measures

At the second stage of the CIRC's supervisory review process, supervisory measures are imposed on the basis of the assessment outcome derived from the on-site and off-site activities conducted at the first stage. The supervisory measures taken by the CIRC could be decomposed into three kinds, including preventive measures, corrective measures and disciplinary measures.

Preventive measures aim to make an insurance undertaking aware of its weaknesses and prompt actions to remedy the weaknesses for the purpose of preventing the occurrence of material non-compliances. For instance, Chinese supervisors might communicate significant weaknesses or risks identified to the management of an insurance undertaking, requiring immediate improvements. Additionally, preventive measures are also used to exert supervisory intervention in stressed scenarios to avoid the deterioration in financial conditions or the magnification of adverse impacts. A typical example is that a suspension of underwriting new policies is likely to be imposed in the circumstance where an insurance undertaking is found to be deficient in solvency.[228]

Corrective measures are the supervisory interventions which require insurance undertakings to take counteractive or rectifying actions for the purpose of restoring them to compliance with existing regulations. Requirement to increase capital is a straightforward illustration for corrective measures in the circumstance of inadequate solvency position.[229]

Disciplinary measures are intended to sanction those insurance undertakings violating rules and discipline the responsible executives by penalties of administrative or financial nature, such as a reduction in business lines[230] and a revocation of qualifications.[231]

However, it could be inappropriate to make assertions about the nature of a supervisory measure without due regard for the situation of imposition. As an example, suspension of underwriting new policies would be deemed to be a measure to prevent the assumption of more obligations to new policyholders on the condition that it is inflicted on an insurer unable

---

228 *See* supra note 29, at § 139.
229 *Id.*
230 *See* supra note 29, at § 165.
231 *Id.* at § 173.

to satisfy capital adequacy requirements. Nevertheless, the measure could fall into the category of disciplinary measures when inflicted on an insurer violating the rules in the area of investment. What's more, the boundaries between different kinds of supervisory measures can be hard to delimit in certain circumstances since a proportion of measures have mixed intervening purposes. By a broad categorization in ordinary circumstances, primary supervisory measures exercised by the CIRC are listed in Table 5.

Table 5: Supervisory Measures by the CIRC

Preventive Measures	– Suspension of underwriting new policies
	– Restriction of shareholder rights
	– Restriction of dividend payout
	– Prohibitions on executives (in predefined circumstances):
	  – Request to border control authority for a prohibition of exit from China
	  – Request to judicial authority for a prohibition of free disposal of private assets
	– Communication of risks to the insurance undertakings concerned and request for declarations from the management
	– On-site inspection on a specific risk area
	– A plan to prevent inadequacy of solvency position or improve risk management function

Corrective Measures	– Rectification or taken over by a panel appointed by the CIRC
	– Restriction of business and assets:
	  – Restriction of business expansion;
	  – Restriction of asset growth
	  – Restriction of establishment of affiliations;
	  – Restriction of advertisements;
	  – Restriction of acquisition of fixed assets;
	  – Restriction of operational cost
	– Change of business or asset structure
	– Change of transactional counterparties
	– Change of executives
	– Ceding exposures to reinsurers or transfer of portfolios
	– Auctioning assets of which the holding results in large losses
	– Capital increase
	– Specific measures against operational risk, strategic risk, reputational risk and liquidity risk contingent on causes of risks

Disciplinary Measures	– Transfer of equity – Fines – Withdraw of authorization – Reduction in business lines – Revocation of professional qualifications

	– Restriction of scope or proportions in relation to investments – Restriction of executive compensations

Source: The Insurance Act of China 1995, CIRC department rules and normative documents.

2. The Mechanism of Supervisory Intervention in China

In the CIRC's supervisory review process, an on-site or off-site assessment is followed by the imposition of one or more types of supervisory measures on an insurance undertaking of which the deficiencies or non-compliances are identified. The supervisory assessments ended with classification outcomes are distinguished from those without classification outcomes in regard to the basis underlying the determination of supervisory measures. Among the various kinds of supervisory review methods, a few appraisals classify insurance undertakings in accordance with their conditions and capabilities in the evaluated areas.[232] As far as these appraisals are concerned, the classification outcome assigned to an insurer serves as the indicator of the severity of the deficiencies or violations the insurer has, which is translated into the intensity of supervisory measures. An insurance undertaking, once deemed problematic in certain risk areas, is subject to one or multiple supervisory measures tailored to its classification level. The interventions imposed could be a combination of different types of supervisory measures determined based on the risks and deficiencies inherent in its insurance business. The intensity of supervisory measures would escalate where deteriorating conditions cause a downgrade in classification. Under that circumstance, the insurance undertaking will face tougher measures tailored to the inferior classification level.

The classification outcome hence constitutes the basis for the determination of the supervisory measures in the abovementioned supervisory appraisals. Unlike them, the supervisory assessment methods without classification outcomes, i.e. on-site examinations, ongoing evaluations and some of the theme-focused evaluations,[233] involve supervisory judgments in

232 For instance, the integrated risk rating, the evaluation of governance system as well as the evaluation of the internal control and compliance in regard of investments.

233 The theme-focused evaluations without classification outcomes include, for example, the evaluation of the level of solvency risk management and the evaluation of the overhaul of misleading sales.

reaching the decisions on what supervisory measures to impose. Supervisory judgments are used to determine the severity of deficiencies and the intensity of supervisory measures since nothing else is available to provide useful indications in these aspects. Supervisors judge the riskiness, deficiencies or non-compliances, exercising supervisory measures thereafter. Conventionally, for insignificant problems identified, insurance undertakings would be demanded a correction within a defined time frame. If the problems identified are deemed significant, disciplinary measures would be imposed alongside the requirement for remedy. Supervisory measures will become more rigorous in case the insurance undertaking concerned fails to remedy deficiencies in a timely manner. Under the situation, it is highly likely that tougher corrective and disciplinary measures would be imposed.

3. Similarities and Dissimilarities of the Supervisory Measures between the EU and China

After the comparison between China and the EU of the manner in which supervisory measures are exercised, it is found that shared practices exist in some aspects. The supervisory measures applied in the EU, as provided in the pertinent guidelines, could be categorized as preventive and corrective measures of which the definitions have no material differences with the counterparts in China.[234] Moreover, for the NCAs in the EU, supervisory judgment is relied on to assess the significance of weaknesses or non-compliances in order to match the intensity of supervisory measures with the firm-specific riskiness,[235] identical to the way in which supervisory measures are normally determined following an evaluation without a classification outcome in China. Further, a ladder of interventions is required in the EU's insurance legislation to be established for varied treatment of distinct levels of non-compliances and for necessary escalation in intervention in case less rigorous measures fail to rectify problems. In China, the mechanism is also maintained in place, which has been introduced previously.

As regards the disparities in supervisory measures between the two jurisdictions, they arise mainly in two aspects. Firstly, the supervisory measures imposed under the EU guidelines are better tailored to the idiosyncrasies

234 *See supra note* 211 (Guidelines), at §§ 33-42; *see also* Solvency II Directive, § 36 (5).

235 *Id.* (Guidelines) at §§ 34, 36, 42.

of insurance undertakings as compared to those imposed in accordance with China's supervisory rules. An additional stage is incorporated into the supervisory review process of the NCAs in the EU, namely the detailed review stage. Supervisory measures are supposed to be determined based on the outcome of the detailed review activities. By virtue of in-depth undertaking-focused analyses, the EU supervisors would be able to scrutinize the particularities surrounding the risk areas of an individual insurer exceeding the level of the assessments made at the prior stage. The outcome of risk-profile identification is hence calibrated, which makes the supervisory measures more specific to the nature and characteristics of the risks inherent in the business of a targeted insurance undertaking. The CIRC's supervisory review process lacks a component which could extend in greater detail the evaluation of the risk areas analyzed in the previous stage or could examine other risk areas that are not covered in previous assessments. In fact, the concerns of either the integrated risk rating or the theme-focused evaluations are confined to predetermined areas where Chinese insurance undertakings are commonly considered to possess risk exposures. Consequentially, firm-specific risk areas are prone to exclusion from the scope of these off-site appraisals conducted across all insurance undertakings. Besides, the appraisals essentially measure the alignment with criteria or requirements using sets of indicators, but do not deliver complete analysis of specified risk areas or the interplay between them. Owing to the factors above, the appropriateness, specificity and effectiveness of the intervention exercised by the CIRC cannot be superior to their EU counterparts.

The other disparity resides in the characteristics of supervisory measures. The measures exercised by the CIRC exhibit, by and large, the attribute of restriction. A majority of the supervisory measures involve restraints placed on various respects of business operation. Resorting to tough intervention, the CIRC intends to deter insurance undertakings from acting in a way that deviates from supervisory requirements. The rigidity of the measures often tends to be in excess of what mitigation of risks or rectification of violations actually requires. Relatively, more supervisory measures of higher aptness and flexibility are exercised by the EU supervisors despite the use of tough measures against severe non-compliances. In the EU, flexible supervisory measures instead of restrictive means are always exercised at the first attempt to help withstand adverse conditions. In light of the severity of the measures, they are not intended to deter non-compliances ex ante by arousing insurers' concern for being subjected to severe restraints, but aimed to restoring compliance ex post by providing a resolution. A common approach is to align the supervisory methods with the firm-specific risk characteristics. For example, in order to tackle a significant deviation of risk profile from the assumptions underlying standard formula, previous to a capital add-on imposed as the last resort, the insurance undertaking concerned would be initially required to substitute standard parameters with undertaking-specific parameters or to use an internal model in line with relevant requirements.[236] According to the C-ROSS rules, a large proportion of parameters used in the calculation of capital requirements are prescribed as standard parameters, but there exist no supervisory measures allowing the adaptation of them to individual conditions.[237] The CIRC is inclined to design supervisory measures in such a way that elaborate arrangements would not be involved. The formulation of flexible interventional mechanism is nevertheless a demanding rule-making task, which inevitably entails complicated technical details because the supervisory measures should balance the need to provide insurers with room for rectification against the necessity of due supervisory control. Oversimplified rules in this regard hence result in rough supervisory measures imposed on insurance undertakings or the management thereof, giving rise to hefty regulatory costs for Chinese insurance undertakings.

IV. Conclusions

Above all, a striking disparity in the supervisory review process between the two jurisdictions resides in the constituent stages. The inclusion of a detailed review stage in the Solvency II process permits a further evaluation of a particular insurance undertaking exceeding the level of analytical detail delivered by the risk assessment made in the previous stage, which leads to more apt supervisory measures determined relative to those imposed by the CIRC which bases the determination on a general assessment

236 Solvency II Directive §§ 37, 110, 119.

237 For calculating capital requirements for different risk modules, each type of exposures within a risk module is assigned risk coefficients which show the degree of risks. However, the seemingly exhaustive list of standard risk coefficients does not suffice for an appropriate indication of riskiness because insurance undertakings are likely to experience substantially different level of loss frequency and severity owing to the factors specific to asset or loss exposures. None of the supervisory measures enables a modification of coefficients according to the idiosyncratic riskiness of certain exposures possessed by an insurer. It would otherwise serve as a technical intervention to prevent or correct deficiencies in a less restrictive manner.

of confined risk areas without undertaking-focused scrutiny for outcome calibration.

Two differences arise from the absence of a detailed review stage in the CIRC's supervisory review process. Firstly, the risk areas that are involved in the theme-focused analyses made at the Solvency II detailed review stage could vary depending on the outcome of previous risk assessments. To the contrary, the theme-focused evaluations carried out by the CIRC are limited to a predetermined scope of risk areas, which deprives supervisors of the capability to shift concentration to newly-emerging risk areas. A second difference relates to the supervisory plan. The EU supervisory authorities are required to create a plan for each insurance undertaking to specify the elements of the supervisory activities conducted at the detailed review stage.[238] However, the individualized plan is not necessitated in the CIRC's supervisory review process mainly because of the uniformity of evaluation focuses across all insurance undertakings. The uniformity is rooted in the statutorily defined scope for the risk areas analyzed by theme-focused evaluations. Firm-specific risk areas are thus inadequately factored in the review activities of the CIRC.

Besides, an evaluation of the impacts or importance of an insurance undertaking, particularly with respect to the impacts of its failure on stakeholders and the market, is incorporated in the assessment framework of the Solvency II supervisory review process. However, the analyses from this perspective are not applied in the corresponding process of the CIRC.

Finally, the supervisory measures imposed in the two jurisdictions exhibit distinct features. The supervisory intervention by the CIRC consists of more restrictive measures than those imposed by the EU supervisory authorities. With a high proportion of supervisory measures being restraints, China's supervisory authority is inclined to derive deterrent effects from severe restrictions at the very beginning of the occurrence of a non-compliance. Whereas, its EU counterparts tend to exercise more flexible supervisory measures facilitative to the rectification of a non-compliance before severe measures are resorted to.

---

238 *Supra note* 211 (Guidelines), at §§ 20-22; *see also* Solvency II Directive, § 36 (6).

B. Adjustments to Workings of CIRC's Supervisory Review Process

I. Incorporation of Detailed Review Stage and Supervisory Plan: Advantages and Adaptations

In preceding sections, the benefits brought about by a detailed review are discussed. Meanwhile, the disadvantages attributed to the lack of a functionally equivalent component are analyzed. The situation calls for the inclusion of a detailed review stage in the CIRC's supervisory review process, in order for the disadvantages to be eliminated.

The new review stage could be positioned between the two existing stages comprising the entire supervisory review process. In the Solvency II review process, on-site inspections and theme-focused analyses are conducted at the detailed review stage. However, it would be unnecessary to make the CIRC's supervisory review process identical with its EU counterpart by abrogating all the inconsistent procedures and approaches. A cost-efficient way is to have two rounds of theme-focused evaluations and on-site inspections respectively at the supervisory assessment stage and the newly introduced detailed review stage, with the risk areas being divided between the first-round activities and the second-round ones. The theme-focused evaluation addressing those statutory risk areas can be retained at the supervisory assessment stage, which is supposed to be the first-round theme-focused evaluation in the whole supervisory review process. Subsequently, new risk areas emerging as a result of the supervisory assessment stage should be assigned to the second-round theme-focused evaluation conducted at the detailed review stage. On-site inspections could be adapted in a similar manner that the inspections carried out at the supervisory assessment stage are supposed to examine the issues prescribed in the supervisory rules, whereas the second round of inspections conducted at the detailed review stage should address the new risk areas exposed at the supervisory assessment stage. In essence, the first-round activities are concerned with the prescribed risk areas, leaving the risk areas that are newly identified to the second-round activities. Thus, an overlap of evaluated risk areas between the existing supervisory assessment stage and the added detailed review stage could be avoided.

If the change is effected, the purpose of the supervisory assessment stage would be reoriented such that it is no longer used to determine supervisory measures but to make a preliminary identification of new risk areas or problematic insurers. On-site and off-site evaluations are conducted to give a general assessment of insurer risk profiles. The initial assessment outcome derived after the first stage would then serve as the basis for the undertaking-focused and theme-focused evaluations at the detailed review stage. The undertaking-focused evaluation gives analysis to those undertakings identified as having severe deficiencies or complicated risk profiles, while the theme-focused evaluation is intended for the analysis across all insurance undertakings of the emerging risk areas identified at the previous stage. Eventually, the outcome of the detailed review activities will be taken as a crucial factor in calibrating the supervisory measures to be exercised.

To ensure the coherence and effectiveness of the reorganized supervisory review process, establishing a supervisory plan is indispensable. In the Solvency II supervisory review process, the plan constitutes a nexus between the risk assessment framework stage and the detailed review stage. The NCAs in the EU are required to utilize the supervisory plan to lay down the arrangements of the supervisory activities conducted for each insurance undertaking at the detailed review stage based on the outcome of risk assessment framework and other relevant information.[239] A number of issues will be set out in the plan, such as key risk areas to be reviewed, analytical methods to be used as well as time and resources to be allocated.[240]

As far as the CIRC's supervisory review process is concerned, the utilization of the supervisory plan is unlikely to lead to incompatibility with other mechanisms. The functioning of the supervisory tools and activities involved in the existing supervisory review stages will not be undermined by the effects of the planning. As a matter of fact, the decision-making quality with regard to supervisory activities would be improved with the use of a delicate plan.

Evidently, integrating the supervisory plan into the process brings great benefits for the conduct of supervision. Above all, it enhances the appropriateness of the frequency and intensity set for the subsequent supervisory activities. Assuming that the decisions on the supervisory activities to be conducted at the detailed review stage are made on the basis of general judgments without specific details given, the uncertainties are liable to lead to the detailed review activities being incommensurate with the degree of the risks facing an insurance undertaking. For instance, an arbitrary exercise of inspections or application of methods is likely to occur. The prominent advantage of a supervisory plan is that it clearly specifies the essential elements of prospective review activities and individualizes supervi-

239 *Id.*
240 *Id.*

sory activities according to the particular risk characteristics of an undertaking. The specificity of supervision is thus raised to a higher level. Besides, a supervisory plan contributes to the consistency of the treatment of the insurance undertakings with similar risk profiles. In the course of planning, supervisors from different function units inside the supervisory authority would form a shared view as to how to match the intensity of further review activities with the degree of the risks identified, which is conducive to the adoption of a standardized approach to determining the supervisory activities conducted at a later stage. In addition, the utilization of a supervisory plan promotes the efficiency of supervisory resources. By clearly defining the aims and scope of supervisory tools, follow-up actions and time frame, finite supervisory resources are placed under strict control to ensure that they are allocated to the detailed review activities for specified risk areas or undertakings in a proportionate manner. The issues that entail higher risks should be addressed with more time and efforts relative to those of lower riskiness. Excessive review activities could be prevented by a precise plan beforehand.

II. A Supplementary Perspective for Supervisory Review

1. The Grounds for Inclusion of an Assessment of Impacts of Insurer Failure

The impact classification which measures the impacts imposed by an insurance undertaking on related entities is combined with the risk classification in the Solvency II supervisory review process in order for a complete assessment of the risks inherent in insurance business.[241] As opposed to the practices in the EU, the potential impacts of insurance undertakings are outside the scope of the supervisory assessment in the CIRC's supervisory review process. The assessment tools applied only address the risks an undertaking is exposed to, but do not involve an analysis of the potential costs an undertaking poses to its stakeholders. Indeed, a big insurer with sound governance system and abundant capital resources tends to face a

---

241 *See supra note* 211 (Guidelines), at § 15; *see also* Solvency II Directive, § 36 (6) (providing the legal basis for the regulatory instruments aimed at implementing a proportionality-based supervisory review process that appropriately aligns the frequency and intensity of supervisory review activities with an insurer's individual conditions, such as risk profile and failure impacts).

lower level of risks than a small one with poor conditions in the two foregoing dimensions. Nevertheless, if both types of insurers fail, the economic cost posed by the insolvency of the former would far exceed that of the latter. Although the degree of risk is related to the likelihood of failure, the outcome for risk-profile evaluation gives few clues about the extent of impacts of an insurer failure. Without taking into account the potential impacts of an insurer insolvency, supervisors are prone to misjudgment in regard to the frequency and intensity of the supervisory activities and measures exercised on the insurers with low risks but high impacts and those with high risks but low impacts.

a) From the Standpoint of Policyholders and Beneficiaries

Where an insurance undertaking fails, the interests of policyholders and beneficiaries would be at stake. If the insurer goes insolvent, the remaining assets might be inadequate to meet the insurance obligations because of the impaired financial position and massive surrender of policies at the sign of insolvency. The remaining insureds are therefore likely to be deprived of covers and claimants might be unable to access full indemnifications for their losses or expected benefits.

In China, it is prescribed that the life insurance policies of an insolvent insurer should be assigned to another sound insurer.[242] The Insurance security fund would provide financial assistance to the assignee on condition that the liquidated assets of the assignor are insufficient to fulfill contractual obligations.[243] As to non-life insurance policies, if the liquidated assets of the insolvent insurer cannot meet its obligations, the insurance security fund would directly reimburse the residual losses of policyholders.[244] However, the transfer of policies will inevitably consume much time since the completion of the transfer involves negotiations between insurers and a mediation by the supervisory authority. Seeking compensation from the insurance security fund is no easy work as well, which concerns the planning by the supervisory authority, the consultation with relevant govern-

242 The assignment is supposed to be achieved through negotiations and agreements between insurers. In case a failed insurer is unable to secure such an agreement, the CIRC will appoint an insurer to take over the policy portfolios. *See* the Insurance Act of China 1995, § 92.

243 The Administrative Rules on the Insurance Security Fund 2008, § 21.

244 *See Id.* at § 19.

ment departments, and the approval by the State Council.[245] From the occurrence of insolvency till the completion of policies transfer or the receipt of reimbursements from the insurance security fund, it is likely that the insureds undergo a loss of cover in the interim, with indemnification and other benefits being denied to policyholders and beneficiaries. In fact, the insurance security fund, following the indemnification made using the liquidated assets, offers reimbursements up to 80% of the excessive claim amount for corporate policyholders and up to 90% for individual policyholders,[246] which means policyholders would have to incur partial losses in case of shortage of assets backing the settlement of claims as the consequence of an insurer insolvency.

Besides a loss of cover and the unavailability of policy benefits in the intervening period, ensuing effects on policyholders will be triggered, which vary across different lines of insurance business by nature and degree. In China's life and health insurance sector, endowment insurance and annuity insurance policies constitute the largest portion in the policy portfolios of most insurers.[247] The endowment insurance products favored by Chinese consumers typically provide coverage against death due to disease or accidents, grant periodic payouts, distribute profits, and return premiums on maturity date.[248] An insurer failure could hence result in a reduction in the income of policyholders. For those that are in need of a large quantity of funds, worse scenarios might be present as it becomes difficult to obtain policy loans or retrieve the premiums for mature policies. As to policyholders and beneficiaries under annuity policies, their life quality will be materially affected by the loss of stable benefits stream. The amount and frequency of benefits granted under annuity policies are mostly much higher than those of the benefits to which endowment policyholders are

245 *Id.* at § 17.

246 *Id.* at §§ 19(2), 21(1), (2).

247 As disclosed by the several biggest life insurers, the insurance products which contribute most to the total premium incomes mainly consist of endowment insurance and annuity insurance products. The Insurance Association of China has the disclosure documents of all insurance undertakings on its electronic platform, *see* 'Annual Information Disclosure of Insurance Companies' (Insurance Association of China) <www.iachina.cn/hysj/ndxxplnew/rsxgsnew/> accessed 18 June 2015.

248 The features of different endowment insurance products vary. Nevertheless, they are not much distinct from each other with respect to the aggregated benefits measured by cash inflows.

entitled, which leads to annuity policyholders' higher susceptibility to the suspension in benefits payment.

In China's property and casualty insurance sector, car insurance, commercial property insurance, liability insurance and accident insurance basically comprise the biggest proportion of the policy portfolio at most insurance companies.[249] Before discussing the idiosyncratic effects of an insurer failure on policyholders that take out the sorts of covers noted above, a common disadvantage need be mentioned. In the event of a failure, it is not mandatory for an insolvent non-life insurer to assign policies to another, which means policyholders might need to seek new covers provided by another insurer on their own. Non-life insurance policyholders are therefore exposed to the risk of being unable to secure similar cover terms at the cost close to original premium rate.[250] The replacement of a cover would take a period of time since comparing coverage conditions and quotes among insurers is demanding.

As regards car insurance, the absence of an effective coverage following an insurer failure could make policyholders refrain from driving because they need otherwise retain losses themselves until the insurance security

---

249 For some property insurance companies, the credit and guaranty insurance ranks among the most important business lines. Expectedly, the loan guaranty insurance will assume an even more important role in the business of non-life insurers. The failure of a loan guaranty insurance provider will affect the cooperative bank since the bank relies on the insurer to repay the loans defaulted on by the borrower who takes out the guaranty insurance policy. In-depth analyses of the issue are given in the section E of Chapter 3.

250 A number of papers mention the affordability of a replacement cover from the position of the policyholders deprived of coverage due to an insurer failure. In particular, the papers raise the concern that the life insurance policyholders with a loss of coverage might be subject to an unaffordable premium rate demanded by insurers due to their ageing or health conditions. But, as far as China's market is concerned, life insurance policyholders are highly unlikely to face the tough situation given the fact that reserves for their policies will be fully transferred to the new insurer and the insurance security fund would make payments to complement the reserves in case of the inadequacy to meet obligations. Regarding the discussion on the affordability of a replacement cover, *see e.g.*, The Technical Study led by Prof. Kevin Davis, *Study of Financial System Guarantees* (Commissioned Report, 2004) para 5.20 (noting that "premiums are determined at the date that the policy is taken out and remain fixed 🕛 Policyholders may be unable to find replacement cover at the same price🕛"); *supra note* 140, at 217 (presenting that "This may be particularly important for life insurance where the policyholder's life expectancy may have reduced considerably since the original policy was taken out, meaning that life insurance premiums on a new contract would be much higher.").

fund is accessible or a replacement of cover is completed.[251] It exemplifies the deterrent effects of an insurer failure - a policyholder's life could be disrupted due to the discontinuity in the provision of coverage.

The failure of a non-life insurer with considerable loss exposures in the business line of commercial property insurance could result in liquidity shortages at the corporate policyholders which incur losses owing to natural disasters or incidents, if the insurer insolvency disables a prompt indemnification. At a time when the premises, stock or equipment are damaged as the consequence of a natural disaster or an incident, a business entity which is insured against those perils would demand an immediate indemnification in order to be restored to what it previously was. If the rebuilding, repair or replacement of the damaged objects is not made at the earliest possible time, larger losses would be incurred by the business entity. The underlying reason is that businesses might encounter a disruption in production, a forced exit of the market or a financial distress that causes difficulties in business maintenance and loan repayment. As far as an insolvent insurer is concerned, it is likely that the insurer no longer has adequate financial capacity to settle big claims by corporate policyholders, or at least, is unable to settle them without delay. The simultaneity of the claims made by the corporate policyholders from the same disaster-struck region further reduces the likelihood of a prompt and full indemnification. The insolvent insurer might default on the indemnification for both direct and indirect losses. A typical example of indirect losses could be the shortfall in income due to a business interruption in the wake of a natural disaster, which is usually insured against as an extra cover on top of a basic cover against the risk of commercial property losses.[252] For small- and medium-sized businesses in China, it is difficult for them to secure financing at times of normal operation, let alone in distressed situations. Therefore, a default by an insurer on indemnification would especially hinder the recovery of their production and business activities. If own funds that are originally intended for other purposes are appropriated for restoration, much financial pressure could be exerted on the business entity, leading to a liquidity shortage abruptly. The adverse effects would not be confined to

251 *See supra note* 140, at 217.

252 *See* 'Business interruption insurance' (*Association of British Insurers*, 13 Nov 2014) <www.abi.org.uk/Insurance-and-savings/Products/Business-insurance/Business-interruption-insurance> accessed 22 June 2015 (introducing the features of business interruption insurance, including the circumstances under the coverage, reimbursement of losses, etc.).

the business entity affected by a natural disaster or an incident, but will be spread to its related entities, which are exposed to high counterparty risk owing to the impaired financial position of the corporate policyholder.[253]

With respect to liability insurance, where an insolvent insurer is unable to meet the obligations, the interests of the insured and the third party could be harmed simultaneously since the insurer is supposed to indemnify the third party for the bodily injury or property damages on behalf of the insured. In China, few individuals or households purchase personal liability insurance. Liability insurance policies are normally taken out by large corporations of which the production or services concern public interests.[254] On the occurrence of incidents, the insured would be held liable for the compensation for the damages it causes to the members of the public or the environment. Under the circumstance where neither the insured nor the insolvent insurer is able to make compensations, the harmed would have to bear losses. At the same time, damages could be exacerbated due to the fact that restoration is not fulfilled in a prompt manner. In terms of the liability insurance, the costs posed by an insurer failure will be elevated with more harmed individuals or entities being involved as the third party.

---

253 If the production capacity and financial position of the company is not restored to the normal level prior to the occurrence of the loss event, the stakeholders of the company could also incur adverse factors. The income of the employees might be reduced, delayed or even suspended. The suppliers might encounter a default on the payment for the goods delivered and the size of the orders from the company might be curtailed. The company might request to the buyers for an extension to the delivery period of the products, which would give rise to a disruption in the buyers' business. Creditors, like the suppliers, might face a default on debt repayment. Given the negative impacts on various stakeholders, the economic costs arising from the failure of the company to access insurance benefits against large losses are considerable.

254 Public liability and product liability coverage, among all kinds of liability insurance products, generate most premium income for Chinese insurers. Basically, transportation carriers and food manufacturers take out the largest portion of the total liability insurance policies underwritten by an insurer. For the materials on the current and future developments of China's liability insurance sector, *see* 'The Special Issue on Liability Insurance' *China Insurance News* (Beijing, 28 Oct 2014).

b) From the Standpoint of Other Entities Exposed to Insurer Failure

Apart from underwriting activities, there exist other important activities through which insurance undertakings exert influence on various entities in the financial market or the real economy. The issues discussed below overlap, to some extent, with the analysis of the systemic relevance of Chinese insurers in the section E of Chapter 3, owing to the fact that the discussion of systemic relevance involves the evaluation of a broader range of activities. However, the subsequent analyses will be made from a different perspective given the specific concerns in this context.

Firstly, investment activities constitute a primary activity with the attribute. In China's insurance sector, the largest portion of insurer assets is held in the form of bank deposit. A number of medium-sized banks in China have developed strong reliance on the deposits of the insurers that are related parties of the banks or maintain close business relationship with the banks.[255] It is unclear to what extent an insurer withdrawal would impact on those banks and their resilience thereafter. Expectedly, the banks would experience high liquidity pressure under that circumstance. Without an analysis of the scale and distribution of the funds deposited by an insurer, the supervisory authority will not be able to determine its importance to particular credit institutions. The second largest class of assets in the investment portfolios of Chinese insurers is securities, namely bonds and stocks. An insurer, in response to a financial distress, might be prompted to implement a fire sale of the securities positions, which in turn amplifies market fluctuations. Some big insurers are significant investors for the bonds issued by financial institutions. The failure of such an insurer could bring about declined market liquidity, and heightened transactional cost for other market participants as the ease with which the bonds are traded is lessened. The size and distribution of each insurer's holding of securities is thus indicative of an insurer's importance to a segment market or the market as a whole. In addition, a rising proportion of insurer funds are allocated to the assets which are not traded in the stock

255 In China, the related-party status is usually derived from either the fact that the insurer and the bank are affiliated to the same group, or the fact that the insurer owns significant shareholdings in the bank. Certainly, there exist other factors that cause the two entities to qualify as related parties. For the definition and scope of related parties, *see* D Christian and N Lüdenbach, *IFRS Essentials* (1st edn, Wiley 2013) 203-204. The close relationship refers to the association which is mainly built on long-term cooperation in important aspects of business.

exchange or the principal bond market.[256] They are mainly composed of financial products and debt investment plans, with a focus on infrastructure and real estate projects.[257] By holding the assets, insurers obtain periodic inflows of interest payment. A clear tendency is exhibited that Chinese insurers become increasingly interested in infrastructure-oriented investment plans since steady and lucrative returns could be yielded.[258] For this reason, the investment in the class of assets is expanding dramatically, accounting for an increasingly larger proportion in the overall portfolios. Needless to say, the greater an insurer's provision of funding resources is, the more impacts it has on the wider economy. For this reason, the criteria used to measure the importance of an insurer should always take into account the extent to which an insurer assumes the role of financier for the economy. Further, the subsidiaries and long-term shareholdings acquired or established specially for engaging in real estate business and financial

---

256 In China's financial sectors, these assets are designated "non-standard debt-based assets" (NSDB assets). The name of the assets reveals its two primary characteristics. Firstly, because these assets are not traded in the stock exchange or the inter-bank bond market, they need not be standardized qualitatively or quantitatively to adapt to the requirements on traded instruments. Secondly, by holding the assets, financial institutions actually make debt investments instead of equity investments. *See* Yaohua Tang, 'The Origin and Evolvement of NSDB Assets' *Securities Times* (Shenzhen, 22 Nov 2013) A5; Junling Huang, 'CIRC Poised to Permit Unit-Linked Insurance Plans to Invest in NSDB Assets' *National Business Daily* (Beijing, 10 Oct 2014) 16. 'The Dangers of Debt: Shadows Lengthen' *The Economist* (Hong Kong, 13 Apr 2013).

257 A wide range of items are included in the class of assets, for example, credit asset-backed securities, infrastructure and real-estate debt investment plans, trust, asset management program, etc. Among them, the debt investment plan is the most favorable investment vehicle for Chinese insurers. Essentially, the vehicle channels insurer funds to infrastructure development. The structure of the debt investment plan approximates to trust, given the fiduciary relationship existing in the transaction. In the setting of a typical infrastructure debt investment plan, the insurance asset management company is entrusted to finance an infrastructure project on behalf of the insurer, transferring the interest payments to the beneficiary, namely the insurer. There exist two relevant rules on this issue. *See* CIRC, *Notification on Insurer Investments on Financial Products Concerned* (Normative Document, No 91, 2012); CIRC, *Provisional Administrative Rules on Infrastructure Debt Investment Plans* (Normative Document, No 92, 2012).

258 Given the fact that Chinese insurers are prohibited from investing in infrastructure on their own, they have to rely on the arrangement with a trustee to make investments (usually debt investments) on their behalf. The prohibitive provision is laid down in a normative document, *see* CIRC, *Administrative Rules on the Pilot Scheme: Indirect Investments of Insurers in Infrastructure Projects* (Normative Document, 14 Mar 2006).

services merit consideration in the evaluation of aggregated exposures associated with the insurer.

Secondly, the financing activities of insurers are accompanied by the risks facing the market players that provide liquidity or capital. Chinese insurers conduct repo transactions to meet the demand for short-term liquidity while seeking debt capital to strengthen financial position in the long run.[259] The lending institution which extends credit to the insurer is exposed to counterparty risk. The impairment in the financial conditions of an insurer would increase the likelihood of a default on the payments it owes to creditors. The financial soundness of an insurer is thus of significance to all institutions extending credit to it. Without ascertaining the details of an insurer's credit-borrowing activities, for example, the components of its lenders and their respective credit exposures to the insurer, it will be impossible to derive a reliable conclusion as to how market players will be adversely impacted by its insolvency.

Thirdly, related party transactions are likewise a critical channel through which the importance of the insurer can be perceived. Increasingly, Insurance undertakings in China evolve into financial conglomerates with extensive acquisitions and establishment of diverse types of financial institutions.[260] The transactions between group members rise substantially in quantity on a yearly basis. Since the insurance subsidiary is the central entity in which the assets of a group are concentrated, it is deemed to be an indispensable source of business for other group members and expected to grant financial support to them as well. Simultaneously, for the insurance subsidiary itself, the assistance from and the cooperation with other group members are manifestly necessary. There exist a variety of transactions between them, including liquidity provision, assets assignment, capital rais-

---

259 Currently, the subordinated debt is the major debt capital instrument that Chinese insurers rely on. In January 2015, the PBC and the CIRC jointly released a notification that insurance undertakings are allowed to issue capital-supplementing bonds which will be traded in the inter-bank bond market. Expectedly, it will become another important way for insurance undertakings to replenish capital in the future. *See* PBC and CIRC, *Issues Relating to Insurance Undertakings' Issuance of Capital-Supplementing Bonds* (Normative Document, No 3, 2015).

260 Large Chinese insurance groups usually have subsidiaries operating in most financial sectors. Take Ping An Insurance group which possesses the most diversified business portfolios among all insurers as an example, its numerous group members operate business covering the following areas: insurance, bank, securities, trust, futures, investment funds, asset management, financial lease, venture capital and financial assets exchange.

ing and business dealing, to name a few. In case the insurance subsidiary runs into crisis, the remaining group members would inevitably be affected. The transactions and agreements in progress could be revoked, with the financial resources pledged being unavailable to the associated group members. In light of the size of intra-group transactions, the fall of an insurance subsidiary will certainly result in a serious shock to the rest of the wider group. The insurer's impacts in this regard shall hence be included in the scope of the relevant assessment.

2. Role of Impact Classification After Adoption

The importance of Chinese insurance undertakings to policyholders and other stakeholders could be demonstrated by the negative effects triggered subsequent to their failure. The entities affected by an insurer failure are not confined to those contractual parties, but extend to include a wider range of entities which are impacted indirectly. For this reason, the evaluation of the economic costs of an insurer failure should take account of the adverse factors that all of its stakeholders incur.

The impact classification will enable the CIRC to be informed of the differences in importance between insurers, so that high-impact insurers could be identified. The allocation of supervisory resources, the intensity of supervisory activities and the severity of supervisory measures would thus not only be aligned with risk classification outcomes, but also be in alignment with impact classification outcomes. The proportional approach on the basis of insurer importance shows the supervisory authority's regard for the interests of insurance consumers and the financial stability, underlain by the thinking that higher economic costs would be caused by the failure of an insurer with more exposure units and linkages. A higher-impact insurer would be subject to more rigorous oversight which involves the use of more complicated assessment methodologies in relation to a lower-impact one. At the same time, the CIRC will be capable of calibrating the level of supervisory measures to avoid excessively tough measures that could undermine the interests of massive individuals and organizations connected with a high-impact insurer.

In light of the purpose of the impact classification, it should be integrated into the off-site appraisals made at the supervisory assessment stage, along with the existing appraisal mechanisms. The addition of the new appraisal component will not result in any conflict or overlap arising among the constituent parts of the supervisory review process, as it is complementary to the analytical perspectives provided by other evaluations.

The outcome of the impact classification, parallel to those of other evaluations, will have a profound effect on the elements of the supervisory plan and the activities conducted at the detailed review stage. The impact classification assigns insurers to different impact-level groups. The classification outcome serves as an indicator of the intensity of the supervisory activities to be exercised on an insurer. Unless an insurer with low impacts has a complicated risk profile or is exposed to high degree of risk, the supervisory intensity would be consistent with its impact level. High intensity of supervisory activities would be applied to high-impact insurers. It is absolutely necessary to apply the undertaking-focused evaluation to the review of the risk profiles of those high-impact insurers identified. The other consideration is that the impact classification reveals the impact areas where greatest losses could be incurred if an insurer fails. Those significant impact areas could be included in the scope of theme-focused evaluations to facilitate a comparative study of the cause, pattern and distribution of the losses experienced by a particular group of stakeholders. In the formulation and determination of supervisory measures, the study outcome should be taken into account to make the measures designed have the effects of mitigating the potential negative impacts. Additionally, the supervisory authority can make use of the outcome to improve the mechanisms for safeguarding policyholders and beneficiaries in the event of insurer insolvency, which would contribute to an orderly resolution regime with insignificant disruption to the stakeholders in the insolvent insurance undertaking and to the functioning of the financial market.[261]

---

261 In this context, resolution is defined as the process by which the authorities can intervene to manage the failure of a financial institution. A resolution in an orderly manner means that the failed institution is resolved without excessive disruption to the financial system, without avoidable interruption to the critical economic functions it provides, and without exposing taxpayers to losses. At the end of a resolution, the institution concerned might be wound down, absorbed or restructured. *See* BoE, *The Bank of England's approach to resolution* (Publication, October 2014) paras 1-9, 93-96. *See generally* FSB, *Key Attributes of Effective Resolution Regimes for Financial Institutions* (Policy Document, 15 October 2014) (presenting the core principles and elements in twelve aspects which underpin an effective resolution regime).

III. Amelioration of the Supervisory Intervention Mechanism of CIRC

As have been analyzed, the shortcomings of the supervisory measures by the CIRC lie in the lack of specificity and flexibility. The former shortcoming will be much mitigated as a result of the incorporation of detailed review activities, which could promote the aptness of supervisory measures by calibrating the evaluation outcome of the previous stage.

This part is intended to address the latter shortcoming, deriving implications from the supervisory measures designed by the EU regulators. In the Solvency II system, supervisory measures are mostly concerned with the intervention imposed against the risks, deficiencies and non-compliances identified in accordance with quantitative requirements, in particular capital requirements. The supervisory measures against the risks, deficiencies and non-compliances of insurance undertakings in the areas of pillar II and pillar III are not set out in detail. In fact, the Solvency II supervisory measures for the non-compliance with the capital requirements are composed of sophisticated mechanisms which well balance flexibility, proportionality, cyclicality and stringency. Given the fact that ensuring capital adequacy is a core element of insurance supervision, the supervisory measures serving this purpose are most important among all intervention by supervisors. For the abovementioned reasons, the supervisory measures against the breach of capital requirements, which typify the way supervisory intervention is exercised in the EU, merit an in-depth study. In the following sections, a comparison of capital requirements between the EU and China will be drawn to reveal the similarities between the Solvency II Solvency Capital Requirement (hereinafter referred to as "SCR") and the C-ROSS minimum capital standard (hereinafter referred to as "MCS"). Then, it will be analyzed how to improve the supervisory intervention against the breach of the MCS taking account of the mechanisms employed in the Solvency II with regard to the supervisory measures against the non-compliance with the SCR. Lastly, the criteria and principles utilized by the EU regulators and supervisors in the formation of supervisory intervention are summarized, which will be followed by a discussion on the application of these factors underlying supervisory judgment.

1. The Relationship and Disparities between Capital Requirements in EU and China

It is of significance to grasp a concept that the MCS stipulated in the C-ROSS corresponds to the SCR prescribed in the Solvency II,[262] whereas there exists no counterpart in the C-ROSS for the Solvency II minimum capital requirement (hereinafter referred to as "MCR").

a) On the Aspect of Definition

The calculation of the SCR takes into account 'all quantifiable risks to which an insurance or reinsurance undertaking is exposed' on the presumption of 'a going concern'.[263] The definition of the MCS is akin to that of the SCR, defined as 'the amount of capital which insurance undertakings should have in order for an appropriate level of financial resources used to make provision for the potential adverse impacts on solvency arising out of various quantifiable risks, as required by the CIRC pursuing prudential regulation and supervision'.[264] The emphasis of the definition for the MCR is nevertheless distinct from that of the foregoing notions. The MCR, as defined in the Solvency II, is the level of capital resources 'below which policyholders and beneficiaries are exposed to an unacceptable level of risk were insurance and reinsurance undertakings allowed to continue their operations'.[265] Inferred from the definitions of the three notions, it is established that the sensitivity of the capital requirements to actual risk profile is the disparity between them. The premise of a going concern reveals that the SCR is supposed to be such a necessary level of capital position as to ensure that insurers above the level are able to absorb all losses and sustain a normal operation of business. Likewise, in view of the keyword 'appropriate', the MCS is not intended to set an absolute threshold below which the authorization of an insurance undertaking will be im-

262 The MCS constitutes the only insurance capital requirement exiting in China, which is different with the situation in the EU where there exist two-tier capital requirements, namely the SCR and the MCR. The discussion made herein will address the question as to which one of the capital requirements in the Solvency II approximates more to the MCS in the C-ROSS conceptually.

263 Solvency II, § 101 2 and 3.

264 CIRC, *The Supervisory Rules on the Solvency Position of Insurance Undertakings No 2: MCS* (Normative Document, No 22, 2015), § 3.

265 Solvency II, § 129 1 (b).

mediately withdrawn. Instead, it aims to prescribe a sufficient but not overly stringent level in line with the scale of the aggregate risk exposures of an insurance undertaking. In essence, by imposing the two capital requirements mentioned above, regulators stipulate a suitable capital position which is expected to be exactly commensurate with the degree of the risks facing insurance undertakings. Further, compliance with them will lead to sustainable operation, preventing the insurer from collapsing in the event of a sudden adverse change or market movement. The MCR exhibits different characteristics. Its definition does not convey any element related to the dimension of risk sensitivity, which implies that the calculation methodology of the MCR might not embody the characteristics of risk sensitivity to a great extent. Moreover, non-compliance with the MCR is deemed completely unacceptable, which indicates there is no margin for error for an insurer merely meeting the MCR.

b) On the Aspect of Basic Calculation Principles

Notwithstanding some differences in the details of the requirements, the SCR and the MCS have similarities in the general structure and methodologies of the calculation.[266] Either of them requires the risks incurred by insurers to be decomposed into modules and sub-modules in which loss exposures are captured in the formula and respective capital requirements are derived. The total capital requirement is hence imposed by aggregating the capital requirements specific to risk categories. Alongside the resemblance, the two capital requirements both involve the utilization of a scenario-based approach which determines the capital required to absorb loss-

266 The calculation method of the SCR refers to the approach of standard formula. The partial or full internal model is not involved in the comparison, given that Chinese insurance undertakings are only allowed to use the approach of standard formula and parameters as prescribed in the regulations. *See supra note* 264, at § 8 (providing that the uniform method and parameters shall be applied across the insurance sector in determining the minimum capital position an insurance undertaking should possess; *See* CIRC, *Notification of the General Framework of China's Second-generation Solvency Regulation and Supervision Regime* (Normative Document, No 42, 2013) sec 4.6.3 (noting that the standard model is the only applicable method for deriving capital requirements and the method of internal model might be introduced in due course).

es on the premise of assumed adverse conditions.[267] The risk categorization and the scenario-based approach show that capital requirements in conformity with the notions of the SCR and the MCS are formulated and calibrated in line with the dynamic risk profile of insurance undertakings. Unlike the SCR and the MCS, the formula for the MCR does not involve the measurement of exposures to various risk categories. The approach used to derive the MCR is far less complicated than the way to measure the SCR or the MCS on account of the simple formulas as well as the few constituents thereof. The constituents of the formulas refer to some variables which are determined statically such that they are determined by an estimation of obligations, cash flows and other metrics on a ceteris paribus presumption that the financial position of an insurance undertaking is solely affected by the developments in business conditions in respect of underwriting and settlement.[268] Moreover, the calculation of the MCR relies

267 In deriving the SCR or the MCS, the risk-factor method is also used in the calculation, complementing the scenario-based method. As far as the SCR is concerned, it is mostly calculated using the scenario-based method. Whereas, the calculation of the MCS for all risk categories, except for life underwriting risk, uses the risk-factor method. The level of granularity of the risk factors stipulated in China's regulatory rules is high in that the factors are specified for various classes of exposures within each risk module or sub-module in proportion to the riskiness of the exposure. In the subsequent part, the MCR will be compared with the foregoing two capital requirements. Here, it should be pointed out in advance that the calculation of the MCR entirely relies on risk-factor method. Nevertheless, the risk factors are merely a revelation of the linear relationship between the MCR amount and several variables associated with underwriting and settling activities. Unlike the risk factors used in the calculation of the MCS, the MCR risk factors are not intended to serve as the indicator of the riskiness of various exposures arising from all kinds of activities by an insurer. Due to the discrepancy, the MCS has a much higher level of sensitivity to the changes in riskiness than the MCR does.

268 The MCR formula does not capture the impacts on insurer's financial position as a result of the adverse changes in various risk categories including underwriting risk, market risk, counterparty risk, etc. Because the formula components, i.e. technical provisions, premiums and capital at risk, are all calculated with underlying factors being unchanged. For example, the technical provision for a life insurance segment is calculated using a certain level of mortality rate. However, the mortality rate underpinning the calculation might increase materially, in which case the technical provision would no longer be sufficient to cover the increased claims by policyholders or beneficiaries. The risk of increase or decrease in the value of those factors underpinning the calculation of quantitative requirements is not taken into account. As to risk category except for the underwriting risk, they are not involved in the calculation of the components of the MCR formulas as well.

on risk factors which are assigned to the variables as multipliers, rather than the scenario-based method as adopted in the calculation of the SCR or the MCS. In sum, the calculation method employed affirms the low sensitivity of the MCR to the risks insurance undertakings are exposed to.[269] In addition to the feature of low risk-sensitivity, a defining attribute, which distinguishes the MCR from the other two, lies in the existence of floor and fixed range for the capital requirement. Under the provisions of the MCR, absolute minimums of capital amount are imposed on insurers in different segment sectors while the MCR is prescribed as a level between 25% to 45% of the SCR of an undertaking.[270] Clearly enough, the MCR requires a much lower capital position relative to the SCR, serving as the ultimate threshold for the continuation of an authorization. Non-compliance with the SCR or the MCS basically does not trigger such severe consequence as a withdrawal of an authorization, but leaves scope for supervisors to intervene in and for insurers to remedy problems on a going concern basis.

2. Overhaul of Supervisory Intervention in the Breach of MCS

The preceding analyses lead to a clear conclusion that the MCR of the Solvency II and the MCS of the C-ROSS are completely different in all dimensions, although they resemble each other in the name. It will thus be inappropriate to draw a parallel between them on the supervisory measures against non-compliances. The SCR, as the counterpart for the MCS, should be the appropriate target for comparison in regard to the nature and severity of the supervisory measures in the event that a breach of capital requirements occurs.

a) The Downsides of Intervention during Rectification

Essentially, an insurance undertaking failing to comply with the capital requirements is treated more toughly under the C-ROSS. The insurance un-

269 The MCR is a risk-based capital standard, given the risk factors diversifying across lines of business and the extreme conditions envisaged for the capital at risk. Nevertheless, relative to the calculation methods of the SCR and the MCS, its risk-sensitivity is much lower.

270 Solvency II Directive, §§ 129 (1)(d), (3).

dertaking of which the capital position falls below the MCS will be demanded to re-establish compliance and simultaneously subjected to other supervisory measures which inflict restrictions or material changes on the business of the undertaking concerned.[271] As claimed by the CIRC, the supervisory measures will be imposed on the basis of the cause for non-compliance. In its opinion, tough intervention should be implemented at the outset of the occurrence of a non-compliance in parallel with the remedial measures taken by the undertaking.

It is undisputed that apt supervisory intervention should be exercised by the authority in appropriate circumstance in order to restore compliance and protect the interests of policyholders. The complexity arises around the aptness of the intervention and the appropriateness of the circumstance where intervention is exercised. In analyzing the way in which Chinese insurance undertakings failing to meet the MCS are treated under the provisions of the C-ROSS, the dissertation identifies the demerits of imposing intervention during the rectification process. Since the supervisory measures imposed involve restrictions, prohibitions or structural changes, they will inevitably put a great strain on an insurance undertaking that already incurs a financial distress. The overall business and financial activities of the insurer will be disrupted to certain extent depending on the stringency of the measures imposed. The rectification progress of the insurance undertaking, which would have been able to fully rely on own remedial measures to re-establish compliance, could be impeded. For example, there exists a supervisory measure in the C-ROSS which requires an insurer to change executives or managers in responsible positions.[272] The non-compliance might be ascribed to poor decisions or operations by the management. However, the dismissal at the very beginning of the rectification process could not make the insurance undertaking better off in view of the

271 According to the C-ROSS integrated risk rating, the insurers with a non-compliance with the MCS are classified into the level C or D, which means the oversight activities and supervisory measures will be exercised with the intensity and methods prescribed for the C or D level group. As provided in the relevant C-ROSS rules, the quantitative indicators for the measurement of solvency adequacy include the core solvency ratio (core capital / MCS) and the aggregated solvency ratio ((core capital +supplementary capital) / MCS). The threshold for the former is 50%, while that of the latter is 100%. *See supra note* 215, at § 20 (3) (4), 27 and 29; CIRC, *China Risk Oriented Solvency System Conceptual Framework* (Policy Paper, 5 March 2014) sec IV (1); Secretariat of the CIRC, *Notification about the Consultation on the Supervisory Rules on Solvency Position of Insurance Undertakings (Public Consultation Version)* (Notification No 374, 2017).

272 *Supra note* 215, at § 27 (6).

fact that nobody is better informed of the root cause for the financial difficulty and the firm-specific factors than the existing managements. They should at least be given an opportunity to try to navigate the firm through the crisis within a specified time frame. If the attempt fails within the given period of time, alternative candidates for the management position should then be considered.

The other demerit stems from the intrinsic nature of supervisory measures. Supervisory measures are conventionally directed at problems or deficiencies in specific areas. An insurance undertaking would be required by the supervisory authority to focus on the implementation of those measures addressing the authority-targeted problems intensively. Such a practice might lead to unfavorable consequences. Intensive implementation of supervisory measures is likely to cause unintended adverse effects in a longer term, resolving short-term problem notwithstanding. Structural change as required by the authority, in particular, could bring about adverse by-products, impairing the business development in the long run. For instance, a Chinese insurer with inadequate solvency position might be required of a change in the asset structure where the CIRC holds the opinion that the decline in solvency position mainly results from heightened riskiness or actual losses arising out of certain asset categories in which an insurer has a concentration.[273] Certainly, the insurer will have to follow the mandate by selling off the assets and reallocating funds. The structural change might relieve the insurer of the present financial pain, but concurrently, it is liable to be accompanied by a maturity mismatch between the assets and liabilities. Despite the potential or actual fall in market price, the original assets might correspond well to the nature of the insurance business in terms of maturity. Under the pressure of the authority, the insurer must effect the change within short time frame, which is conducive to hasty reallocation decisions and operations. A mismatch between assets and liabilities tends to arise in such circumstance, increasing liquidity risk. Therefore, a likely by-product brought about by the requirement of asset structure change is the asset-liability mismatch that is detriment to an insurer's financial position over a long time horizon.

To sum up, the preceding analyses are not intended for a disapproval of imposing supervisory measures to resolve the situation, but proposing that they should be imposed where a fact is established that the insurer's own rectification leads to no improvement or an even worse solvency condition. The insurers that fail to meet the MCS should be entitled to restore

273 *Id.* at § 27 (3).

financial soundness free from supervisory measures within a reasonable period of time during which remedial measures can be implemented based on their own arrangements with the firm-specific factors being allowed for. The self-directed rectification will reveal the insurer's resilience to adverse conditions and examine the efficacy of the mechanisms the insurer designs to re-establish capital adequacy. More importantly, it creates a sound environment for the rectification to the extent that any undesired effect arising from restrictions, prohibitions or changes is avoided. If the insurer is able to recover financial viability in a timely manner, it will be prevented from incurring stringent supervisory measures which might produce unintended impacts on its business and financial conditions in a longer term.

b) Dual Supervisory Approach to Capital Inadequacy

A dual approach is supposed to be adopted by the NCAs in the EU in tackling the breach of the SCR. The treatment of the insurance undertakings that have non-compliance with the SCR is differentiated depending on whether the solvency position of the undertaking continues to deteriorate subsequent to the initial non-compliance.[274] If further deterioration does not occur, the insurer would be allowed to remedy the non-compliance itself on the basis of the approved recovery plan within a specified period of time, and more importantly, without incurring additional supervisory measures.[275] In the circumstance where a deterioration arises after the initial non-compliance with the SCR, the insurance undertaking will be subjected to tough supervisory measures comprising restrictions, prohibitions or alterations that are aimed at reducing its risk profile and preventing a reduction of financial resources.[276]

274 Solvency II Directive, § 141.

275 *Id.* at § 138 (2) (3).

276 *Id.* at §§ 140 - 142. In addition to the materialization of a financial deterioration, there exists another exception that 'In exceptional circumstances, where the supervisory authority is of the opinion that the financial situation of the undertaking concerned will deteriorate further, it may also restrict or prohibit the free disposal of the assets of that undertaking'. *See id.* at § 138 (5). As for the specific supervisory measures under deteriorating financial conditions, a draft regulatory technical standard (hereinafter referred to as "RTS") provides important examples. *See* EIOPA, *Consultation Paper on the Advice to the European Commission in response to the Call for Advice on recovery plan, finance scheme and supervisory*

The duality of the supervisory treatment shows the EU insurance regulators' inclination that severe supervisory measures should not be employed as the first tactic to deal with the insurers violating the SCR. It is consistent with the proposition made previously in the dissertation. The mechanism of the supervisory measures by the CIRC need be restructured for the sake of insurer's sustainable financial soundness in a longer-term. The dual approach, as adopted in the EU, is suitable for the CIRC's supervisory review process in view of the relatively independent status of the supervisory intervention stage. Differentiated arrangements for supervisory measures have no collision with other mechanisms in the CIRC's supervisory review process.

On account of the more drastic market movements in China as compared to mature economies, it is in the interests of policyholders to adopt a more prudent manner in determining the circumstances where supervisory measures should be put in place. It is advisable that stringent supervisory measures become applicable where no sign of improvements is observed after the lapse of two-thirds of the rectification process, even if a deterioration in solvency position does not occur during the process.[277] The reason is that the failure to make any progress in reverting to an adequate capital position within the larger portion of the time frame for a rectification suffices to prove that the remedial measures planned and implemented by an insurer are insufficient or inappropriate. Proceeding with those remedial tactics to go through the remaining course of the rectification could hardly bring about a desired outcome for the financially impaired insurer, and meanwhile it will put the interests of policyholders and beneficiaries at great stake given the accumulation of adverse factors and intensification of market reactions with a further lapse of time.

For the purpose of reaching a due judgment of the rectification condition, the CIRC shall conduct closer surveillance of the rectification progress of the insurers concerned. Insurers would therefore be subject to more stringent reporting requirements during the rectification process.

---

powers in deteriorating financial conditions (Consultation Paper, EIOPA-CP-14/062, 2014) 12.

277 The length of the rectification process mentioned herein should also include any extension permitted.

c) Advice on Effective Rectification Mechanism

In accordance with the Solvency II, a supervisory authority is empowered to take all measures necessary to protect the interests of policyholders in case the insurer has a deterioration in financial conditions after the initial non-compliance with the SCR. It means that a supervisory authority can use its discretion in setting the severity of supervisory measures, which will not be confined to a predetermined scope. Obviously, the stringency of the supervisory measures exercised in deteriorating financial conditions under the solvency II approximates that of the supervisory measures for an initial breach of the MCS under the C-ROSS. It exposes again the shortcoming of the intervention mechanism in China's insurance supervision, namely the absence of flexible supervisory measures with due regard for firm specificities. Owing to the lack of such supervisory measures, Chinese insurance undertakings are often subjected to restrictive or prohibitive measures once a non-compliance with capital requirements materializes.

aa) Essential Elements of the Recovery Period under Solvency II

As far as the Solvency II is concerned, the flexibility of the intervention exercised against the breach of the SCR resides in the recovery mechanism built on the trade-off between an insurer's business autonomy and the need for supervisory oversight. An insurance undertaking will not receive instructions from the supervisory authority as to what actions shall be taken, but will be required to work out the resolution on its own. The undertaking is vested with the freedom to decide on the tools and approaches for restoring its financial position. Apart from that, an extension arrangement underpins the flexibility of the recovery mechanism as well. The recovery period could be prolonged by three months.[278] For major insurance market players, in exceptional adverse situations, the prolongation could be up to seven years.[279] Of course, the course of recovery is not fully at the discretion of an insurer, otherwise the recovery mechanism cannot be categorized as a supervisory measure. The supervisory authority steps in to exert control over the recovery at times when it is necessary to determine if the insurer is on the right track to restoration. Before an insurer can take any action to remedy its non-compliance, it is required to submit to the au-

278 Solvency II Directive, § 138 (3).
279 *Id.* at § 138 (4).

thority a recovery plan presenting mandatory information about critical aspects of the recovery, which is mainly intended for making projections of its financial conditions and specifying prospective remedial measures.[280] The authority would evaluate the recovery plan and make a decision on an approval. The plan is therefore the principal means by which the authority can exercise an ex ante control over the adequacy of the remedial measures devised by the insurer. In the course of a recovery, the authority collects information and oversees the progress so that it could reach an appropriate judgment about the developments of the insurer's financial conditions. Where an actual deterioration or an evident tendency of deterioration in solvency position is identified, more severe supervisory measures will be imposed. With the recovery period approaching an end, the supervisory authority will make an assessment of the situation faced by the undertaking in order to determine whether to grant an extension to the recovery period.

In essence, the recovery mechanism qualifies as a flexible supervisory measure which leaves sufficient room for the insurance undertaking to devise and implement remedial measures autonomously to great degree. Supervisory intervention is reduced to a low level such that the substance of the remedial actions taken to re-establish compliance is not defined by the supervisory authority, which only conducts technical control of the efficacy and duration of the recovery.

bb) Weaknesses of Existing Rectification Arrangement

In the C-ROSS system, there exists only one provision in relation to the rectification, which shortly lays down that the insurer concerned will be required to rectify problems within a specific time frame.[281] It is greatly different from the recovery mechanism of the Solvency II in two aspects. Firstly, for a Chinese insurer breaching the MCS, the rectification will be carried out along with the implementation of other supervisory measures consisting of restrictions or disciplines. However, a European insurer will

280 Apart from these main issues, there are other elements required to be presented in the recovery plan, including overall reinsurance policy, the methods and assumptions used in deriving the estimations, own analysis of the causes for non-compliances, as well as the supporting evidence of the internal approval and of any outside commitments. *See id.* at § 142; *supra note* 276 (Consultation Paper), at 8.

281 *See supra note* 215, at § 26 (3).

not be subjected to any additional supervisory measure while making attempts with remedial actions to improve the inadequate solvency condition, provided that its financial conditions do not continue to deteriorate. Secondly, as opposed to the high particularity of the rules on the recovery mechanism embedded in the Solvency II, there is not even a basic frame provided in the C-ROSS with regard to the rectification process, which gives rise to an uncertainty in the length of the process and an absence of supervisory control over the rectification.

The first difference above results from a lack of differentiation in treatment between the non-compliant insurance undertakings without financial deteriorations and those with continued financial deteriorations. As analyzed in previous sections, the adoption of a dual approach will be beneficial to an insurer's restoration to compliance, contributing to the sustainability of its financial soundness. On condition that the supervisory intervention mechanism under the C-ROSS is adjusted in alignment with the dual approach, the difference will no longer be present. The second difference shows a serious lack of implementing details about an insurer's rectification process in China, which implies insufficiency of supervisory control before and during the rectification process. Without a due involvement of the supervisory authority, independent evaluation and control, which is used to ensure the adequacy of the rectification measures by an insurer and determine the systemic impacts of those measures, is unavailable. The unspecified provision on insurer rectification also results in the absence of essential principles for the duration and prolongation of the rectification process, which is likely to cause inconsistent treatment of the insurers with similar degree of non-compliance.

cc) Reshaping Rectification Process in Alignment with Solvency II Recovery Mechanism

In view of the downsides, the provision on rectification should be expanded on to develop into an elaborate mechanism balancing flexibility with intervention. The recovery mechanism of the Solvency II is viewed as a paragon of such a balance on account of the tools, procedures and methods employed to bolster the recovery in normal or exceptional situations.

The recovery plan is critical to an orderly functioning of the Solvency II recovery mechanism. It serves as the basis for a re-establishment of compliance given that an insurer will keep to the self-formulated plan to implement remedial measures. Concurrently, the plan is made use of by the supervisory authority to intervene in the recovery process in light of the elements required to be included alongside the supervisory approval. Seeing that the plan plays a major role in shaping a sound recovery mechanism, the rectification process under the C-ROSS should likewise incorporate a rectification plan so as to assess ex ante the viability of the rectification measures and identify potential deficiencies of those measures. It will otherwise lead to a higher likelihood of a failure to rectify non-compliances due to the fact that the supervision in the course of a rectification would then have to be solely based on the ex post information or reports on the measures which the insurer has already taken and the effects thereof. A rectification plan will allow the supervisor to intervene in a proactive manner in an insurer's course of actions, instead of taking a reactive approach to dealing with the problems exposed in the process of rectification. In the formation of the requirements on the rectification plan, the characteristics of China's insurance market and the accounting practices of Chinese insurers shall be taken into account.

Another important quality of the Solvency II recovery mechanism is the time schedule for the procedures following the observation of a non-compliance with the SCR. As a matter of fact, the current C-ROSS rules give no clue about the span of the rectification. There exist two possibilities under the current situation. The first possible scenario is that no specified time limit is imposed and a rectification is expected to be completed within a reasonable period of time. If it is the case, the divergence in regard to the definition of reasonableness might arise between the supervisory authority and the insurers. The other possibility is that the CIRC would specify the time limit in each particular case. If true, it will be viewed as an instance of low supervisory transparency since the grounds on which the duration is determined are not made public. It suffices to say that specific rules should be put in place in regard of the time frame for all the required activities related to a rectification process. At least, the time limit for the submission of a rectification plan, the rectification period and the extension thereof should be laid down with clarity in the relevant provisions. Provided that there is a scope for supervisory judgment under some circumstances, the time frame that would normally apply shall be explicitly provided for in the provisions, accompanied by the factors on which the supervisory judgment is based.

Last but not least, a special extension arrangement is provided in the Solvency II regime. The arrangement is intended to further extend the recovery period for the major insurance market players affected in exceptional adverse situations for the purpose of reducing the potential pro-cyclical effects on the financial system or the insurance market which could be caused by the remedial measures of those insurers.[282] On account of the considerable length of the maximal extension to the six-month normal recovery period,[283] namely seven years, collective pro-cyclical behavior for reducing risk profile or increasing eligible own funds within a short period among the major insurers distressed by adverse market movements is less likely to materialize. Importantly, the flexibility of an extension arrangement is subject to supervisory control throughout the course of the extended recovery period. The supranational and national insurance supervisory authorities in the EU are responsible for determining and proclaiming the existence of an exceptional adverse situation, which constitutes the grounds of the extension granted.[284] As to the duration of an extension, the supervisors base their decisions on the estimation of the financial market developments and might make adjustments according to the actual changes of market conditions.[285] Over the extended period, the recovery progress is placed under close oversight. The failure to achieve notable progress will result in the withdrawal of the extension.[286] In China, the downside of the absence of such a mechanism has been exposed during the financial crisis erupting in 2007. At the time, several big Chinese insurers incurred deteriorations in financial conditions, faced with the risk of or actual capital inadequacy due to the sharp downturn in the financial markets.[287] In order for restoring the capital position within a short period as well as being relieved of stringent supervisory measures, the financially distressed insurers had to take drastic actions with high pro-cyclical effects. The already poor market conditions were further worsened by the intensive capital-raising activities of the big insurers which issued a massive amount of new shares, convertible bonds and other financial instruments.[288] Another notable fact calling for the establishment of the special

282 Solvency II Directive, § 138 (4); EIOPA, *Consultation Paper on the draft proposal for Guidelines on the extension of the recovery period in exceptional adverse situations* (Consultation Paper, EIOPA-CP-14/046, 2014) para 1.7.

283 Solvency II Directive, § 138 (3).

284 *Id.* at § 138 (4).

285 *Supra note* 282 (Consultation Paper), at para 1.9.

286 *Supra note* 284.

287 The solvency position of a large proportion of insurers in China declined sharply during the financial crisis in 2008 according to their financial statements. Most insurers ascribed the sizable fall in the solvency ratio to the bearish capital market.

288 As an example, the large-scale capital-raising plan of Ping An put a great strain on the market which was undergoing financial crisis at the time, causing a fur-

extension mechanism is that China's economy begins to experience a slowdown, which will last in the long run. China's financial markets would be periodically impacted by the falls in major economic indicators. Given the susceptibility of Chinese insurers to the adverse market developments, their solvency position will be materially affected at times of the materialization of significant slowdowns. If an adequate rectification period is unavailable, those big insurers of which the solvency ratios fall below the required level would be forced to make tremendous sell-offs or raise vast amount of capital in the market during the market downturn for the sake of restoring compliance within a short time frame and avoiding the escalation in the intensity of supervisory measures. Definitely, it entails great systemic risk for China's financial system as a whole. Therefore, it is absolutely necessary to integrate the special extension mechanism into the rectification process of the C-ROSS. In other words, insurance undertakings with significant market share generally or in a specific line of business, if fail to meet the capital requirements owing to an exceptional adverse condition which causes substantially negative effects on the whole or a specific segment of the insurance sector, should be entitled to a longer time frame to restore solvency adequacy than the rectification period permitted under normal economic situations. The definition of the insurers and circumstances, which qualify for the special extension, can be adapted to cater for the economic and institutional idiosyncrasies in China. In addition to the three situations laid down in the Solvency II,[289] other likely scenarios which can give rise to financial hardship need to be included within the scope of the exceptional adverse situations in the C-ROSS, such as an unanticipated plunge in non-financial asset price and a significant policy change in the financial sector.

---

ther plummet of the stock index. *See* Jason Leow, 'Ping An to Test China Markets For Resilience' *The Wall Street Journal* (Beijing, 18 February 2008).

289 Exceptional adverse situations are defined as the three conditions as follows: an unforeseen, sharp and steep fall in financial markets, a persistent low interest rate environment, and a high-impact catastrophic event. *See* Solvency II Directive, § 138 (4).

3. Factors, Judgments and Conclusions

a) The Considerations Factored in Determining Supervisory Measures

Through the discussion on the supervisory intervention against the breach of the SCR, the important factors forming the basis for the decision on the supervisory measures become apparent. Some of the factors are implied by the arrangements of the recovery mechanism embedded in the Solvency II, while others are explicitly referred to as the principles which the NCAs in the EU should take into account in formulating the supervisory measures for an insurer incurring a financial deterioration after the observance of a non-compliance with the SCR.[290] The factors are set out as follows. (i) trigger for the non-compliance; (ii) level of riskiness, deficiencies or non-compliance; (iii) actions an insurer has taken; (iv) possibility of a more flexible supervisory measure; (v) applicability of the standard approach; (vi) adequacy of the supervisory measure to avoid another non-compliance in the short term; (vii) pro-cyclical effects of the supervisory measure; (viii) level of supervisory reporting required for the implementation of the supervisory measure; (ix) intensity of the oversight of the progress of implementation and restoration to compliance (x) long-term impacts on the insurance business.

b) Flaws in Formation of Supervisory Measures and Root Causes

As far as the CIRC's supervisory practices are concerned, in view of the fact that the supervisory measures against the non-compliances with quantitative and qualitative requirements are basically determined on the basis of the classification outcomes which reveal the causes and the extent of the non-compliances,[291] the abovementioned factor (i) and (ii) are the major

290 *Supra note* 276 (the Consultation Paper), at 12-13.

291 The supervisory measures provided for in the C-ROSS integrated risk rating constitute the essential part of the whole intervention mechanism of the CIRC. The rating incorporates a classification that is utilized to indicate an insurer's solvency risk profile. Supervisory measures are prescribed accordingly. As introduced in previous sections, there exist other supervisory assessments of which the outcome would lead to supervisory measures being imposed. Some of those assessments contain a classification, while others give the evaluation outcome without a classification. However, none of them is deemed more significant than the C-ROSS integrated risk rating because the latter encompasses the eval-

considerations taken into account in reaching the decision. Among all the factors, (iv), (v), (vi), (vii), (ix) and (x) are not made adequate allowances for in determining the supervisory measure to impose in a particular situation, mainly as the consequence of the supervisory activities centering around classification outcomes. An insurer with deficiencies, at the end of the supervisory review process, is subjected to the supervisory measures associated with its classification level. However, the insurers classified into the same level according to their riskiness are mutually different in asset-liability and business structure. The linkage between the supervisory measures and the classification level therefore diminishes the scope for tailoring the intervention to the idiosyncrasies of a particular insurer. In spite of the disadvantage, as far as the supervisory authority and the supervised entities in China are concerned, classification outcomes have become the center of attention insofar as most efforts of both sides are dedicated to maintaining or raising the classification level. From the standpoint of the authority, sound classification outcomes across the insurance sector signify the effectiveness of supervisory rules and an accomplishment of supervisory objectives. As to the insurers, a fine classification outcome represents financial soundness and prevents the imposition of severe supervisory measures. The purpose of the supervisory intervention is somewhat distorted as a result of the classification outcomes being made as the priority, which actually leads the intervention to be directed at inducing a prompt elevation of the classification level. This entails the repercussion that the need to improve the classification level overrides the consideration given to other aspects, including the effects on the insurance business in a longer term. However, pro-cyclical effects being insufficiently factored in the determination of supervisory measures is ascribed to the lack of awareness of insurers' systemic importance in China, which is associated with the scant regard for financial stability in setting supervisory objectives.

c) Generalization about Amelioration of CIRC's Supervisory Intervention

Dissociating supervisory intervention from the classification level will be conducive to factoring the absent considerations in the determination of

uation of almost all major risk factors associated with the core issue of insurance supervision, namely the solvency. The CIRC attaches great importance to the integrated risk rating to the extent that the approaches and intensity of supervisory approvals and reviews are premised on the outcome of the rating.

supervisory measures. Ideally, the decision on the measures should be based on the conclusion of a deep and focused analysis of individual insurers like the analyses supposed to be carried out at the detailed review stage in the Solvency II supervisory review process. However, a restructuration of the basis for supervisory measures would involve extensive changes to the existing rules and prompt a concern for the coherence of the rule-making because the classification-based supervision is regarded as the keystone of China's insurance supervision. For this reason, it will be better to adopt a more cost-effective approach to enable a partial dissociation by bringing in mechanisms complementary to the classification-based intervention. The mechanisms to be put in place shall consist of two parts. One is to provide for a rectification mechanism prior to the imposition of tough supervisory measures that are associated with the classification level. That is to say, an insurer shall be granted a period to rely on its own course of action to remedy non-compliances arising in any supervisory area. The substance should be identical to the proposed rectification process in the case of the non-compliance with the MCS. Given the advantages of such a mechanism, the failure to allow for those necessary factors in making intervention decisions can be counterbalanced to some extent. Only on the occurrence of a deterioration in pertinent conditions or at the conclusion of a failed rectification should the supervisory measures connected with the insurer's classification level be imposed for drastic intervention.

Where the classification-based intervention is set to be exercised, the findings of the analysis made at the detailed review stage shall assume a critical role in forming the concrete supervisory measures. This is envisaged as the other part of the complementary mechanisms referred to in the preceding paragraph. Evidently, the prerequisite is to put in place the detailed review stage. The findings of the detailed review shall be used to help adapt supervisory intervention to the business, financial and risk characteristics of a specific insurer.[292]

It is absolutely necessary to take account of the potential pro-cyclical effects in reaching the decisions on intervention, especially when it comes to

292 Deeper analyses and evaluations are developed at the detailed review stage. The intensity and direction of those analytical activities is determined by the outcome of the various assessments conducted at the former stage. In other words, the detailed review activities take into account the outcomes of all previous assessments, making calibration and refinement. The outcome of a detailed review can accurately reflect an insurer's overall conditions and highlight its distinctive facets. The detailed review outcome therefore serves to calibrate supervisory measures.

the intervention decisions concerning those major insurers of which the behavior could bring about market-wide impacts. An effective way of avoiding undesirable pro-cyclical consequences is to evaluate the all-round effects of the planned supervisory measures case-by-case and redesign them on the grounds of any material pro-cyclical effects foreseen. In parallel, pro-cyclical effects should be factored into supervisory decisions on any other issues, not limited to supervisory measures. This again calls for the inclusion of the element in the scope of supervisory objectives, as pointed out in the section E of Chapter 3.

C. Chapter Conclusions

The CIRC's supervisory review process is comprised of two stages - supervisory assessment and supervisory measures. At the supervisory assessment stage there are on-site inspections along with off-site appraisals directed at the supervisory areas which are statutorily specified. A majority of the off-site appraisals will conclude with classifications for insurance undertakings. Each classification is linked to several supervisory measures specified in relevant regulations. An insurer with risk of or actual non-compliances is therefore subjected to one or more supervisory measures according to the classification it is assigned as a result of the appraisals.

Insofar as the supervisory assessment by the CIRC is concerned, emerging problems and adverse factors that come into existence in the insurance sector and the wider financial system cannot be adequately taken into account due to the fact that the assessment only covers the predetermined areas prescribed in the regulations. As for the supervisory measures, the close association between classifications and intervention has a negative effect on the specificity of the intervention imposed on insurance undertakings because even the undertakings with an identical classification result would have distinct risk profiles.

The comparison with the relevant parts in the Solvency II system reveals an important element embedded in the supervisory review process of the NCAs in the EU, namely the detailed review stage, which distinguishes the CIRC's supervisory review process from that of its European counterparts in terms of the level and quality of assessments. The stage lies between the risk assessment stage and the supervisory measures stage, which draws a marked contrast to the procedures of the CIRC's supervisory review process. As the main benefits of the detailed review activities, the theme-focused and undertaking-focused analysis based on the findings of the risk assessments at the previous stage would be performed to examine in depth and detail the weaknesses and deficiencies of insurance undertakings. By the application of a detailed review, new risk areas identified in the previous assessments will be dealt with using a theme-focused analysis of all the insurers. Firm-specific problems will be exposed in the undertaking-focused analysis and the conclusion of this analysis could make the subsequent supervisory measures more tailored to the actual conditions of the undertakings concerned. Incorporation of the detailed review stage is hence deemed to be a solid approach to the shortcomings of the CIRC's supervisory review process as referred to in the previous paragraph.

Another emphasis of the chapter is placed on the CIRC's intervention mechanism against the non-compliance with capital requirements, i.e. the breach of the MCS. The supervisory measures exercised by the CIRC show scant specificity and undue severity. A full dissociation of supervisory measures from classification results is not advisable, because China's insurance supervision is devised as a classification-based system and dissociation requires fundamental changes to a large number of legal acts. The specificity of supervisory measures could be enhanced providing that a detailed review stage is integrated into the supervisory review process. The outcome of the detailed review activities can help calibrate the supervisory measures which are initially determined according to the classification result of an insurance undertaking. As for the flaws related to severity, the chapter calls for a dual approach to the non-compliance with the MCS, in alignment with the way adopted in the EU for tackling the non-compliance with the SCR. That is to say, in the event of a non-compliance without further deterioration in financial conditions, an insurer could be given a time frame to restore to compliance free from additional supervisory measures. In the other case, if a continued deterioration occurs, severe supervisory measures would be imposed. For the purpose of the implementation of the dual approach, an effective rectification mechanism should be put in place. The application of the dual approach shall not be limited to the non-compliance with capital requirements, but extended to non-compliances arising in other supervisory areas as well.

Chapter 5. An Analysis of CIRC's Supervisory Transparency

Transparency is one of the essential qualitative aspects of a supervisory regime. Supervisory transparency reflects the extent to which the component elements of a supervisory system are made known to the public.[293] The manner in which the supervision is conducted has material impacts on the quality of the discharge of the supervisory responsibilities and on the public confidence in the supervision.[294] The level of supervisory transparency is dependent on the accessibility and clarity of the substantive, procedural and methodological elements comprising the supervisory system.[295]

---

293 *See* Christine Kaufmann and Rolf H Weber, 'The Role of Transparency in Financial Regulation' (2010) 13(3) Journal of International Economic Law 779, 782 (noting that information is the essential element of transparency, with making information public being its institutional dimension); Alberto Alemanno, 'Unpacking the Principle of Openness in EU Law Transparency, Participation and Democracy' (2014) 39(1) European Law Review 72, 77 (analyzing that the Article 15 (3) of the TFEU actually provides the concrete essence of the principle of transparency to which the EU institutions should conform: citizens are entitled to the access to the documents of all EU institutions); Alan S. Blinder, *The Quiet Revolution: Central Banking Goes Modern* (Yale University Press 2004) ch 1 (defining that " a central bank is transparent if its actions are 'easily detected,' its policies are 'readily understood,' and its pronouncements are 'free from deceit'."); Franka Liedorp *et al.*, 'Transparency of Banking Supervisors' (2013) 61(2) IMF Economic Review 310, 313 (presenting that transparency in supervision means the degree to which the information involved in the supervisory process is disclosed by the supervisor).

294 *See* Monika Bauhr and Marcia Grimes, 'What is Government Transparency: New Measures and Relevance for Quality of Government' (2012) The Quality of Government Institute at the University of Gothenburg Working Paper Series 2012: 16, 20-23 (presenting that 'transparency increases the likelihood of detecting malfeasance①thereby deter the abuse of public power', leading to a lower level of corruption and enhanced quality of government.); Rex Deighton-Smith, 'Regulatory transparency in OECD countries: Overview, Trends and Challenges' (2004) 63(1) Australian Journal of Public Administration 66, 68 (analyzing that transparency can effectively promote the trust in government given the stakeholders' ability to scrutinize the administrative actions and decisions.).

295 *See* Elia Armstrong, 'Integrity, Transparency and Accountability in Public Administration: Recent Trends, Regional and International Developments and Emerging Issues' (2005) Publication of the Department of Economic and Social Affairs at the United Nations, August 2005 <unpan1.un.org/intradoc/groups/pu

A secretive supervisory culture is certain to cause great concerns of the public for the credibility and legitimacy of the rules or decisions made by the supervisors on account of the insufficiencies of informational accessibility and participation rights. Moreover, secretiveness is conducive to a supervisory capture.[296]

---

blic/documents/un/unpan020955.pdf> accessed 20 January 2016 (conceptualizing transparency as public accessibility to timely and reliable information about the decisions and developments in the public sector). Some papers argue that the judgment about the transparency of a public actor should be based on the availability of the information about the actor which enables outsiders to monitor its internal workings and activities. *See* Stephan Grimmelikhuijsen et al., 'The Effect of Transparency on Trust in Government: A Cross-National Comparative Experiment' (2013) 73(4) Public Administration Review 575, 576; Albert Meijer, 'Understanding the Complex Dynamics of Transparency' (2013) 73(3) Public Administration Review 429, 430.

296 Regulatory capture is the result or process by which regulation is, at least partially by intent and action of the sector regulated, consistently or repeatedly directed away from a defeasible model of the public interests and towards the interests of the regulated sector. The attempt made by regulated entities to capture regulatory agencies is grounded in the fact that the public agencies are empowered to coerce. The regulated sector mainly seeks policy benefits from regulators in four dimensions: subsidy, entry control, substitutes or complements, and price-fixing. In the setting of supervision, the public and the supervisory agency interact in a principal-agent relationship. The cost for the public to monitor the moves of a supervisory agency plays a key role in determining the viability of public scrutiny, which in turn impacts on the extent to which a supervisory agency would act in the interests of the public. The monitoring of a supervisory agency is premised on an adequate level of transparency in the supervision. Without due supervisory transparency, monitoring becomes overly costly and public participation would be impeded. In the absence of information directly available from the supervisory agency, monitoring has to be made on the basis of the observation of supervisory outcomes and the information from non-official sources. Secretiveness in supervision is therefore likely to prompt supervisors to cater to the demands of the supervised entities for private benefits at the expense of the public interests which supervisors are supposed to represent. *See* Daniel Carpenter, 'Detecting and Measuring Capture' in Daniel Carpenter and David A Moss (eds), *Preventing Regulatory Capture: Special Interest Influence and How to Limit It* (Cambridge University Press 2013); David A Moss and Daniel Carpenter, 'Conclusion: A Focus on Evidence and Prevention' in Daniel Carpenter and David A Moss (eds), *Preventing Regulatory Capture: Special Interest Influence and How to Limit It* (Cambridge University Press 2013); George J Stigler, 'The Theory of Economic Regulation' (1971) 2(1) The Bell Journal of Economics and Management Science 3, 4-6; Michael E Levine and Jennifer L Forrence, 'Regulatory Capture, Public Interest, and the Public Agenda: Toward a Synthesis' (1990) 6 Journal of Law, Economics, & Organization 167, 172-174.

The importance of supervisory transparency lies in the fact that it serves as the prerequisite for participation and accountability which are crucial factors underpinning the openness and legitimacy of the supervision alongside transparency.[297] Instead of merely being the basis of the two factors, supervisory transparency interacts with them in the shaping of the openness of a supervisory system since one factor tends to be reinforced as a result of the improvement of another, or weakened following the worsening of another.[298]

A. Critical Thinking about CIRC's Supervisory Transparency

China's policy decision makers have established the objective of building a rule-based public administration.[299] In other words, laws are expected to become the keystone of the governance in the future, accompanied by fewer instructions given at the discretion of the officials in charge. Openness is defined as one of the important factors leading to a rule-based administration.[300] The legal standards in relation to the transparency of administra-

---

297 *See e.g.* Teresa M Harrison and Djoko Sigit Sayogo, 'Transparency, participation, and accountability practices in open government: A comparative study' (2014) 31(4) Government Information Quarterly 513 (analyzing that an open government can only be achieved through the measures and efforts in regard to transparency, participation and accountability, which presupposes public accessibility and represents democracy.); *supra note* 293 (Kaufmann and Weber) at 791-792 (noting that without the mechanisms ensuring the access to reliable information, members of the public are unable to have an informed participation in regulatory decision-making or hold actors accountable); Joana Mendes, *Participation in EU Rule-Making: A Rights-Based Approach* (Oxford University Press 2011) ch 5.4.1 (presenting that 'the right of access to information is a fundamental prerequisite for an effective exercise of participation rights.').

298 *But see* Sanjeev Khagram et al., 'Overview and Synthesis: The Political Economy of Fiscal Transparency, Participation, and Accountability around the World' in Sanjeev Khagram, Archon Fung and Paolo de Renzio (eds), *Open Budgets: The Political Economy of Transparency, Participation, and Accountability* (Brookings Institution Press 2013) 39 (presenting that in the realm of public finance they find 'the links between fiscal transparency, participation, and accountability are often weak, interrupted, incomplete, or, in the best of cases, difficult to unearth and explain and dependent on idiosyncratic factors and conditions.').

299 The Central Committee of the Communist Party of China and the State Council, *The Implementing Framework for Establishing a Rule-Based Administration (from 2015 to 2020)* (White Paper, 2015).

300 *Id.* at para 30.

tion are released in order for a uniform and consistent implementation across the government departments and agencies in China.

As the single government agency exercising oversight of China's insurance sector, the CIRC adopts transparency mechanisms and determines the scope for disclosure in conformity with those standards. The supervisory openness of the authority is governed by a self-formulated department rule transposed from an administrative regulation on governmental information publication which is issued by the State Council.[301] The foregoing department rule serves as the legal basis for the particular responsibilities fulfilled by the authority for the sake of supervisory openness. It defines the principles, scope, tasks and rules of procedure for the work related to supervisory transparency, conferring the right to supervisory information on the public.

Generally, information is made known to the public through electronic publication, press briefings and supervisors' presentations delivered at conferences.[302] The information is by and large released on a voluntary basis, but individuals are entitled to solicit for undisclosed information as well.[303] Where a member of the public files a request for the access to information, it will be subject to a supervisory evaluation of the need for secrecy and consent from the entities involved.[304] It is noteworthy that the openness of the supervision at the local level is congruent with that at the national level as the regional supervisory agencies around the country stick to the approaches used by the central supervisory authority.

In the following parts, the main facets of China's insurance supervisory transparency will be analyzed. The analytical emphasis is placed on the particularity of the published information, the transparency mechanisms and the weaknesses thereof.

I. Transparency of China's Insurance Supervisory Rules

The fundamental facet of the openness of a supervisory regime lies in the accessibility and clarity of the rules. From the perspective of the CIRC, the

301 *See* the Rules on the Publication of Administrative Information at CIRC 2008; *see also* the Regulations on the Publication of Government Information in China 2007.

302 *Supra note* 301 (the Rules) at § 14 (1).

303 *Id.* at § 16.

304 *Id.* at § 19.

rules, in functional terms, can be broadly categorized into two sorts: the rules for control and the rules for scrutiny. The rules for control denote the statutory provisions whereby the supervisors exercise authority to exert control proactively or reactively for the sake of insurers' compliance. In the context of China's supervisory rulebook, they mainly refer to the provisions on supervisory approvals required for specified activities by an insurer and the supervisory intervention in the event of a (potential) non-compliance. The rules for scrutiny are the provisions whereby the authority continually monitors and assesses the overall conditions of an insurer, which encompass the restrictive standards imposed all around and the assessment approaches employed by the CIRC.

1. Accessibility and Clarity of CIRC's Supervisory Rules

The rules for control are soundly accessible given the fact that the substantive requirements governing the authority's decision-making with reference to its supervisory approvals and intervention are explicitly available in the relevant department rules and normative documents.[305] The procedural elements pertinent to its supervisory decisions are laid down in parallel.[306]

The interested parties are able to be well informed of the way Chinese supervisors exercise judgments and of the factors the supervisors take into account in arriving at a decision on a specific issue, as long as the applicable provisions existing in the relevant regulations are properly ascertained. The ascertainment is facilitated by the assembling of the statutory requirements on supervisory approvals and measures. The entirety of statutory requirements pertinent to the supervisory approvals for a range of issues is recapitulated in an integrated manner in a special section on the electronic platform of the CIRC. Inside the section, all of the issues subject to the au-

305 The requirements in relation to supervisory approvals are usually laid down in a separate section of a regulation on condition that the regulation concerns an issue subject to approval. The provisions on supervisory measures are mostly stipulated inside the section titled oversight and administration or the section titled legal liability in most regulations.

306 The procedural elements regarding a supervisory approval basically refer to the set of procedures an insurer should follow and the materials required to be submitted to the supervisory authority.

thority's approval are enumerated,[307] accompanied by the guidance on the pursuit of approvals which specifies the legal basis, required documents, review criteria and process. The integration of the provisions relating to supervisory approvals is definitely conducive to the lucidity of the decision-making mechanism of the authority. As a matter of fact, the documents and conditions relevant to an approval decision on a specific issue could be stipulated in more than one legal act owing to the fact that supplementary requirements are likely to be prescribed in implementing regulations or other regulations with an overlap in that issue.[308] By assembling the rules regarding supervisory approvals, the supervisory authority effectively draws the provisions applicable to a specific issue from all pertinent regulations, giving integrated instructions with respect to the essential elements involved in the pursuit of a supervisory approval. As for the provisions on supervisory intervention, they are assembled in the final chapters of the Insurance Act of China,[309] including the measures against the non-compliances of insurance undertakings and the legal liability of the management. From the perspective of stakeholders, the assembling of the rules enables a global view of the essentials of the supervisory measures imposed under different situations, delineating the boundaries between permitted and prohibited activities as well as clarifying the discrepancies between varying levels of non-compliance in regard to the intensity of supervisory measures.

In terms of the rules for scrutiny, they show sufficient accessibility, but scant clarity. All the thresholds, ratios and limits in quantitative and qualitative aspects above which insurance undertakings are expected to reach are explicitly stipulated in different forms of regulations. Meanwhile, the criteria, tools and methods that the supervisory authority employs to exercise on-site inspections and off-site appraisals are disclosed as well. The

---

307 There exist altogether eighteen issues subject to supervisory approval as required by the authority. Those issues could basically be categorized as: establishment and wind-up of (re)insurance business, major changes in business operation (articles of incorporation, place of business, split/merger, etc.), forms and rates, qualification of executives, capital increase, investment in new asset categories and establishment of insurance intermediaries. *See* CIRC, 'The Catalogue of the Issues Subject to CIRC's Administrative Approval' (CIRC Website, 11 December 2014) <www.circ.gov.cn/web/ site0/ tab5177/> accessed 4 May 2016.

308 As contrasted with supplementary requirements, general requirements on a supervisory approval for a specific issue are covered in the regulation which specifically deals with the issue. In the foregoing regulation, other requirements relating to various aspects of the issue are laid down in parallel.

309 The Insurance Act of China 1995, §§ 136-179.

clarity of these rules poses a major drawback, while they are publicly available. The clarity stated herein does not refer to the wording or the intelligibility of the provisions. Instead, it means the supervisory rules as a whole are arranged in a way that renders the rule system disorderly and ambiguous to some extent. A larger part of the problem has been analyzed in the section B of Chapter 2. There exist dozens of department rules and hundreds of normative documents in force. Each department rule or normative document is issued as an independent regulation. Different aspects or situations relevant to a supervisory issue are addressed separately in multiple regulations. The regulated entities are liable to unintentionally disregard the supervisory requirements as the unsystematic rule-making undermines the ability to be informed of the existence of special rules applicable to a particular situation. As opposed to the way that the rules for control are presented, the rules for scrutiny are not assembled on the basis of the connections between the rules. The dearth of such an arrangement as to have the effect of rule assembling leads to the deficiencies in clarity, notwithstanding the sound accessibility.

2. Deficit in Rationale behind Requirements

In addition to the accessibility and clarity, another important factor, which needs to be weighed in the assessment of the transparency of supervisory rules, is the extent to which the rationale behind the changes of statutory requirements and the introduction of new rules is openly provided. Press interviews are deemed to be the principal means by which the supervisory perspectives on newly issued regulations are communicated to the outsiders. Notably, only part of the newly issued regulations are analyzed in the press interviews while the remaining ones are not addressed by the authority through any open channel. The basis for the selection of the regulations on which the CIRC will publicly extend opinions remains opaque. Insofar as the opinions delivered in press interviews are concerned, they are focused on the background, desired effects and substance of a new regulation.[310] The points made with respect to the background are aimed at clarifying the factors that prompt the formulation of a regulation, which usually relate to the regulatory needs stemming from insurance market developments. The clarification of the rule-making background contributes

---

310 For transcripts of the news conferences, *see* CIRC, 'Policy Briefings' (CIRC Website) <www.circ.gov.cn/web/site0/tab5227/> accessed 4 May 2016.

to the understanding of what underpins the formulation of a new regulation in general, but reveals few clues about the motives and considerations for specific important requirements in the regulation. As for the desired effects and the substance of a new regulation, the analysis of these elements does not involve the revelation of the grounds for specific requirements as well. Based on the actual practices the CIRC adopts, it is evident that the rationale behind a particular requirement is not subject to public dissemination. The lack of reasoning impairs the transparency of China's insurance legislation.

II. Transparency of CIRC's Functioning

Among the determinants of the level of supervisory transparency, the functional transparency of a supervisory authority stands out as being best indicative of an agency's willingness to embrace openness. The transparency of supervisory functioning could be determined by a measurement of the particularity with which the organizational and operational details are conveyed to the interested parties and the public.

The organizational and operational details concern the way in which the agency is run internally and the activities the agency conducts to discharge its supervisory responsibilities. Internal workings relate to the arrangements serving the needs for a consistent and effective basis for the day-to-day running of the agency. They are concerned with the structures and processes maintained inside the agency. Complementarily, the performance of supervisory duties is directed at satisfying the demands of external entities. Policyholders rely on the agency for protection, with the government expecting it to ensure financial stability and insurers calling for due supervisory stringency. In short, internal workings and supervisory activities make up the dual dimensions of the functioning of a supervisory agency. The transparency of the CIRC in both dimensions is discussed below.

1. Obscurities in Internal Organization and Procedures

In regard to internal workings, there is much room for the CIRC to ameliorate transparency. The publicly accessible elements include the composition of internal departments,[311] the profiles of the chairpersons, the rule-making procedures,[312] the budgets,[313] and the geographical distribution of regional bureaus.[314] These elements are however insufficient to amount to a complete and clear picture of the internal structure and procedures of the supervisory agency.

The primary deficiencies lie in the lack of information about the governing bodies responsible for decision-making, administration and monitoring within the agency, as well as in the absence of the procedural rules of such governing bodies. The only relevant clue is actually derived from the provisions stipulating the rule-making process, which provide that proposed rules with significant impacts should be approved by the 'chairman administrative meeting'.[315] Nevertheless, the composition, function and procedural issues of the 'chairman administrative meeting' are not made

311 The CIRC has sixteen internal departments of which the functions are respectively made public, including secretariat, department of development and reform, policy research center, department of solvency supervision and accounting, consumer protection bureau, department for the supervision of property and casualty insurance and reinsurance undertakings, department for the supervision of life and health insurance undertakings, department for the supervision of insurance intermediaries, department for the supervision of insurer's investments, international department, legal department, department for statistics and information, department for investigation, department for human resources and education, commission for discipline inspection and the publicity department of the party committee.

312 The set of procedures involved in the making of department rules and normative documents are disseminated to the public through the issuance of two separate regulations. *See* Rules on the Rule-making Procedures of CIRC Department Rules 2006; CIRC, *Administrative Rules on the Formulation of Normative Documents* (Normative Document, No 101, 2013).

313 The budget based on a forecast and the outturn based on the budget implementation are broken down by revenue and expenditure items. Both the budget statement and the outturn account show how the figures change by comparison to those of the preceding financial year and provide explanations for the changes. *See* CIRC, *The Consolidated Budget of CIRC (2016)* (Financial Statement, April 2016); CIRC, *The Consolidated Outturn Accounts (2014)* (Financial Statement, July 2015).

314 There exist thirty-six local bureaus and five sub-bureaus in charge of insurance supervision at provincial or municipal level. The CIRC has revealed their locations, functions and organization.

315 *See supra note* 312 (formulation of normative documents), at § 20 (prescribing that a proposed normative document should be submitted to the chairman administrative meeting for review and approval before issuance if it would significantly impact on the rights and obligations of the entities concerned, on insurance sector developments, or on supervisory practices.); *see also supra note* 312

public. It remains unclear whether other governing bodies or mechanisms run in parallel with the abovementioned meeting. Another question is whether other members of staff are mandatorily involved in the decision-making or charged with the duty to manage the agency alongside the chairpersons. A secondary deficiency that leads to the ambiguity of the organizational picture resides in the unavailability of the information as to how important supervision-related tasks are carried out. The tasks in question include, for instance, the administration of the regional bureaus, the coordination with other financial authorities domestically or internationally, etc.

2. Operational Transparency

All sorts of the information concerning the CIRC's supervisory activities is published in a section titled 'working briefing' on the electronic platform of the agency. A general categorization is implemented according to the intention of the information disseminated to stakeholders and the public. The components of the section as the result of the categorization include press releases which provide materials for the media, public notices which solicit advice or applications, notifications which inform insurers of tasks and requirements, bulletins which feed some statistical and inspection results, along with reports on the activities and speeches of the agency's chairpersons.

a) Availability of Information about Supervisory Activities

Essentially, the information about the CIRC's supervisory activities is not soundly conveyed. The information disseminated to the public is mainly about the supervisory activities that are completed, while the ongoing and future activities are revealed to a much lesser extent.

As far as the completed supervisory activities are concerned, individual pieces of information relating to diverse facets of insurance supervision mingle with each other, shown in different parts of the 'working briefing' section. Since the information is not sorted according to supervisory task

---

(making of department rules), at § 30 (laying down that all draft department rules require a final review and consent by the chairman administrative meeting).

or area of activity, it becomes difficult to determine the state or effects of a supervisory activity. What exacerbates the problem is the limited scope of the released information - only partial supervisory activities are actually made public. It is partly demonstrated by the range of the unfolded supervisory activities, which is much narrower than that of the activities provided for in the rules defining supervisory means. As a matter of fact, the majority of the information on supervisory moves is restricted to the meetings held and the new rules issued. In addition to the low diversity of the unfolded activities, the insufficient revelation of supervisory activities is likewise demonstrated by the obscurity of a notable portion of the supervisory projects or tasks since the actual actions taken to deliver the supervisory projects or tasks along with the results thereof are unspecified. The obscurity in the operational aspects of these projects and tasks implies some degree of inclination and arbitrariness in making the decisions on informational release.

As for the supervisory activities in progress and those in future, few revelations are provided in regard to their operational substance. It is merely possible for the stakeholders to speculate the direction where the supervision is heading on the basis of some accessible information, i.e. the medium- or longer-term goals and the tasks referred to in press releases which are typified by a summarization of a chairperson's speech at a conference. The supervisory goals and tasks stated therein are described shortly and generally. The material activities that the supervisors intend to engage in for the purpose of accomplishing the goals or tasks are not made public. With such a level of transparency, the way and timeframe in which the tasks on supervisory agenda would be tackled tend to be outside the scope of informational disclosure. The interested parties have little access to elements such as the frame of approaches, tools, measures and schedules to be employed in the fulfillment of a longer-term goal. Without the provision of such information, stakeholders have to lean on what the agency discloses ex post to derive the clues about supervisory activities. The opacity of ongoing and prospective activities thus increases the scrutiny cost of stakeholders and the public, hindering their capacity to form informed judgments about supervisory developments.

b) Transparency of Consultations

Among the supervisory activities, consultations are deemed to be a nexus between transparency and participation in that the comments by different stakeholder groups are invited in the course of a consultation, which presupposes a dissemination of adequate information allowing interested parties to appropriately understand the issue at the center of a consultation. Suffice it to say that the quality of consultations, inter alia, reflects the level of openness of a public agency which is empowered to make and implement policy decisions with profound impacts. Based on the considerations above, the consultations initiated by the CIRC are singled out for a closer examination, especially in terms of transparency.

aa) Procedures of Consultations

As noted earlier, the regulations issued by the CIRC are comprised of department rules and normative documents. The stages of consultation are laid down in the rules of procedure for rule-making.[316] The consultation on a proposed regulation is conducted by a CIRC's internal department which has drafted the regulation within its areas of competence.[317] Contingent on the purpose and content of the regulation, various groups including market players, experts, public agencies or the general public could be solicited for advice and comments.[318] A consultation can take place in various forms, such as workshop, hearing and written feedback,[319] at any stage of a draft formulation. A consultation is conducted at the discretion of the drafting department in proportion to the potential impacts of a prospective regulation.[320] It is explicitly provided in the procedural rules that a summary of the feedback received should be included as a part of the materials submitted to the legal department of the CIRC for a review.[321] The review by the legal department is applicable to all department rules and the normative documents that will substantively affect the rights and duties of legal entities.[322] As for a consultation on draft normative documents, the submission of relevant materials to the legal department marks the end of a consultation process. In contrast, further consultations will be

316 The making and issuance of department rules and normative documents are respectively subject to specific procedural rules. *See supra note* 65 and *supra note* 86.

317 *Supra note* 65 § 13; *supra note* 86, § 3.

318 *See supra note* 65, §§ 19, 20, 21, 25, 26, 29; *supra note* 86, § 12.

319 *Id.*

320 *See id.*

321 *Supra note* 65, § 23; *supra note* 86, § 15.

322 *Supra note* 86, § 14.

conducted on draft department rules after the submission on account of their greater importance. In reviewing draft department rules, the legal department is obligated to solicit more interested parties for feedback on the proposed texts,[323] which is followed by a publication of the approved draft on the CIRC's website for the purpose of seeking the views of the general public.[324]

bb) Unrevealed Consultation Practices and Results

The paragraph above intends to present the procedural aspects of a consultation. By and large, the consultation process exhibits low transparency given that the activities the authority opts for and the outcomes thereof are unrevealed in practice. Throughout the whole process of a normal consultation, the only publicly accessible information is the authority's call for comments on a fully-fledged draft. Such requests are made to the general public in most cases, which is maintained as a routine prior to the release of a regulation. In fewer cases, the request for comments is referred to all the stakeholders in specified categories that will be directly affected under the proposed regulation.[325] For example, all property and casualty insurers would be designated as the sole group of respondents to a draft regulation which in its entirety concerns their interests. In fact, as implied in the procedural rules for rule-making, consultations could take place with diverse entities on different scales, through various channels and in several rounds, if necessary. Nevertheless, it remains unknown in each case whether selected insurers, associations, experts or members of the public are consulted under unpublicized requests from the authority in the course of rule-making. It therefore results in incomplete information about the entities participating in a consultation and about the way in which a consultation is carried out.

The obscurity is not restricted to the proceedings of a consultation, but also lies in the outcome thereof. The comments by consultation partici-

323 *Supra note* 65, § 25, 26.

324 *Id.* § 29.

325 The categories here include but are not restricted to the local bureaus of the CIRC, life and health insurers, property and casualty insurers, reinsurers, insurance asset managers, insurance intermediaries, insurance associations and insurance institutes. In the event of a call for comments from the authority to a specific category as a whole, all the entities belonging to that particular category are expected to give responses.

pants together with the authority's reaction to them are not made public in almost all cases.[326] It is certain that the consultation entails supervisory analysis of the feedback following the collection of it from the consulted entities, which can be inferred from the procedural provisions on the components and content of the materials required for the CIRC's internal review.[327] However, owing to the fact that those analytical documents are merely disseminated internally, it is unlikely for the interested parties and the wider public to ascertain the dominant views among feedback providers on critical issues and the authority's position on the advice received. The obscure consultation outcomes have adverse impacts on public confidence in the efficacy of the consultation since the stakeholders and the public are unable to judge the extent to which the rule-makers have taken into account feedback and made changes accordingly.

III. Analysis of Statistical Disclosure

As far as the statistical data is concerned, it is disclosed by China's insurance authority through a few channels. Above all, the supervisory statistics for the insurance sector are undated on a monthly basis on the CIRC's electronic platform.[328] Besides, two special reports are issued by the authority annually, releasing figures in crucial aspects. One of them gives a review of the insurance market developments and the supervisory work in the previous year,[329] while the other one reveals the amount of work the authority carries out for the sake of information openness.[330] Lastly, as an auxiliary source, bulletins are published in order to feed the statistical information about specific issues, in contrast to the main channels mentioned above which are dedicated to broad-ranging issues. The bulletins, depending on the issue addressed, are published on a periodical or an ad hoc basis.

---

326 Only in exceptional cases, a draft regulation would be accompanied by an explanatory document which contains some of the feedback received from previously consulted parties and the authority's opinions about that.

327 *See supra note* 65, §§ 22, 23; *supra note* 86, § 15.

328 CIRC, 'Statistical Data' (*CIRC electronic platform*, monthly update) <www.circ.gov.cn/web/site0/tab5179/> accessed 15 March 2017.

329 CIRC, *Annual Report of the Chinese Insurance Market 2015* (1st edn, China Finance Publishing House 2015).

330 CIRC, *Annual Report of the Activities about Administrative Information Publication 2015* (Report, March 2016).

The data disclosure is focused on the conditions of (re)insurance undertakings and on the activities of the authority at aggregate level, whereas the statistical information about insurance groups is not available. As an increasing number of insurers evolve into larger conglomerates which manage risk-taking and deploy resources at group level, the unavailability of the group-wide data would potentially cause the results of risk-profile analyses made by the outsiders who rely solely on the supervisory data to materially deviate from the actual situations.

1. On the Aspect of Supervised Entities

In regard to the statistical data on the (re)insurance undertakings, the authority makes a detailed disclosure of the insurance market developments and insurer business conditions, but gives a vague picture of the solvency position of the insurers in general. The particularity of the former is demonstrated by the variety of the measures used to indicate the business conditions of insurance market segments, which include premium scale, benefits paid, insured amount, investment allocation, profitability, asset size, distribution of market share and number of undertakings. These measures are shown in both aggregate amount and percentage of change to facilitate the comparisons between financial years and between market segments. A balance sheet of China's insurance sector as a whole is also provided. [331] As far as the solvency position is concerned, the supervisory data available to the public is the average or median solvency ratio of the insurance sector, the aggregated sector solvency surplus and the number of insolvent insurers.[332] But, the figures about the essential components of the solvency ratio and other important elements associated with financial adequacy are not published. The capital base, for example, qualifies as such an essential issue requiring quantitative specification with regard to its constituents, distribution among risk categories, add-ons, the utilization of instruments for capital increases, etc. The current statistical disclosures fail to bring about a sufficient revelation of the full solvency profile of insurers in distinct segment markets. The identification of the risks with respect to

331 *See supra note* 329, at 75-76.

332 *See id.* at 31; the department for accounting and solvency supervision at the CIRC, *the Bulletin on Solvency Supervision in the First Half of 2015* (Notification No 196, 2015) <www.circ.gov.cn/web/site0/tab5218/info3976555.htm> accessed 10 May 2016.

capital quality, asset-liability structure or funding pattern is hindered to a large degree in the absence of numerical specifics of solvency issues. For the stakeholders, it could lead to a misjudgment about the industry-wide movements of loss-absorbing capacity.

2. On the Aspect of Supervisory Authority

Alongside the data about the conditions of the (re)insurance undertakings, the statistical facts about the authority's activities are released, the results of supervisory review activities in particular. The accessible statistical information about the supervisory activities can be broken down into the data on on-site activities and the data on off-site activities. As far as the on-site activities are concerned, the numbers of inspection panels, the inspected entities and the supervisory measures imposed are conveyed to the public.[333] A few important theme-focused inspections are disclosed in detail insofar as the specific actions involved are revealed.[334] However, it is not made public in regard to the respective proportion of the regular inspections and the ad-hoc ones in all on-site inspections.

As for the off-site activities, the published figures relate to the spheres ranging from supervisory scrutiny, supervisory control to information release. In the sphere of supervisory scrutiny, the statistical disclosure features the outcome of the integrated risk rating and a summary of consumer complaints. As a vital component of the supervisory review process, the integrated risk rating is able to expose the distribution of risk areas across the various aspects of insurance business. Nevertheless, the figures about the rating outcome are restricted to the number of insurers in each classification level,[335] without statistical revelation of the loci of prevalent risk areas. Additionally, the outcome of the theme-focused evaluations that are in parallel to the integrated risk rating in the supervisory review process is not publicly available. With regard to the consumer complaints,[336] a

333 *Supra note* 329, at 32.

334 *Id.*

335 *See supra note* 332.

336 As pointed out in a paper by Wandt and Bork, the complaint statistics allow the supervisory authority to evaluate insurers' market conduct. As far as potential insurance consumers are concerned, they could make informed decision on insurance purchase on the basis of the complaint rate of an insurer. The consumers are likely to deem the success rate particularly indicative of an insurer's general attitude towards its policyholders. *See* Manfred Wandt and Kevin Bork,

number of elements surrounding the issue are detailed in a monthly bulletin, including the number of cases, the mediums of complaints, ranking of insurers according to complaint amount and the problems in dispute.[337] Alongside the statistical bulletin on consumer complaints, the supervisory authority releases the result of an annual evaluation of the complaint-handling capacity of each insurer.[338] In the sphere of supervisory control, the aggregate amount of supervisory approvals and supervisory measures is respectively disclosed. However, the statistical disclosure lacks in detail because a breakdown of the aggregate of the supervisory approvals or measures is unavailable. The supervisory approvals differ with each other in the approved issue, while the distinction between supervisory measures lies in the interventional means and the deficiencies directed at. Notwithstanding the application of supervisory approvals and measures to broad-ranging circumstances, the data specific to each circumstance is not provided. Making public the number of supervisory approvals and measures for each predefined circumstance is certain to enhance the informativeness of the statistical disclosure.

When it comes to the statistical data on the activities about information release, the authority publicizes separately the number of news releases, news conferences, notifications, instances of responding to public concerns, instances of disclosure made on request, administrative reviews and lawsuits.[339]

B. *Enhancing Supervisory Transparency through Reinforced Mechanisms*

In relation to China's insurance legislation, the EU's Solvency II regime imposes tougher requirements on supervisory transparency given the

---

'Transparency in German Insurance Supervisory Law' in Kyriaki Noussia and Pierpaolo Marano (eds), *Volume I "Transparency in insurance law and regulation: the insurance undertakings, intermediaries and the supervisory authorities"* (forthcoming).

337 *See e.g.* CIRC, *the Bulletin on Insurance Complaints in Q1 2016* (Notification, 2016) <www.circ.gov.cn/web/site0/tab5218/info4027855.htm> accessed 10 May 2016.

338 The consumer protection bureau of the CIRC, *the Bulletin on the Evaluation Outcome of Complaint-Handling Practice of Insurance Undertakings 2015* (Notification No 23, 2016).

339 *See supra note* 330. The administrative reviews and lawsuits mentioned here only refer to those arising from the disputes over information disclosure.

wider statutory scope and a higher level of detail in terms of information dissemination. In this subchapter the transparency mechanisms adopted by the EIOPA will be taken as the main point of reference to facilitate the seeking of the ways to enhance the CIRC's supervisory transparency.[340] It is grounded in the fact that the transparency standards and practices of the EIOPA, which is charged with advising, overseeing and coordinating the EU-wide insurance supervision, are consistent with or even better in some ways than the level of transparency required of the EU national authorities.

In the following parts, a proportion of the analyses will be given to the EIOPA's transparency mechanisms and practices in the areas where the CIRC is found to have inadequacies. By drawing comparisons, the institutional disparities leading to a contrast in transparency in crucial aspects are exposed. Alongside, the dissertation would propose how the CIRC's existing transparency arrangements should be altered or supplemented taking account of the alternative approaches presented by the EIOPA. The aim of the discussion is twofold. Firstly, to seek the toolkit vital to ensuring supervisory openness which is nonetheless not utilized by Chinese supervisors. Secondly, to determine a necessary level of transparency which should be in place for China's insurance supervision.

I. Approaches to Promoting Transparency of Regulatory Rationale and Supervisory Methodologies

The shortcomings of the supervisory rules in transparency have been exposed. One of the shortcomings arises out of the discreteness of interrelated normative documents, and the other shortcoming results from the fact that the grounds for requirements are not provided. The former concerns the way in which supervisory requirements are formulated or amended, which is an issue falling into the scope of Chapter 2. The remedy for the shortcoming has been put forward in the part C of Chapter 2, which is conducive to a more transparent system of rules in China. It is restated shortly as follows. In essence, it is proposed that each administrative regulation or department rule should be accompanied by a single implement-

340 It should be noted that the practices of the NCAs, instead of the EIOPA, are used as the benchmark in the discussion on the way to improve the transparency of the CIRC's statistical disclosures. Except for that, the EIOPA's practices are taken as the points of reference.

ing regulation in which all the pertinent normative documents are incorporated and coordinated in structure. The consolidated implementing regulations are supposed to bear resemblance to the level-2 delegated regulation of the Solvency II, which systemically sets out requirements on diverse aspects of the upper-level directive. Since the approach to this shortcoming has already been provided, the subsequent discussion would focus on the other one – unavailability of the rationale behind supervisory requirements.

1. Transparent Consultation as a Key to Clarity of Regulatory Rationale

As for the other shortcoming, namely the lack of reasons given for the regulatory requirements imposed, the preceding chapters have not involved it in the scope of analyses. A contrast between the CIRC and the EIOPA can be easily perceived in regard of the transparency of the rationale for rule-making. In China, it is not a customary practice for the rule-makers to make a case for the requirements they formulate either prior or subsequent to issuance. As pointed out in a previous part of this chapter, there does not exist an effectual means by which a rationale is revealed to the public insofar as China's insurance legislation is concerned.

a) Causality between Consultation and Rationale Clarity

By contrast, in proposing rules, the EIOPA publicly conveys the rationale behind envisaged regulatory changes to the interested parties in detail. Basically, the causes for the changes are provided in the course of public consultations instead of other supervisory activities. The fundamental tools employed by the EIOPA to inform stakeholders of a rationale consist of the papers and reports it issues during a normal consultation process, and herein lies another contrast between the two supervisory bodies. The CIRC conducts the consultation in a much less transparent way than the EIOPA does given the fact that the draft regulation itself is the only material made publicly available throughout a consultation by the CIRC. As far as a consultation held by the EIOPA is concerned, far more materials are published alongside the draft rules, which include a theoretical analysis, an explanatory text, an impact assessment, a feedback statement and a resolution of comments. In the course of a consultation, some of these consultative materials are presented in the discussion paper or the consultation paper while others are addressed in the final report.

Table 6: The Effects of EIOPA's Consultative Materials on Clarity of Rationale behind Rules and on Transparency of Consultation

Consultative Materials	Input to Rationale behind Rules	Contribution to Transparency of Consultation
Theoretical Analysis	A priori and a posteriori illustration of the factors and economic considerations underlying possible regulatory options and approaches	– Informing stakeholders of rule-makers' preliminary thoughts on regulatory options and positions on the issues concerned – Enabling stakeholders to provide opinions on regulatory options and the underlying factors thereof before the options are solidly decided on.
Explanatory Text	– Making no direct input to rationale – Reducing the vagueness of requirements by expounding application details and exemplary practices, which in turn makes stakeholders better able to infer the reasons behind specific provisions.	Providing concrete information about what the entities concerned are supposed to perform in practice in accordance with the rules, which leads stakeholders to reach more informed judgments about the rules consulted on.
Impact Assessment	Presenting concrete reasons for the adoption of a specific policy option based on a cost-benefit analysis of each option and a comparison of the effects on different stakeholder groups between envisaged policy options	Giving interested parties an insight into the grounds on which the regulators determine a preferred option while reject others, which enables consultation participants to form opinions more apposite to current supervisory context.
Feedback Statement	Giving reasons to defend regulators' own policy decisions or to accept respondents' advice about the changes	– Publicizing the representative opinions received – Showing exactly how the stakeholders' opinions have impacted on the prospective rules

Resolution of Comments	Same as above	– Identifying all the interested parties responding to a consultation – Making public all the comments submitted, unless secrecy is requested – Disclosing regulators' reaction to each piece of advice by each respondent – Indicating one by one, either the changes to draft rules in case of agreement to a comment, or the reasons in case of disagreement

Table 6 illustrates in which ways the EIOPA's different consultative materials are instrumental in bringing about the clarity of a rationale and the transparency of a consultation. The findings show that the giving of reasons specific to requirements is entailed as an indispensable part in a consultation by the EIOPA.

For the sake of regulatory transparency, it is sensible to provide rationales in the course of a consultation prior to the issuance of rules. The incorporation of reasons into consultative documents allows the interested parties to perceive and judge the legitimacy of regulations. In the circumstance where flaws in legitimacy are identified, disapproval would be expressed in feedback on the grounds of those flaws, which consequently promotes the quality of a consultation. Even if the regulatory legitimacy is found to be flawless, giving of reasons is still beneficial. The rationale provided is able to help ensure the acceptability of proposed rules and a smooth implementation afterwards given that the rationality and practicality of draft rules would be solidly established through the interpretation of the motives for ratios, limits, conditions, etc. If a rationale is only provided after rules become effective, consultations would be conducted without the reasons behind rules being revealed. The interested parties would have to derive the rationales based on their own inferences when being consulted, which could result in a diversion of their cognizance away from actual regulatory considerations. The perception of the rationale for a rule has an effect on the way in which the intention and legal application of that rule would be construed. A faulty perception of rationales is hence likely to cause fallacies in the comments by consultation participants. In addition, impaired legitimacy of rule-making is to be exposed as another weakness in case the rationale for rules are made available after the rules take effect.

Because the regulators, by behaving in that way, make an impression that the rules would be imposed regardless of whether the reasons are adequate or how the stakeholders perceive the reasons. Assuming that reasons are given subsequent to issuance, stakeholders would be divested of the ability to evaluate the reasonableness of a proposed rule through the examination of the underlying factors. And there remains little practicability of amending rules right after issuance even if stakeholders deem that the reasons given are somewhat inadequate or unfair.

Based on the analyses above, a conclusion is drawn that the clarity of the rationale behind rules will be best served by means of a transparent consultation. It is likewise appropriate the other way around, i.e. that the transparency of a consultation is best served with the inclusion of clear rationales behind rules. For the CIRC, the optimal way of achieving rationale clarity is through establishing transparent consultations, in view of the interplay between the two elements. Transparent consultative mechanisms can bring about high-quality consultations alongside clear rationales for rules.

b) Consultative Procedures and Mechanisms Providing Justification for Rules

The dissertation advises for a two-stage proceeding of the consultation, which is an extension of the existing consultative procedures. Under the existing procedures, the CIRC issues a call for comments on a draft regulation on the electronic platform seeking opinions from either the general public or all the stakeholders bound by the regulation. The draft is the only document available to consultation participants. The dissertation hereby recommends that the CIRC publicize supplementary materials which include, among other things, analysis of the necessity and practicality of rules, advice received in previous consultations conducted on a small scale, reaction to the advice received and an impact assessment. These materials should be made available accompanying the draft regulation in order for an informed participation in the consultation. In short, at the first stage a draft regulation and ancillary consultative materials are supposed to be issued concurrently with the request for comments.

Such ancillary materials, at the moment, are merely circulated within the CIRC according to the procedural rules for its rule-making. As provided in the foregoing rules, the ancillary materials are intended to shed light on numerous aspects of a proposed regulation: background, underlying principles, major elements of the regulation, necessity and practicality of specific requirements, likely effects and the advice received from stakeholders.[341] Through a study of the exceptional cases where ancillary materials are made public together with draft regulations, it is found that only part of the intended aspects are actually addressed and the aspects addressed differ between cases.[342] What's even worse is that some of the aspects addressed are insufficiently analyzed with few discussions given. It is uncertain whether the ancillary consultative materials publicized in those exceptional cases are identical to the internal version of the materials used inside the authority. However, the CIRC should ensure that in each case the published ancillary materials contain adequate analyses made to at least the following aspects: necessity and practicality of requirements, advice received in previous consultations conducted on a small scale, reaction to the advice received and an impact assessment.

The dissertation's approach to the content of ancillary consultative materials is similar to the EIOPA's, but differs from it in some ways. As far as the EIOPA is concerned, the composition of its consultative documents remains uniform across the legal acts of same type.[343] The necessity of requirements is not available as a component aspect incorporated in the EIOPA's consultative document. Instead, as illustrated by Table 6, the rationale behind rules is delivered through the explanations and discussions made on other aspects: theoretical basis, explanation of draft rules, impact assessment, summary of advice and reaction to advice. Under the approach of the dissertation, the analysis of the theoretical basis or the explanation of rules is not necessarily included in the scope of consultative materials, whereas the necessity and practicality of requirements constitutes a vital analytical aspect of those materials. The distinctions in analytical aspects between the dissertation's approach and the EIOPA's arise out of the following factors. Firstly, the EIOPA's theoretical analysis is aimed at present-

---

341 *Supra note* 65, at § 22; *supra note* 86, at § 15.

342 See e.g. CIRC, *Notification on the Consultation on Draft Administrative Rules on Nuclear Catastrophe Reserves* (Notification No 506, 2015); CIRC, *Notification on Draft Administrative Rules on the Capital Increase of Insurance Companies* (Notification No 422, 2014).

343 There are several types of legal acts that the EIOPA is empowered to draft or issue, including level-2 implementing measures (the delegated regulations), ITSs, RTSs and guidelines. After the EIOPA draws up the draft of a legal act and before the draft is submitted to the European Commission or formally adopted, a public consultation will be conducted. *See* the Regulation Establishing EIOPA, § 8 (1)(a), 10, 15, 16.

ing preliminary thinking at an early consultation stage where the draft is not yet developed. Whereas, the CIRC would not publicly solicit advice before a draft is completed, which renders a theoretical analysis pointless. Secondly, the explanation of draft rules, which is a component of the EIOPA's consultative materials, brings about little revelation of rule-making reasons but the application of the rules in practice. Since the CIRC is accustomed to issuing normative documents to serve the clarity of rule application, it is unnecessary to incorporate such an explanatory text. Thirdly, an analysis of the necessity and practicality of requirements is statutorily provided for as one of the essential components of the CIRC's internal consultative materials. Provided the internal materials are publicized, the analysis would be substantially beneficial to the clarity of the rationale behind rules.

Based on the approach of the dissertation, at the first consultation stage a summary and a resolution of the feedback which the CIRC receives before completing the draft of a regulation should be publicized along with other materials. The need for the publication of the feedback summary and resolution stems from the existence of earlier consultations that are conducted with selected entities prior to the public solicitation of comments.[344] That is to say, the CIRC has collected advice and factored it in rule-making before engaging in a consultation with the wider public or with all the entities affected by a proposed regulation. The reaction to the feedback collected as a result of earlier consultations would be reflective of the considerations influencing the authority's decisions on specific policy options and its attitude towards the advice which might contain widely shared views among industry participants on some crucial policy issues. For the interested parties who intend to provide opinions in response to the public call for comments, a revelation of the earlier interaction between the authority and a small group of entities would grant an insight into the factors underlying the proposed regulatory requirements and help

344 The earlier consultation involves the participation by a limited number of stakeholders, who are invited by the CIRC, in an event whereby the authority is able to seek advice and exchange opinions with the invited participants about the formulation of a draft regulation. Such an event could be held in various forms, such as workshop, hearing and written-form exchanges. It is at the discretion of the authority to decide on the composition of the participants in the consultation, while the criteria for such a decision are unrevealed. The earlier consultation is usually conducted on a small scale, contrasting with the broad consultation at a later stage which is aimed at the participation of the general public or all the entities affected by the proposed regulation.

preclude the opinions identical to those that have already been weighed by the rule-makers.

The paragraphs above made discussion on the first consultation stage under the approach of the dissertation, in particular the consultative materials involved. As for the second stage under the approach, it is intended to publicize and explain the results of the consultation. The dissertation advises that the CIRC adopt the EIOPA's practices, i.e. releasing a report, at the last stage of a consultation. For the EIOPA, the final report for a consultation is essentially used to convey how the authority deems the feedback and what changes are made. It contains the summary and resolution of the comments received, along with the amended version of draft rules and that of the impact assessment. Such a responsive mechanism is at present not employed by the CIRC as no information is publicized subsequent to the issuance of the request for comments on a draft regulation. The withholding of information about results is responsible for the low transparency of the consultations by the CIRC. For this reason, it is definitely necessary for the CIRC to introduce an additional consultative stage in which a revealing report is released in reaction to the comments following the public solicitation made at the first stage. The report is supposed to summarize all the comments received, clarify the CRIC's positions on the comments, present the reasons for acceptance or disapproval of stakeholders' advice, and specify changes. Additional aspects could be included in the report, but none should be given priority over the abovementioned ones. The justifications for reassessed regulatory decisions provided in the report allow the interested parties to have a deeper understanding of the rule-makers' reasoning beyond the level of the first consultative stage. Provided that other materials, such as a modified impact assessment, is integrated into the final report, the explanations for the changes presented therein would lend additional perspectives to stakeholders' interpretation of the rationale behind rules.

2. Role of Publications in Transparency of Supervisory Tools and Methods

The resolution to the discreteness of interrelated normative documents and the deficit in rationales, which are identified as the major shortcomings detrimental to the transparency of regulatory rules and approaches, has been discussed above. In studying the differences in regulatory practices between the EIOPA and the CIRC, the dissertation finds a beneficial routine of the EIOPA which strengthens regulatory transparency, namely releasing advisory and expository publications.[345] Whereas, the CIRC does not engage in such activities.

a) Benefits of EIOPA's Advisory and Expository Publications

A majority of the foregoing publications are intended to present the EIOPA's points of view as to how the supervision of a wide range of issues should be conducted. Typically, a publication would analyze the concepts, prevailing theories and common practices with respect to a supervisory issue, advocating good practices that the EIOPA expects the NCAs to adopt.[346] Besides, a certain proportion of the publications are devoted to fact-finding of the supervisory methodologies of different member states, giving recommendations based on the findings. There are also a few publications that are aimed at recommending ideal practices to insurance market participants.

By means of the advisory and expository publications, the convergence of supervisory approaches and culture across the EU member states is fostered. The publications complement insurance legislation in harmonizing the way in which supervision is conducted in the home country of an undertaking with that in other host countries in the bloc. In addition, insurance undertakings and other stakeholders are able to better understand the actual practices and prospective developments with regard to the instruments and methodologies that the supervisory authority employs. The in-depth knowledge of supervisory mechanisms will consequentially prompt the stakeholders to make proactive adaptations so as to ensure that their operational policies and strategies are aligned with the criteria and measures which are used at present or to be used in the near future by the supervisors. Furthermore, the publications convey the EIOPA's positions

345 For these publications, *see e.g.* the reviews, surveys and other analytical documents in the section titled 'reports' on the EIOPA's electronic platform. <eiopa.europa.eu/publications/reports> accessed 7 September 2016; *cf.* Solvency II Directive, § 31 (2)(b).

346 The good practices put forward are not legally binding on the NCAs or market participants. The comply-or-explain mechanism for guidelines is not applicable to the good practices recommended in a publication. Essentially, the good practices shall be regarded as a complement to the union or national legislations in force. Despite the non-binding and complementary nature of the good practices, the entities concerned are expected to fully adopt the recommendations or at least take them into account in their operations.

on contentious supervisory issues, which serve as points of reference for national supervisors and market participants in carrying out the activities related to those issues.

b) Comparison and advice

In contrast, the China's insurance watchdog does not regard the issuance of publications on oversight tools and methodologies as an item within the scope of its responsibilities. It is uncertain whether expository or advisory publications on this topic are formulated and circulated inside the authority. The established fact is that such publications are unavailable to the stakeholders or the general public in China. Despite the fact, the CIRC publicizes some items serving other purposes. Among them, specific references should be made to two items as they bear functional similarities to certain types of the publications by the EIOPA to a degree. The first item is the non-binding guidance, which is mostly addressed to insurance market participants making recommendations for better operation and management. In terms of effects, it is comparable to the EIOPA's advisory publications targeting market participants in that both are directed to making advice on good practices for market players. The group targeted by the guidance is confined to the supervised entities, instead of the supervising entities, i.e. the CIRC and its regional bureaus across China. None of the guidance is dedicated to explicating sound practices that the supervisory agencies are expected to deliver. The second item is the reply to stakeholders.[347]

347 All replies are published in a special section on the CIRC's electronic platform, <www.circ.gov.cn/web/site0/tab5226/> accessed 7 September 2016. The replies by the CIRC to stakeholders are functionally comparable to the circular letters (*Rundschreiben*) by the BaFin to insurers. The circular letters are used to represent the supervisory authority's decisions on the issues raised by a specific insurer. Such issues referred to the authority usually relate to the interpretation of a specific stipulation and the admissibility of the conduct of business. The circular letters were intended to provide guidance for all insurers facing the same situation as the insurer that raises an issue, enhancing the predictability of supervisory decisions and actions. However, after the Solvency II came into force, the guiding effects of the self-binding decisions of the authority is lessened because of the principle-based approach of the legislation. That means the insurers facing the same situation, under the current supervisory regime, cannot have the equivalent degree of legal certainty to what they would have by ascertaining the decisions available in the circular letters before the inception of the Solvency II regime. *See supra note* 336.

The regional bureaus affiliated to the CIRC and various kinds of insurance market players, on encountering issues that are difficult to determine, would request for the authority's perspective on the issues and act in accordance with its opinions. In the reply to a request the CIRC bases its opinions on the rules apt for the issue in question, sometimes with an interpretation of the specific requirements applicable to the situation. The reply demonstrates the authority's attitude towards the legal application of the rules with respect to some issues. Given that the EIOPA's publications partially aim to clarify the supervisors' views on diverse issues, the common ground between these publications and the replies by the CIRC lies in the revelation of the authority's stance. However, the common ground is overshadowed by the disparities between them. The EIOPA's publications are largely devoted to expounding the way in which oversight should be conducted, whereas the replies by the CIRC do not serve that purpose at all. Insofar as the replies to the regional bureaus affiliated to the CIRC are concerned, the legality of a complicated issue facing the local supervisors is determined alongside the explanation of the legal basis for the determination, but little direction would be given with respect to the particular measures, tools or methods which the local supervisors are supposed to employ in tackling that issue. In short, neither the guidance nor the reply plays a role in serving the transparency of the CIRC's supervisory approaches.

On the basis of the discussions above, the dissertation calls on the CIRC to make the publications on supervisory methodologies openly available. Provided the supervisory methodologies for an issue is not clearly set out in the insurance legislation, papers or reports detailing the instruments and mechanisms which the authority utilizes at present or plans to employ are necessitated to be publicized for the sake of supervisory transparency and convergence. The supervisory convergence stated herein refers to the uniformity of the oversight methodologies, criteria and practices among the CIRC's regional bureaus which are charged with performing supervisory tasks locally. With such publications released as a supplement to supervisory rules on a regular and an ad hoc basis, the vagueness of the oversight methodologies arising from the insufficiencies of the implementing details of various issues could be alleviated. All categories of stakeholders ranging from regional supervisors to insurance market participants will be better able to behave in alignment with the authority's explicit requirements and implicit expectations.

II. Addressing CIRC's Functional Transparency

1. Measures against Low Transparency of Internal Organization and Procedures

The EIOPA exhibits a higher level of transparency in internal structure and procedures relative to the CIRC, which can be ascribed to a union regulation forming the legal grounds for the functioning of the EU insurance watchdog.[348] The supervisory institution is propelled to transparency by the founding regulation which lays down comprehensively the EIOPA's component entities and the operational procedures of its essential activities. The regulation further stipulates that the EIOPA should publish detailed rules defining the rules of procedure for internal bodies and make public important information about the internal workings.[349] The interested parties are granted the access to the inner structure and mechanisms of the EIOPA on the grounds of the regulation and the elements published accordingly.

As far as the CIRC is concerned, its status as the insurance regulatory and supervisory body is conferred by the Insurance Act of China. The empowering legislation is entirely different from the founding regulation for the EIOPA, because the legislation stipulates merely the powers and tasks of the CIRC while leaving other aspects undefined. The CIRC is explicitly mandated to issue rules related to the oversight of market entities, nevertheless the legislation does not impose on the agency an obligation to publish the rules governing its internal workings. It is up to the agency itself to decide whether and to what extent the rules about inner organization and working procedures shall be made publicly available.

At present the CIRC has separately issued its rules of procedure regarding, inter alia, rule-making, supervisory information publication and administrative appeal.[350] The existence of the set of rules renders it meaning-

---

348 Regulation (EU) No 1094/2010 of The European Parliament and of The Council of 24 November 2010 establishing a European Supervisory Authority (European Insurance and Occupational Pensions Authority), amending Decision No 716/2009/EC and repealing Commission Decision 2009/79/EC OJ L331/48.

349 *See id.* at §§ 44, 45, 55, 60.

350 The Rules on the Rule-making Procedures of CIRC Department Rules 2006; CIRC, *Administrative Rules on the Formulation of CIRC Normative Documents* (Normative Document, No 101, 2013); the Rules on the Publication of Administrative Information at CIRC 2008; the Rules on the Administrative Appeal at CIRC 2010.

less to amend the Insurance Act of China by inserting an additional sub-chapter defining the organizational and procedural issues of the CIRC. It will be less costly to complement the CIRC's rules than to introduce a major amendment to the framework legislation at the parliamentary level. On the basis of the considerations above, it is inadvisable to amend the Insurance Act of China in such a way as to incorporate the elements contained in the regulation establishing the EIOPA.

a) Rules of Procedure for Critical Entities and Arrangements

A sensible way of enhancing the CIRC's organizational and procedural transparency starts with the issuance of the rules of procedure for all governing bodies of the agency. It has been pointed out that these bodies are currently invisible in the organizational structure and their workings are found secretive in the absence of procedural rules. The supervisory agency is therefore expected to explicitly define the essential dimensions of each body that presides over or steers the agency in some ways. The rules of procedure for the EIOPA's internal entities could be regarded as a point of reference,[351] which provide extensively the important facets relevant to the functioning of a component entity, such as composition, tasks, voting modalities, decision-making and meetings. The foregoing facets should be embraced in the prospective procedural rules for the CIRC's governing bodies. Predefined rules of procedure covering extensive facets serve a threefold purpose: to avoid an arbitrary exercise of powers, to reduce the secrecy of internal entities and their working processes, and to hold actors accountable for violation of procedures. Besides the workings of the governing bodies, the interaction between the CIRC and its regional bureaus, which falls into the scope of internal workings as well, has been identified as an area where rules of procedure are not in place. The regional bureaus constitute integral parts of the whole supervisory network in light of the

351 *Cf.* Solvency II Directive, § 31 (2)(e), (3); *see* the Regulation Establishing EIOPA, §§ 40-53; *see generally* the Board of Supervisors of EIOPA, *Rules of Procedure* (Internal Procedure, EIOPA-BoS-11/002-Rev 2, 2015); the Management Board of EIOPA, *Rules of Procedure* (Internal Procedure, EIOPA-MB-11/002, 2011); the Board of Supervisors of EIOPA, *Decision of the Board of Supervisors concerning the Rules of procedure of the Mediation Panel pursuant to Article 41 of Regulation (EU) No 1094/2010 of the European Parliament and of the Council of 24 November 2010 establishing a European Supervisory Authority (European Insurance and Occupational Pensions Authority)* (Internal Procedure, EIOPA-BoS-12-032, 2012).

significance of the supervisory tasks assigned. The nationwide branches or subsidiaries of insurance undertakings, insurance intermediaries and insurance-related organizations are subject to the oversight by the regional bureaus on a broad range of issues. Though the tasks of the bureaus conducting supervision regionally are explicitly prescribed,[352] there is no clue about the way in which the central authority directs and coordinates the work of the regional bureaus, or conversely, how their work could influence the decisions by the central authority. The CIRC shall publicize the rules of procedure specifying these absent elements and processes to afford the interested parties an insight into the agency's institutional arrangements and relationship with the local supervisors.

b) Improvements to Web-based Disclosure

Alongside the complements to the existing rules of procedure, a strengthened web-based disclosure would be of great use to promoting the functional transparency of the supervisory agency. Currently the CIRC only publicizes the responsibilities of each internal department and introduces briefly the chairperson and vice chairpersons on the electronic platform. Such an amount of information is far from adequate to fit the purpose of transparency since the interested parties are unable to be cognizant of the whole inner structure of the agency. As far as ordinary insurance consumers and the wider public are concerned, using the information accessible on the electronic platform of the supervisory authority is the most practical way to understand the functioning of the institution. Even if the supervisory authority has set out the functional details in some rules or publications, the elements indispensable to the formation of the entire functional arrangements within the authority should be elucidated in a specific section on its website. Because a straightforward statement provided on the electronic platform, instead of sophisticated rules or lengthy reports, would make it easier for the public to have a sense of how the complex agency operates internally. The CIRC could consider enhancing the web-based disclosure of its internal organizational and procedural details in several ways, which will be set out in subsequent subsections.

---

352 The Rules on Supervisory Responsibilities of Local Agencies Affiliated to the CIRC 2016.

aa) Organizational and Procedural Details

At the first place, information should be published in a higher level of detail with regard to the configuration of the agency. The scope of disclosure shall not be restricted to the internal departments, but include the governing bodies that exercise authority over the operations of the whole agency, the working groups which are affiliated to, crossing or independent of the internal departments, and the joint bodies which the CIRC forms with the supervisory authorities in other financial sectors.

As for the governing bodies and the joint bodies, the CIRC is supposed to publish clear statements on their respective responsibilities, composition and essential working rules. In specifying the composition of a certain body, the authority shall make public the curriculum vitae of each component member, particularizing the positions they hold inside and outside the supervisory agency, which could deter key decision makers from taking up a position creating a potential conflict of interests. This has been well put into practice by the EIOPA on its electronic platform since the revelation of the interests represented by different participants is crucial to assuring the stakeholders and the wider public of the confidence in the independence and impartiality of the high-level bodies in functioning. In addition to the background information about the component members of the governing and joint bodies, the rules of procedure for each of these bodies should be briefly summarized to reflect the most essential points of the workings of a body concerned. The synopsis would especially facilitate the understanding of the working mechanisms in place at the highest level of the agency for the ultimate beneficiaries of the insurance supervision, namely policyholders, and they are thus better able to know and judge the credibility and effectiveness of the processes and tools that the supervisory agency employs to ensure the quality of decision-making and policy deliverables.

When it comes to the internal departments and working groups, they can basically be subjected to a lower level of supervisory disclosure in regard of functional arrangements, by comparison with the governing and joint bodies which play vital roles in directing the agency at the top. Although it is likewise necessary for the CIRC to clearly state on the website the organizational information of the various internal departments and working groups, the working procedures thereof are not deemed to be within the scope of obligatory disclosures. The organizational information refers to the responsibilities and objectives of a department or a working group concerned as well as the introduction about the head thereof. The reasons why complete rules of procedure for them are not categorized as obligatorily disclosed items are discussed below. The working rules of an internal department or a working group only reveal the way in which the department or working group is run, and more importantly, the rest of the agency would not be materially affected by the activities of a single component part of the agency. In contrast, the operations of the governing and joint bodies have unparalleled impacts on each constituent part of the agency which will have to align the functioning with the decisions adopted by the superior bodies. The disparity in impacts entails the different importance of their rules of procedure to the effective functioning of the agency as a whole. The transparency of internal workings therefore depends more on the public availability of the procedural details of the principal bodies with overarching impacts than that of the procedural details of the subordinate entities that influence the agency partially.

bb) Organizational Chart

An informative organizational chart will also be a useful tool for the CIRC in the pursuit of functional transparency. Essentially, the degree of informativeness is crucial to the efficacy of the chart. If the chart is formulated in a way that makes the inner structure oversimplified, it fails to serve the intended purpose. And herein lies the flaw of the organizational chart published by the CIRC.

An organizational chart of the agency is available in a CIRC's annual report instead of on its electronic platform.[353] The chart enumerates the internal departments and (vice) chairpersons, corresponding to the textual information on the agency's website.[354] However, the relationship between the entities present on the chart is not illustrated, as the chart does not contain any connecting lines. Due to this, the users of the chart would be clueless about the division of duties, for instance, the way in which the tasks of the superintendence over the work of various internal departments are assigned. Apart from the unavailability of linkages, the CIRC's organizational chart insufficiently reveals the complexity of the agency's structure which comprises more than the departments on an equal footing with each other and the (vice) chairpersons.

353 *Supra note* 329.
354 *See id.* at 29.

By contrast, the weaknesses of the CIRC's organizational chart are not found to exist in the case of the EIOPA. In other words, the chart of the latter exhibits a clarity in relationship and completeness of structure. For the sake of organizational transparency, the EIOPA makes public two separate charts: a chart showing the relations between the internal entities and the other one illustrating specifically the positioning of the working groups in the larger institution.[355] Both charts have a characteristic in common that the make-up of the entire institution is revealed using a multilevel structure, which demonstrates the vertical subordination of an internal entity to another as well as the horizontal alignment between the entities in parallel.[356] It draws a sharp contrast to the extent to which the organizational arrangements are disclosed by the CIRC's chart. With the current level of details shown by the CIRC's organizational chart, it is impossible to perceive the allocation of powers or the relational patterns inside the institution. Additionally, the oversimplified structure as is shown in the CIRC's chart gives rise to the obscurity in organizational structure because it fails to reflect the route through which the mandates and controls are exerted from top to bottom. By comparison, the multilevel structure revealed by the EIOPA's charts lends more transparency to the internal organizational pattern demonstrating clearly the foregoing route across the entities at different levels of the institution.

Based on the preceding discussion, three recommendations aimed at improving the CIRC's organizational transparency are provided below. The first one is simple but important: making the organizational chart available on the electronic platform. Suffice it to say that a chart published directly on the website will receive wider dissemination than that incorporated in a report as is the case with the current practice. The second recommendation relates to the revelation of the relations and the division of

---

355 *Cf.* Solvency II Directive § 31 (2) para 3; *see* the Regulation establishing EIOPA, at recital 64 and § 8 (1)(k); EIOPA, 'EIOPA Organizational Chart' (*Document*, September 2016) <eiopa.europa.eu/Publications/Administrative/2016%2009%20 Organigram%20External%20USE.pdf> accessed 2 November 2016; EIOPA, *Annual Report 2015* (Publication, 2016) Annex III.

356 The multilevel structure is explained as follows. According to the EIOPA's charts the organizational structure can be divided into five levels. The institutional arrangements are specified for each organizational level, with the information being given about the functions of the various entities at each level and the corresponding persons in charge. From the top to the bottom of the five organizational levels they are chair, executive director, departments, units, and sub-units or working groups.

responsibilities between internal entities. The CIRC's organizational chart is meant to be illustrative of the functional affiliations of all the entities involved in the chart. Typically, connecting lines are used to form the linkages. The last recommendation centers around the completeness of the organizational structure. The organizational chart is expected to illustrate the entities above, affiliated to, crossing or independent of the internal departments. It is akin to the multilevel model as presented by the EIOPA's organizational chart. By making visible these de jure and de facto entities which serve as regular mechanisms for directing the entire or part of the operations of the agency, the CIRC is able to inform the public of the actual way in which it is organized. To give a concrete example of an entity above the internal departments: a regular meeting mechanism, attended by a vice chairman and the heads of some closely-related internal departments, specifically for the decision-making in specified supervisory areas, shall be deemed to be a body superior to the relevant departments and made visible in the organizational chart. In this example, the regular meeting mechanism is equivalent in nature to a decision-making body which mandates the way of supervision in predefined areas of competence. Insofar as the entities affiliated to, crossing or independent of the internal departments are concerned, they refer to the working groups performing supervisory tasks which involve, inter alia, producing policy deliverables, making analyses and conducting supplementary oversight. Depending on the nature of a working group, its activities are exercised under the direction of, based on the coordination between, or without the involvement of the internal departments.

cc) Assembling Rules of Procedure

Last but not least, it will be beneficial for the CIRC to incorporate all the rules related to its internal workings in a specific section on the electronic platform. It is observed that on the EIOPA's platform there exists a section containing the rules of procedure for internal entities in combination with other internal governance rules.[357] As a matter of fact, the CIRC applies

357 *Cf.* Solvency II Directive, § 31 (2) para 3; *see* the Regulation Establishing EIOPA, recital 64; EIOPA, 'Legal Framework' (*Website Section*, 2016) <eiopa.europa.eu/about-eiopa/legal-framework> accessed 2 November 2016. It includes the founding regulation for the EIOPA, the rules of procedure for important internal entities, a set of internal operational rules alongside external procedures.

thematic integration to the rules in force in some supervisory areas, such as supervisory approvals and supervisory measures. The CIRC should equally apply such an integrated approach to the internal rules of procedure as to put together in a section on its electronic platform all the stipulations on the workings of its governing entities and critical administrative operations. This would definitely reduce the cost for the interested parties to seek information about the organizational and procedural details of the supervisory authority, which could translate into an escalation in supervisory transparency.

2. Measures Aimed at Strengthening Transparency of Supervisory Activities

Following the preceding discussions on how to enhance the CIRC's organizational and procedural transparency, this part will proceed with the analysis of the way of improving the authority's operational transparency, namely the transparency of supervisory activities.

Before the analyses are given, it is necessary to clarify an issue. In the first subchapter the mechanisms and flaws are examined in regard to the transparency of the CIRC's supervisory activities in general and the transparency of the consultations in particular. The consultation, as a sort of supervisory activities, is singled out for a focused discussion on its transparency due to its close relations with supervisory transparency and public participation. In the second subchapter, in presenting the approach to the lack of rationales behind rules, the dissertation sets forth the view that 'the clarity of the rationale behind rules will be best served by means of a transparent consultation' and 'transparent consultative mechanisms can bring about high-quality consultations alongside clear rationales for rules'. And therein, concrete proposals are laid down as to how the transparency of the consultations by the CIRC could be enhanced. In light of this, it will be unnecessary to develop the approaches to the low transparency of the CIRC's consultations again in this section.

The following parts will thus focus on an analysis of the means by which the CIRC could ameliorate the transparency of its supervisory activities taking into account the methods the EIOPA utilizes. More considerations would be given to cost-effectiveness. The advice put forward would therefore reflect the specificities of China's supervisory environment.

a) General Approach

It has been noted that one major flaw of the CIRC's supervisory disclosure lies in the unmethodical publication of the completed, ongoing or future supervisory activities, which makes it difficult for stakeholders to form a consistent and clear view of the supervisors' moves. In comparison, the EIOPA makes available a better organized supervisory disclosure characterized by a categorization of activities according to supervisory issue or project and by a use of timeline showing the full records of all the activities that the authority conducts to accomplish a particular task. Perceiving the contrast between the supervisory disclosure of the CIRC and that of the EIOPA, the dissertation advises that the CIRC's electronic publication be altered in such a way as to categorize activities by supervisory area, ensure the informational completeness and reveal key facts about an activity.

These effects can be materialized by the establishment of a specific unit for the disclosure of supervisory activities inside the section on 'working briefing'. The existing units in the section would be retained, but subject to minor changes in content. The prominent advantage of the creation of a new unit resides in that it avoids a reorganization of the entire supervisory disclosure system. As far as the new unit is concerned, supervisory activities therein ought to be categorized on the basis of the relevance to specific supervisory issues. In each category the authority should make public the completed supervisory activities, the ongoing supervisory activities and the prospective ones that are fully planned. The activities that do not qualify as supervision or regulation in nature should not be included. The information about the progress or results of the non-supervisory activities that the authority engages in could be published in other units. Meanwhile, it shall be ensured that all sorts of important supervisory activities conducted by the CIRC are disclosed in the new unit. Arbitrary decisions on supervisory disclosure, which results in partial revelation of activities, should be prevented. In addition to the widening of the scope for supervisory disclosure, the particularity of the disclosure need be heightened. In other words, the CIRC should ensure an adequate level of detail in publicizing its supervisory activities. Specification of the operational elements across key dimensions will be instrumental in making the disclosures informative. The key dimensions of a supervisory activity comprise time frame, operations, tools, products and outcome.[358] As far as the completed supervisory activities are concerned, all the dimensions should be clearly specified. As for the ongoing supervisory activities, the disclosure is expected to be aligned with the actual operational conditions because the timeliness of information publication is crucial to the authority's operational transparency. A timely supervisory disclosure would be indicative of an authority's readiness to be placed under public scrutiny and to be responsive to the demands of stakeholders. For this reason, a disclosure will have to be revised and augmented where actions deviate from a prearranged plan or where a product becomes deliverable in the course of a supervisory activity. When it comes to the future supervisory activities, the disclosure measures provided herein would be applicable to the supervisory activities satisfying two criteria: being thoroughly devised and being conducted within the following six months.[359] The main reason for imposing the criteria is that there are great uncertainties surrounding a supervisory activity which is supposed to take place after a long period of time. It might not be put into practice or subject to material changes due to numerous external factors. By contrast, the supervisory activities occurring in the short term exhibit greater predictability, and correspondingly, the operational specifics of this kind of activities are more likely to be settled. The CIRC shall therefore disseminate the plans devised for the supervisory activities that will be conducted in the short run. Except the products and outcomes, which are unavailable at the time of dissemination, the operational dimensions of the foregoing activities must be publicized in the new unit prior to the implementation of a plan.

The discussions above set out the treatment of independent supervisory activities, i.e. the activity which neither depends nor impacts on the occurrence of another one. The authority, however in some cases, delivers sig-

358 Operations denote the procedures and actions involved in a supervisory activity, and tools mainly refer to the technical approaches employed. Products and Outcomes have different meanings. The former generally relates to legal instruments and documents which are formulated to regulate or review the insurance sector, whereas the latter concerns the ensuing effects of a supervisory activity.

359 Essentially, the future supervisory activities subject to the proposed disclosure measures actually refer to the activities that will take place in the short run, as opposed to those that will be carried out in the long run, i.e. after a long period of time. 'Six months' is an optional length of time for the definition of the activities in the short run. Alternative length of period can be adopted as long as the supervisors are certain about the arrangements for all the supervisory activities taking place during that period.

nificant supervisory products through supervisory projects or programs over a lengthy period. Each of the supervisory projects or programs consists of a series of related supervisory activities which are proceeded with in sequence. The supervisory projects or programs should be made public and arranged in pertinent categories inside the new unit in parallel with the independent supervisory activities. All the supervisory activities within the scope of a project or program shall be revealed in combination, instead of being separately shown as an independent activity. The component activities of a supervisory project or program are expected to be disclosed in the same way as the independent supervisory activities, which means the disclosure standards for the independent ones are likewise applicable to the activities comprising a supervisory project or program. As an extra disclosure measure, the framework and the general arrangement of a supervisory project or program shall be made public to enable a global view by the interested parties of its structure and developments.

In short, under the proposal laid down above, the CIRC's disclosure of supervisory activities would be subject to thematic categorization. It is actually an important feature of the EIOPA's disclosure practice, leading to a more methodical revelation of the actions that the authority takes to advance supervisory agenda. This particular feature is thus drawn on to introduce adjustments to the mechanism whereby the supervisory activities are publicized in China. In shaping the proposal, cost-effectiveness is prioritized. The proposal is hence designed in a way that is meant to balance the cost of reshaping the existing lines of supervisory disclosures with the need for a publication mechanism that demonstrates systematicity, completeness, particularity and timeliness. The proposed establishment of a new unit within the 'working briefing' section, alongside the further approach to the publication of the completed, ongoing and prospective supervisory activities, are the very products stemming from the trade-off. In terms of particularity, the level required under the proposal is even higher than that of the disclosures by the EIOPA.

b) Special Treatment of Supervisory Activities Occurring in the Long Run

Before the end of this subsection, it is necessary to address a remaining issue, i.e. the disclosure of the supervisory activities taking place in the long run. The characteristics and the disclosure of the supervisory activities conducted in the short term have been discussed. As opposed to them, the activities that are planned to be conducted after a long period of time are susceptible to market developments and the operational arrangements are hard to solidly predetermine. On account of the dissimilarities between the two kinds of supervisory activities, it would be impractical to require the activities in the long run to be publicized with a level of detail equal to that applicable to the activities in the short run. Nevertheless, the particularity should not be reduced to such an extent that the stakeholders are unable to form a general idea about the supervisory work to be done in the coming years. The dissertation, after studying the EIOPA's approach to the issue, holds the opinion that the CIRC should consider absorbing the beneficial elements of the EIOPA's approach within the bounds of practicality and making the scheme for the supervisory activities in the long run more instructive. The EIOPA issues a multi-annual work programme to circulate the arrangements for the supervisory activities within the subsequent three-year period.[360] The programming document identifies the objectives, presents the activities serving each objective and sets forth the allocation of human and financial resources across the objectives. By means of the document the EIOPA conveys to stakeholders the prioritization of supervisory areas alongside the planning of deliverables in the future, which renders the supervisory direction and moves more transparent. Comparably, a five-year scheme is devised and published by the CIRC.[361] There exist, however, material differences between the CIRC's scheme and that of the EIOPA. The former serves the purpose of supervision as well as promoting insurance sector development, while the latter is specifically intended for supervision. Besides, the former covers a span of five years, which extends two years more than the latter. Furthermore, the former is mainly confined to setting objectives, whereas the latter combines objective-setting with ensuing arrangements serving the objectives. The last difference actually exposes the most salient shortcoming of the CIRC's scheme. That is to say, the scheme is full of high-level objectives and associated operational objectives, but lacking in road maps to the materialization of the numerous objectives. The reference to road maps does not represent an undue expectation that the authority should make publicly available a precise action plan which gives details in all respects relating to the attainment of an objective. Instead, it conveys that the authority shall ensure that stakeholders

360 *Cf.* Solvency II Directive, § 31 (2)(e); *see* the Regulation Establishing EIOPA, § 8 (1)(k); *see e.g.*, EIOPA, *Single Programming Document 2017-2019 (AWP 2017)* (EIOPA-BoS-16/23, 2016).

361 *See e.g.*, CIRC, *the Outline of the Scheme for Development of China's Insurance Sector from 2016-2020* (Normative Document No 74, 2016).

are able to derive reliable clues as to the main activities devised for an intended area of supervision.

To tackle the shortcoming, the CIRC's scheme could be complemented by an element embedded in the EIOPA's work programme, namely the revelation of prospective supervisory services and products.[362] It means the CIRC ought to incorporate in the scheme the information about the major activities and deliverables which are planned for the pursuit of each objective within the following five-year period. The revelation is by no means expected to be exhaustive, but should specify for each objective the set of activities and products on which the authority's resources specific to an objective incline to be concentrated. Alongside that, the revelation shall not be limited to the name of these essential activities and products. The substance of these activities and products, which denotes the effects, methodologies and procedures, should be given a brief glimpse into. For the sake of practicality, the substantive elements need not be stated in detail. The other beneficial practice in the EIOPA's formulation of a work programme, which deserves being adopted by the CIRC, is the setting of key performance indicator (hereinafter referred to as "KPI") as the targets for the supervisory work in the long term.[363] The need for KPIs stems from the fact that the objectives stated in the CIRC's scheme are qualitative. Ambiguities could arise from the qualitative definition of objectives since the precision or the extent of the issues involved in numerous objectives is evidently difficult to determine. Admittedly, a larger portion of the objectives can only be defined qualitatively in view of the diversity, variability and complexity of the factors which have effects on the fulfillment of the long-term objectives. Even though, there remains room for quantifiable objectives since it is not unfeasible to identify the areas where the effectiveness of supervision can be properly measured by the use of numbers and percentages showing the frequency or degree of desired activities and scenarios. Quantification increases the particularity of an objective and facilitates the evaluation of the supervisory work pertaining to an objective. The CIRC shall ascertain the quantifiability of key areas of activity, establishing numerical targets where appropriate. Another feature of the EIOPA's long-term work programming, i.e. the publication of human and financial re-

362 *Cf.* Solvency II Directive, § 31 (2)(e); *see* the Regulation Establishing EIOPA, § 8 (1)(k); *see* EIOPA, *EIOPA Multi-Annual Work Programme 2015-2017* (EIOPA-BoS-14/109, 2014) Annex I; *see supra note* 360 (Single Programming Document), at 11-19.

363 *See supra note* 360 (*Single Programming Document*), at 8-11.

sources distribution across various objectives, has been made reference to in the previous paragraph. The publication is certain to contribute to the transparency of supervisory work since resource allocation is a constituent dimension of the working mechanism of a supervisory authority. Despite the relevance, the disclosures about the resources assigned to different objectives are not central to the transparency of supervisory work because they would not lead to any clues about what and how specific activities would be performed. The disclosures are hence inferior in importance to those about the arrangements of supervisory activities and products. The dissertation holds that it is unnecessary for the CIRC to adopt the practice, not only for the lesser importance as presented above but also due to the concern for its practicality. As far as China's government agencies are concerned, financial resources are widely regarded as the only sort of resources that requires budgeting and publication. The notion of planning human resources is not well accepted. Moreover, the financial budgets of China's public agencies are aimed at projecting the expenditure on gross functional aspects. To establish a resource allocation as the EIOPA does, it requires a breakdown of the projected expenditure on supervision by specified operational objectives, which is nevertheless not in line with the views held by the regulatory and supervisory agencies in China about the level of particularity that a budget should exhibit.

III. Changes Proposed for a Granular Statistical Disclosure

The deficiencies of the CIRC's statistical disclosure have been identified in the first half of this chapter. The flaws found concern the unavailability or insufficiency of the statistical data on the supervised entities and the authority itself. This section is intended to respond to the prior findings by laying down advice on the approaches to these flaws.

1. Statistics for Insurance Groups

The first flaw to be addressed is the absence of the statistical data on the insurance groups in China. Currently, the statistics for insurer business and financial conditions are published by line of business.[364] The statistics represent the facts about several major segments of the China's insurance market on aggregate and average level, the figures for gross written premiums in particular.[365] The numbers are aggregated and averaged either at the level of solo undertakings pursuing life insurance business or at the level of those that pursue non-life insurance business. The released statistics, however, show no regard for the group-wide situation of the numerous insurance conglomerates across the nation.[366] In China, an entity normally qualifies as an insurance holding company on condition that it has controlling stakes in a range of subsidiaries which operate respectively life insurance, non-life insurance, asset management and other insurance-related business.[367] Suffice it to say that group supervision is one of the most fundamental elements of insurance supervision, given a parent undertaking's influence over subsidiary insurance undertakings, the interconnections between group members as well as an insurance group's impacts on other financial institutions. The significance of group-wide statistical data is iden-

364 The lines of business involved in the publicized statistics do not constitute an exhaustive categorization of loss exposures. Only the most important lines of business are involved in the statistical disclosures by the CIRC, including life insurance, health insurance, personal accident insurance as well as property and casualty insurance which is divided into agricultural insurance, compulsory automobile liability insurance and others.

365 *See supra note* 328.

366 According to the records publicized by the CIRC, there are currently twelve insurance groups in China. CIRC, 'Seeking Information about Insurance Institutions' (*CIRC electronic platform*) <www.circ.gov.cn/tabid/5254/Default.aspx> accessed 15 March 2017.

367 The insurance-related business mentioned herein usually means the services of insurance mediation, rendered by insurance intermediaries including insurance agents, brokers and adjusters. Hence, a group with insurance-related business actually has subsidiaries conducting the foregoing business. Alongside the issue, the regulatory rules do not explicitly require a combination of life and non-life insurance business as a condition for qualifying as an insurance group. The rules, as a matter of fact, stipulate that the parent undertaking in an insurance group should hold over 50% stake in at least two insurance undertakings, without laying down restrictions on the type of the subsidiary undertakings. However in practice, an entity always gains an effective control over both life and non-life insurance undertakings prior to receiving the supervisory approval for a transformation into an officially recognized insurance holding company. It implies the de facto criteria used by the CIRC in making a decision on the approval. For the abovementioned eligibility requirements on insurance groups, *see* CIRC, *Provisional Administrative Rules on Insurance Holding Company* (Normative Document No 29, 2010) § 4.

tical to that of the group supervision, which is exemplified by the EU insurance regulators' approach to this particular issue. With regard to the statistical publication, they basically classify the statistics required for disclosure into three main categories among which there is a category specifically for group-level data.[368] This corresponds to the cornerstone status assigned to the group supervision in the EU Solvency II legislation since group supervision is designated as one of the four major titles comprising the framework directive.[369] It is certain that the significance of group supervision and the necessity for making public the relevant statistics is fully acknowledged by the supervisory authorities in the EU. Insofar as the content of the group-level statistics which the NCAs in the EU are required to disclose is concerned, these statistics are made up of data indicative of the jurisdictional distribution and solvency conditions of the insurance groups subject to a particular group supervisor.[370] The disclosed data on the jurisdictional distribution of insurance groups aims to reveal the numbers of the subsidiary insurance undertakings, which are affiliated to the insurance groups under the supervision at national level, based on where they operate. The other mandatory element, the data on group solvency, serves the purpose of demonstrating the level of group own funds and solvency capital requirements under different calculation methods and shows the amounts with distinct usage of internal models.

The foregoing two aspects contained in the statistical disclosure by the EU supervisors of the insurance groups deserve being factored in the determination of the scope for the corresponding disclosure by the CIRC. The dissertation advises that the CIRC's disclosure of group statistics consist of two elements: business structure and solvency position. The data on the jurisdictional distribution of insurance groups, which is a mandatory com-

---

368 The three categories into which the aggregate statistics are classified are data on insurance and reinsurance undertakings, insurance groups and the supervisory authority. *See* Solvency II Directive, § 31 (2)(c); *supra note* 119 (Solvency II Delegated Regulation) at annex XXI; Commission Implementing Regulation (EU) 2015/2451 of 2 December 2015 laying down implementing technical standards with regard to the templates and structure of the disclosure of specific information by supervisory authorities in accordance with Directive 2009/138/EC of the European Parliament and of the Council [2015] OJ L347/1224, annex I.

369 In the Solvency II Directive, the rules are categorized into six titles. Among them, four titles relate to substantive requirements on key issues, while the others mainly set out miscellaneous and procedural requirements. *See* Solvency II Directive, table of contents.

370 *See supra note* 368 (commission implementing regulation), annex I at 1245-1249; Solvency II Directive, § 31 (2)(c).

ponent of the statistics disclosed by the NCAs in the EU, is nevertheless deemed inapt for their Chinese counterpart. This is largely ascribed to the fact that most Chinese insurance groups have little business presence in foreign markets, with almost all of their premium incomes generated from China's market.[371] Despite increasing investments in foreign assets, the market entry by Chinese insurers through expansion of overseas operations or acquisition of foreign undertakings is uncommon.[372] It draws a sharp contrast with the business pattern in the EU insurance sector where the premium income of the subsidiary undertakings operating outside the home country of their parent undertaking accounts for an important proportion of the aggregate group revenue. Due to the reasons above, the statistical disclosures by the CIRC should instead focus on numerical facts

371 There exist no statistics specific to the premium incomes of the overseas operations of Chinese insurance undertakings and groups. Despite that, the proposition can be corroborated by the facts and views given by a former vice chairman of the CIRC, Yanli Zhou, who discussed the problem in his speech at a forum. According to his speech, all the Chinese insurance undertakings, in total, have only 6 life insurance subsidiaries, 14 non-life insurance subsidiaries and several representative offices in overseas countries and areas. On account of the fact that there are over 110 Chinese-funded insurance undertakings in China, the figures show that most Chinese insurers have not yet established the affiliates providing coverage overseas or acquired controlling stakes in foreign insurance undertakings. Zhou further indicated that the existing overseas operations of Chinese insurers remain small-sized, have imperceptible market share and fail to make profits. For Zhou's speech, *see* Yanli Zhou, 'Opening Remarks' (The Forum on the Globalization of China's Insurance Industry: Challenge and Future - How Can Chinese Insurers Go Abroad, Beijing, 16 January 2017) <pit.ifeng.com/a/20170117/50589467_0.shtml> accessed 17 March 2017.

372 The investment in real estate accounts for the biggest portion of the overall overseas investments by Chinese insurers. Next to real estate, stakes in foreign financial institutions are also favored. However, few Chinese insurers have made investments in foreign insurance undertakings for a controlling status. Anbang and Fosun might be the most active acquirers of foreign insurance undertakings among all Chinese insurance holding companies. *See* Ping An Life, 'The Study of Insurer Overseas Investment' (China Insurance Asset Management Symposium, Beijing, May 2016) (noting that the real estate in major world cities and Hong Kong's capital market most attract the insurers from mainland China in regard of investing abroad); Daochuan Zhou, 'How Do Chinese Insurers Invest Worldwide with Vast Amount of Premiums (Part I)?' (*Wallstreetcn*, 16 January 2017) <wallstreetcn.com/node/285216> accessed 20 March 2017 (analyzing the developments of Chinese insurers' overseas investments and listing the main cases since 2007); *see id.* (presenting that Anbang and Fosun are representative of the few Chinese insurers that entered the insurance markets of developed countries by means of acquisition).

which can help reveal the essential characteristics shared by Chinese insurance groups and are conducive to the identification of the group risk profile.

Among the various factors, solvency position is most critical to the viability of an insurer, either at solo undertaking level or group level. It ought to be included in the scope for statistical disclosure. Due to the importance of the figures for solvency-related issues, the enhancement of statistical disclosure of solvency data will be separately dealt with in the subsequent subsection, which will involve the discussion about the disclosure of solvency conditions at group level.

In parallel with the data on group solvency, the figures revealing the business structure of insurance groups are mentioned as the other set of statistics that are supposed to be publicly disseminated. They are intended to show the scope of the business areas in which insurance groups engage, to measure the financial importance of subsidiary undertakings to the wider group, and to reflect the combined size of the insurance groups. What underlies the dissemination of the statistics for group business structure is that the idiosyncrasies of an insurance group reside in the diversity, scale and interplay of its business. And the study of these idiosyncrasies is central to the interpretation of the group risk profile which is intrinsically different from that of solo undertakings. The statistics for business structure would particularly serve as the basis for a group-wide perspective of risk assessment, enabling stakeholders to derive concrete clues about the extent of impacts of a group member on the remaining entities within a group. Likewise, the statistics will help expose the magnitude of the systemic risks arising from the insurance groups at aggregate level. In practical terms, the CIRC could consider selecting key figures indicative of group business structure from the pertinent supervisory report by each insurance group and publishing the aggregates of those figures.[373] The dissertation, after reviewing the normative document which lays down the requirements on group supervisory reporting, recommends that the CIRC disclose the aggregated data items as listed in Table 7.[374]

---

373 CIRC, *the Rules on Statistics based on Consolidated Supervision of Insurance Groups* (Normative Document No 29, 2016).

374 *Id.*

Table 7: Proposed Statistical Disclosures about the Business Structure of Chinese Insurance Groups

Number of Subsidiary Undertakings per Business Area	– Insurance Area: Life; Property; Health; Pension; Insurance Asset Management; Insurance Mediation – Non-insurance Financial Area: Banking; Securities; Investment Funds; Futures; Financial Lease; Trust – Non-Financial Area
Assets, Liabilities and Revenue	– Combined Group data – Insurance Area: Life; Property; Health; Pension; Insurance Asset Management; Insurance Mediation – Non-insurance Financial Area: Banking; Securities; Investment Funds; Futures; Financial Lease; Trust – Non-Financial Area
Scale of Intra-group Transactions and Exposures	– Intra-group transactions: Between insurance area and non-insurance financial area; between insurance area and non-financial area; between non-insurance financial area and non-financial area – Exposures between the business areas: The exposure of insurance area to non-insurance financial area; of non-insurance financial area to insurance area; of insurance area to non-financial area; of non-financial area to insurance area; of non-insurance financial area to non-financial area; of non-financial area to non-insurance financial area
Linkages with External Financial Institutions	– Exposures of insurance groups to external financial institutions: Deposits at external financial institutions; Short-term lending to external financial institutions in interbank and exchange bond markets; Holding of long-term debt instruments issued by external financial institutions; Holding of equity in external financial institutions – Exposures of external financial institutions to insurance groups: Short-term lending to insurance groups in interbank and exchange bond markets; Holding of long-term debt instruments issued by insurance groups; Holding of equity in insurance groups

The data items in Table 7 should be disclosed aggregating the relevant figures for each insurance group in China. As for the scale of intra-group transactions and exposures, it is unnecessary to break down to such a level of granularity as to show the amount of the transactions and exposures between the various business segments within the three big areas – insurance area, non-insurance financial area and non-financial area. Instead, the authority is only expected to take each big area as a whole in disclosing the statistics for this item. With regard to the means of publishing the data on the business structure of insurance groups, it is advisable to make the disclosures accessible in the section 'statistical data' on the CIRC electronic platform where the figures for the insurance sector in general are provided. With the group-level data in place, the comparison between it and the industry-wide data will be facilitated. The authority can release the group statistics on a quarterly basis, consistent with the frequency with which the insurance groups render supervisory reporting on business and financial conditions.[375]

2. Data on Insurer Solvency

Solvency is most vital to the sustained operation of insurance business. Correspondingly, the data on insurer solvency plays a central role in the assessment of the overall risk profile of an insurer. Insufficient disclosure of solvency-related data by a supervisory authority would definitely translate into low statistical transparency in view of the barriers to the data users seeking the factors underlying insurer capital adequacy and of the potential costs incurred by the entities sensitive to insurance sector movements.

The deficit in solvency-related statistics for insurance undertakings and groups is exposed as one of the major weaknesses of the statistical disclosure by the CIRC, as the analyses in the previous subchapter suggest.[376] The CIRC's disclosures about the solvency profile of the China's insurance sector are found to be far from adequate, as the authority makes public only several figures at a gross level indicative of solvency position and its changes. The disclosures neither give any clues as to how the required capital is distributed across the diverse risks incurred by a particular undertaking, nor bring to light the constituents and quality of the own funds held by an undertaking.[377]

---

375 *Supra note* 373.
376 *See* Chapter 5 Part A III 1.
377 *Id.*

As opposed to the rather limited quantity of macro-level statistical disclosures about solvency, the data collected by the CIRC from each insurance undertaking or group through the supervisory reporting process exhibits nevertheless a high level of detail taking full account of the components or relevant factors in all important dimensions of solvency.[378] There is thus great asymmetry between the input and output of solvency data on the part of the authority. It is certain that the data coverage of an authority's statistical disclosures could be legitimately made narrower than that of the quantitative reports filed by insurance undertakings to the authority, since supervisory needs outweigh the interests of other data user groups. Understandably, part of the data collected by the authority is excluded from the scope of the released statistics owing to its importance, granularity or confidentiality. But, it would be insufficient to amount to a useful statistical disclosure provided that the statistics fail to incorporate the aggregates for undertaking-level data reported to the supervisors on most of the aspects pertinent to capital adequacy. In the absence of a statistical breakdown, a thorough and unbiased evaluation of the solvency risk profile across distinct segments of the insurance sector is impeded as far as the interested parties are concerned. This is not only ascribed to the high cost of private collecting and aggregating data from public disclosures made by individual undertakings, but also due to the unavailability of sensitive data at the undertaking level which is exclusive to supervisors.

A proper level of statistical granularity is exemplified by the disclosure of solvency data by the NCAs in the EU. The data on insurer solvency makes up a major pillar of the EU's insurance statistical disclosures. At union level, the illustration of the EU-wide insurer solvency is provided in the financial stability report and the risk dashboard published by the

---

378 For the relevant statutory requirements and reporting templates specific to the insurance undertakings, *see* CIRC, *Supervisory Rules on the Solvency Position of Insurance Undertakings No 16: Reporting on Solvency Conditions* (Normative Document, No 22, 2015), §§ 7 – 69; CIRC, *Notification on the Issues about the Implementation of C-ROSS* (Normative Document, 25 January 2016) annex 6. For the corresponding requirements and templates applicable to the insurance groups, see CIRC, *Supervisory Rules on Solvency Position of Insurance Undertakings No 17: Insurance Groups* (Normative Document, No 22, 2015), §§ 92 – 100; The Finance and Accounting Department of the CIRC, 'Notification on the Transitional Requirements For the Implementation of C-ROSS' (CIRC Website, 13 February 2015) annex 2 <www.circ.gov.cn/web/site0/tab5216/info3951934.htm> accessed 3 May 2017.

EIOPA.[379] In parallel, at the member state level, the NCAs disseminate aggregate statistics which contain quantitative specifics of the solvency conditions nationwide.[380] In relation to the extent of the CIRC's disclosures, the solvency figures presented in the European counterparts, in conformity with the templates stipulated for aggregate statistical disclosures, demonstrate a greater level of granularity.[381] The macro-level data is broken down into multiple items to enable scrutiny of its composition or distribution. For instance, the eligible amount of own funds is shown for each tier and the SCR under standard formula is specified for each risk sub-module.[382] The level of granularity that the EU's insurance statistics demonstrate is a vital quality that the CIRC will have to embrace in formulating the statistical disclosures about insurer solvency.[383] It means that the CIRC's statistical disclosures should be made more detailed so as to incorporate micro-

379 *See* the Regulation Establishing EIOPA, recital 64. Both of the publications are available on the EIOPA website, inside the section 'Financial Stability & Crisis Prevention' <eiopa.europa.eu/financial-stability-crisis-prevention/financial-stability> accessed 3 May 2017. The financial stability report is published semi-annually, while the risk dashboard is released on a quarterly basis.

380 *See* Solvency II Directive § 31 (2)(c). The aggregate statistical disclosures can be found on the website of a particular NCA, or on the EIOPA website where the combined disclosures for all the NCAs are available. With regard to the latter, *see* EIOPA, *EU/EEA (Re)Insurance Statistics* (Database, EIOPA-FSI-16/025, 2016).

381 *See supra note* 368 (Commission Implementing Regulation); Solvency II Directive, § 31 (2)(c).

382 *Id.* (Commission Implementing Regulation) at 1235-1240.

383 Data quality is crucial to the effectiveness of supervision. Macro statistical data alone is insufficient to give insight into the supervised entities' conditions in diverse aspects and not conducive to the identification of risk areas. With standardized and granular datasets, the supervisory authority is allowed to give deeper analysis of the common risk characteristics across the undertakings in a targeted market category using various measures from different risk perspectives. For other data user groups, abundant micro-level data renders the statistical disclosures informative and transparent, diminishing the cost of private data collection and aggregation. For this reason, the granularity of statistical data is likewise of importance to the interested parties and the wider public. For the references on the use of granular data to financial supervision, *see generally* Klass Knot, 'Granular Data and Macroprudential Policy: Examples and Challenges' (8th ECB Statistics Conference, Frankfurt am Main, 6 July 2016) <www.ecb.europa.eu/pub/conferences/shared/pdf/160705_8th_stats_conference/Knot.pdf?8c24351a2fc6add3c049e74e40f6f4ce> accessed 4 May 2017 (illustrating the benefits of using granular data in shaping macro-prudential policies by way of several concrete examples showing how the utilization of granular data contributes to the fulfillment of financial stability tasks); Benoît Cœuré, 'Opening Remarks: Setting Standards for Granular Data' (3rd the U.S. Office of Financial Research

level figures corresponding in nature to the granular solvency data available in the European counterparts. However, the statistical items adopted by the NCAs in the EU cannot serve as ideal points of reference for the CIRC, mainly due to the differences in the definitions and methodologies used in the determination of capital adequacy.

Based on the comparisons above, the dissertation advises that the aggregate statistics for solvency published by the CIRC be commensurate with the undertaking-level data that it collects from the supervisory reporting by individual insurance undertakings, to the extent that the statistics are made as granular as those disclosed by the NCAs in the EU. The reason why the supervisory reports are perceived as the most suitable points of reference is twofold. Firstly, any items presented in the reports could always be harmoniously integrated into the authority's statistics by means of aggregation or averaging. In this way, the cost of conceptual or methodological transposition is avoided, which would otherwise arise in the case of aligning the CIRC's disclosure with that of an inconsistent system. Secondly, the supervisory reports submitted by insurers have a wider coverage of data on solvency as the provision of information for supervisory purposes is subject to stringent requirements. In terms of the scope and depth of the data involved, a particular undertaking's supervisory report significantly exceeds its public disclosure. Out of these considerations, the optimal approach is to match the scope of the statistical items present in the CIRC's statistical disclosure to that of the mandatory data items included in the individual supervisory reports received by the authority to some degree. The level of granularity of the EU's insurance statistics for insurer solvency could be used as the benchmark for the calibration and determination of the degree to which the statistical items and the undertaking-level data items mutually correspond.

In line with the general arrangements of the data items in the supervisory reports by Chinese insurers, under the topic of solvency there should be several indispensable subtopics that the CIRC's statistical disclosure has to cover. In the context of China's insurance supervision, the subtopics relate

(hereinafter referred to as "OFR") -ECB- Bank of England (hereinafter referred to as "BoE") Workshop on Granular Data, Frankfurt am Main, 28 March 2017) <www.ecb.europa.eu/press/key/date/2017/html/sp170328.en.html> accessed 4 May 2017 (discussing the need for high-quality granular data and corresponding global standards, as well as presenting the progress and challenges on this topic).

to eligible assets, eligible liabilities, capital available and the MCS.[384] Each of the subtopic items should be divided into numerous component items, and for the sake of a necessary level of granularity, further breakdowns should be in place for those component items which are statutorily classified into more tiers or types. Alongside the breakdown of statistical items, the authority is also expected to categorize the insurance undertakings by nature of business in disclosing the statistics for solvency. They could be categorized as life and health insurance undertakings, property and casualty insurance undertakings, reinsurance undertakings, as well as all insurance undertakings. Data shall be shown for all the statistical items across the several categories of entities, except where particular items are not applicable. The CIRC could exercise judgment to determine the form in which different sets of statistical items should be expressed. In relation to other alternatives, the form opted for is supposed to be better able to demonstrate the relative importance of a particular item and facilitate the comparison between distinct categories of entities. As exemplified by the practices of the NCAs in the EU, balance sheet items and own funds are shown in totals, while capital requirements are expressed as percentages.

Among the statistical items about solvency, the most crucial one is the capital adequacy ratio, which serves as a straightforward measure of the solvency conditions of the entire insurance sector or a specified segment thereof. As far as the particular statistical item is concerned, the benchmark would be shifted from the NCAs to the EIOPA since the supranational advisory body utilizes a more granular approach. An important discrepancy between the CIRC and the EIOPA, with regard to the key ratio, resides in the way of ascertaining its representative value. The former employs average to derive the value, whereas the latter relies on median.[385] Given the fact that insurance undertakings are distinct from each other in

384 The four items make up the major pillars of an undertaking's solvency report to the CIRC. The capital available is similar to the own funds as are defined by the EU Solvency II regime, while the MCS is comparable to the SCR under the foregoing regime.

385 The average has different meanings and could be calculated in a number of ways. But, the CIRC's method to derive the average capital adequacy ratio is not made public. The average of a set of data usually refers to the arithmetic mean of the sample, which equals the sum of the values in the data set divided by the number of those values. Nevertheless, in China, the average capital adequacy ratio of a specified insurance sector segment is more likely to be equal to the aggregated capital available of all the insurance undertakings concerned divided by the aggregated MCS of these undertakings. The calculation method here premises that all the undertakings in a specified sector segment are taken as a

asset scale, risk profile, capital quality and capital amounts, the use of averaging is certain to cause a distorted estimation of the typical capital position of a specific segment of the insurance sector. The CIRC's calculation of the ratio, depending on the averaging method which remains unspecified, is largely influenced either by the insurance undertakings with larger balance sheets or by those with a ratio of extreme value.[386] It shall hence convert to median in response to the irregular variance in solvency pattern among the undertakings, since the median is a more accurate measure of central tendency than the average on the occurrence of an asymmetrical data distribution.[387] The asymmetrical distribution of capital adequacy levels holds true for insurance markets in most jurisdictions, which also explains the reason for the adoption of median value by the EIOPA in the measurement of the representative capital adequacy ratio. By taking the middle value of the capital adequacy ratios of all insurance undertakings, the undue impacts of outlier values or the excessive weights given to large-sized undertakings would be avoided. In addition to the median taken as the indicator of the most characteristic solvency condition, the EIOPA makes available multiple percentiles of the capital adequacy ratios of all

---

whole, which has comparable effects to the way of deriving the weighted average. The median is simply the middle value of a data set, separating the higher half of the sample from the lower half. In relation to the average (mean), the median has the advantage of not being skewed by extreme values in a data set. This makes it a better measure of the typical value in the event that a data sample is not normally distributed. For the definitions at issue, *see e.g.* D Anderson *et al.*, *Statistics for Business and Economics* (2nd edn, Cengage Learning EMEA 2010) 68-72, 82-83, 99-100; J Stock and M Watson, *Introduction to Econometrics* (updated 3rd edn (global edn), Pearson 2015) 82, 90. With regard to the concrete statistical disclosures by the EIOPA and the CIRC about the capital adequacy ratios of specified categories of insurers, *see e.g.* EIOPA, *Financial Stability Report* (Publication, EIOPA-FSI-16-016, 2016) ch 2.3; 'C-ROSS Formally Implemented: Positive Effects' (*CIRC Website,* 25 October 2016) <www.circ.gov.cn/web/site0/tab6527/info4047909.htm> accessed 9 May 2017.

386 Under the first circumstance, where the arithmetic mean is taken as the representative value of the ratio, the result would be affected by the excessively high and low capital adequacy ratios of the insurance undertakings involved. Under the other circumstance, where the calculation presupposes that all the insurance undertakings concerned are deemed to be a single entity, the large-sized undertakings would apparently gain more weight in the items on the numerator and the denominator of the ratio.

387 *Supra note* 385.

the insurance undertakings sampled.[388] The approach lends granularity to the disclosure of the statistical item, as the capital adequacy ratios representative of different solvency-level groups are revealed from top to bottom. The benefits of the practice are evident that the interested parties are provided with a broader perspective of the industry-wide solvency picture. The CIRC should consider utilizing a similar method to characterize the patterns specific to high, medium and low solvency-level groups. For this purpose, when giving the statistical facts about the general solvency conditions of a specific insurance sector segment, the CIRC is supposed to make public the quartiles of the capital adequacy ratios of all the undertakings concerned. That means besides the median, the capital adequacy ratios of the insurance undertakings ranking at the level of 25% and 75% among all need be revealed.

Last but not least, the approaches discussed above, which are aimed at the CIRC's aggregate statistical disclosure of the solvency position of Chinese insurance undertakings, can be applied to the authority's statistics for group solvency mutatis mutandis. Distinctive treatment will necessarily be in place for the aggregate statistical data on group capital available and minimum group capital requirements. The distinguishing feature, which differentiates the statistics for group solvency from those for undertaking solvency, lies in that the subtopic statistical items would be broken down in such a way as to reflect the allocation of capital resources and the imposition of capital requirements among subsidiary undertakings of various types.[389] The purpose of the breakdowns is to show the impacts of various group members on the financial standing of a group. However, in the case of the statistics for undertaking solvency, the corresponding breakdowns are implemented mainly on the basis of the quality and risk specificity of capital, rather than by business line or component entity. As stipulated by the CIRC, in the calculation of group solvency, the unsupervised entities which essentially refer to non-financial subsidiaries are not subjected to any capital requirements.[390] Owing to this, the micro-level statistical items, as the result of the breakdowns mentioned above, are supposed to be appli-

388 The EIOPA publicizes in the semi-annual financial stability report the median, interquartile range, 10th and 90th percentile of the SCR coverage ratios sampled EEA-wide. *See id.* (financial stability report). *Cf.* Solvency II Directive, § 31 (2) (c).

389 The subsidiary undertakings subject to capital supervision denote exclusively the entities conducting business in financial sectors. *See infra note* 390, 391.

390 CIRC, *Supervisory Rules on the Solvency Position of Insurance Undertakings No 17: Insurance Groups* (Normative Document, No 22, 2015), § 17 (5).

cable to insurance subsidiaries and non-insurance financial subsidiaries in a group.[391]

3. Disclosures about Off-site Supervisory Activities

The previous subsections have discussed the approaches to the deficiencies of the statistical data on insurance groups and insurer solvency. The discussions are centered on the statistics for the supervised entities. In this subsection, the analytical focus is shifted to the statistics regarding the supervisory authority, i.e. the aggregate data summarizing the activities performed by the authority. In the first subchapter, it is indicated that the CIRC's statistical disclosures about the on-site supervisory activities are generally deemed sufficient,[392] whereas its statistics for the off-site ones fall short of the necessary level of detail with which the disclosures would allow the data users to be informed of the specific actions taken and the results thereof.

The lack of detail is found to exist in two areas of activity, namely the supervisory scrutiny and supervisory control. As previously defined,[393] the supervisory scrutiny refers to the CIRC's employment of tools and approaches for the surveillance and review of insurance undertakings. The activities of scrutiny for which the statistics are considered insufficient include the integrated risk rating along with the theme-focused evaluations. Both of them are essential components of the CIRC's supervisory review process. It should be noted that off-site scrutinizing activities are not with-

391 The non-insurance financial subsidiaries in an insurance group mainly include the entities that engage in the business activities of banking, securities, futures and trust. *See* id. at §§ 17 (3), 25, 106.

392 The statistical disclosure of the on-site supervisory activities is publicly available in the CIRC's yearly market review report. The disclosure revealed the amount of the supervisory work conducted in the main areas of on-site inspections and released the figures concerning the supervisory measures imposed subsequent to the identification of non-compliances. The disclosure shows a lack of quantitative or qualitative information about the weaknesses and risks common to the insurers inspected. The amount of the supervisory measures based on the outcome of the on-site inspections is disclosed according to the means of intervention rather than the circumstance triggering intervention. For the report mentioned here, *see supra note* 329, at 34, 35.

393 *See* the definition of the rules for scrutiny in the first paragraph of Section I of Part A in this chapter, which can be applied to this context mutatis mutandis.

in the scope of mandatory statistical disclosures in the EU.[394] As required by the pertinent ITS, The NCAs are obligated to disclose the data on on-site inspections.[395] Whereas, the quantitative facts about the risk assessment or the detailed analysis, which the NCAs conduct off-site complementary to the on-site inspection,[396] are not subject to disclosure. From the viewpoint of the dissertation, without incorporation of the data on off-site scrutiny into statistical disclosures, the disclosures cannot be deemed to meet a sufficient level of transparency. In relation to on-site activities, far more resources of a supervisory authority are allocated to off-site ones and the majority of the conclusions about insurer riskiness are drawn from off-site reviews. The statistical information concerning the off-site scrutiny could give clues about the workload for each kind of the review activities performed, the differences between the planned and the actual activities, as well as the ensuing findings. It might be argued that the findings of the scrutiny should not fall into the statistical category of the data on a supervisory authority as they represent the situations of the supervised entities in particular aspects. The argument nevertheless fails to take account of the closer relational proximity of the findings to an authority's activities than to the facts about supervised entities. As opposed to the facts about supervised entities which already exist, findings will not come into existence until review activities are carried out. Unlike the statistics showing the facts about supervised entities, the statistics summarizing findings cannot be directly derived through data collection or aggregation. Its derivation requires additional supervisory activities exceeding the scope for the making of statistics. The data on findings, which contain the products and effects generated by the off-site scrutiny, is inseparable from other dimensions involved in the disclosure of scrutinizing activities.

Given that a combination of quantitative and qualitative data would be best conducive to the interpretation of the supervisory activities performed, the statistical disclosure of the off-site scrutiny could be added to the CIRC's annual report on Chinese insurance market,[397] in which the supervisory products and on-site activities delivered are summarized. In

394 *See supra note* 368 (Commission Implementing Regulation) at annex I Template C; Solvency II Directive, § 31 (2)(c).

395 *Id.*

396 The risk assessment and the detailed analysis are part of the supervisory review process of the NCAs in the EU. *See supra note* 211 (Guidelines), §§ 12-32; *see also* Solvency II Directive, § 36.

397 For the annual report, *see supra note* 329. The CIRC could additionally publish the statistical disclosure about the conduct and findings of an off-site scrutiniz-

quantitative terms, the CIRC is expected to explicitly reveal the actual number of each kind of scrutinizing activities performed, the amount of supervisory resources assigned to the activities and the usage of purpose-built review tools and methods which are not applied to regular activities of scrutiny. In parallel with the data on the conduct of scrutiny, the disclosure shall provide the quantitative data conveying the findings of the scrutiny, in particular the indicators for the degree of risk exposures, the extent of compliance and the impacts of the different factors causing non-compliance. In qualitative terms, the disclosure need give a short analysis of the differences between scrutiny plans and actual implementation, the priorities and constraints of the scrutiny in last year, the reasons for the industry-wide risk characteristics and the widespread flawed practices that impair insurers' governance functions or service quality.

Alongside the supervisory scrutiny, the activities of supervisory control are regarded as the other area of off-site activity which lacks statistical disclosure. In line with the definition laid down at the beginning of the chapter,[398] the items involved in this particular area of activity relate to those that the supervisors perform to exert control proactively or reactively for the sake of insurers' compliance. Specifically, the activities of control refer to the supervisory approvals and measures by the CIRC.[399] The only statistical data relevant to the kind of activities is the aggregate numbers respectively for the supervisory approvals and the supervisory measures.[400] As indicated, the shortcoming herein is the unavailability of a statistical breakdown. The necessity of breaking down the aggregate of the supervisory approvals and measures has also been explained.[401] By contrast to the lack of detailed quantitative data on the specific area of activity in China, the aggregate statistical disclosure by the NCAs in the EU contains granular data on insurers' applications, supervisory approvals and supervisory measures,

---

ing activity right after the end of the activity by way of a special bulletin that is published on a periodical or ad hoc basis. Given the different frequencies of the various scrutinizing activities, the data disclosures that fully summarize all types of activities conducted within a calendar year shall in no case be excluded from the yearly report on Chinese insurance market.

398 See the definition of the rules for control in the first paragraph of Section I of Part A in this chapter, which can be applied to this context mutatis mutandis.

399 *See* the first paragraph of the Section I of Part A in this chapter.

400 The aggregate number of both items can be found in the annual transparency report by the CIRC, *see supra note* 330. On the CIRC website individual pieces of information about supervisory approvals and measures are disseminated. However, there exists no statistical analysis of the information.

401 *See* the discussion made in Subsection 2 of Section III of Part A in this chapter.

revealing the usage of supervisory powers in each predefined circumstance where the supervisors are supposed to step in.[402] The foregoing statistical data, which implies the rate of supervisory approval and the frequency of supervisory measures, gives out signals to the stakeholders about the actual severity of an NCA's supervision in general in addition to the methodological preferences and the solvency riskiness of a country's insurance sector.

In order for due transparency of the supervisory activities performed to exert control, the CIRC should provide the breakdowns of insurers' applications, supervisory approvals and supervisory measures in a similar way to its EU counterparts. The relevant statistical data must be disclosed to the extent that the number of insurers' applications, supervisory approvals or supervisory measures is specified for each predefined circumstance where an insurer or the authority is supposed to take such an action.[403] The specification by circumstance is suitable for the disclosure of insurers' applications and corresponding supervisory approvals. Nevertheless, it does not work equally well when being applied to the disclosure of supervisory measures. The reason is that either an insurer's application or a supervisory approval is intrinsically a definite action, while there are a variety of alternatives classified as supervisory measures. It is thus necessary to differentiate between supervisory measures according to means of intervention alongside circumstance of imposition. Statistical breakdown of supervisory measures by interventional means will facilitate the interpretation of supervisory severity as well as the monitoring of the exercise of supervisory powers. In the EU, the statistical disclosure about the supervisory measures adopted is only available in the form of circumstance-based data. The disadvantage is apparent that the number of the supervisory measures of a particular type remains unclear.

In view of the points above, it is advisable that the CIRC make public the breakdown per circumstance of the total number of insurers' applications and corresponding supervisory approvals, and meanwhile, ensure

---

402 *Supra note* 394.

403 Insofar as insurers' applications and supervisory approvals are concerned, the predefined circumstances refer to the scenarios prescribed in the regulations, where an insurer has to submit a request to the supervisory authority for its decision as to whether particular activities or changes the insurer plans could be permitted. With regard to the predefined circumstances for the imposition of supervisory measures, they denote the scenarios where the supervisory authority is statutorily required to intervene for the purpose of preventing the materialization of risks or a deterioration in conditions as well as correcting an insurer's problems identified in order to restore it to compliance.

that the statistics for supervisory measures are disclosed separately according to circumstance and means. The statistics for the activities of supervisory control can be combined with those for the activities of supervisory scrutiny to sum up the performance of off-site supervisory activities in the CIRC's yearly report reviewing the developments in China's insurance sector.

C. Chapter Conclusions

In regulatory terms, the rules for control, which refer to the requirements concerning supervisory approvals and supervisor measures, demonstrate a sufficient level of accessibility and clarity. The rules for scrutiny, which include all the rules other than the rules for control, are soundly accessible, but have a low level of clarity due to the unsystematic normative documents. This weakness is analyzed in detail in Chapter 2 and the approach is also provided therein. Alongside the low clarity of the rules for scrutiny, the absence of rationales for rules is identified as the other prominent weakness of regulatory transparency. The rationale behind important supervisory requirements should be made public before the requirements take effect. The most cost-effective way is to disseminate the rationale during the consultation process. The various analyses provided by the supervisory authority as parts of the consultative documents would give an insight into the rule-making rationale from different perspectives. The clarity of rationales and transparency of consultations fall into distinct categories of supervisory transparency. The former is a matter of rule-making transparency, while the latter is within the scope of functional transparency. A transparent consultation is conducive to the clarity of the rationale behind proposed supervisory requirements, and vice versa. In the course of a public consultation, the CIRC publishes only draft regulations, calling for comments. There is not any other material available. Because of this, it is advisable that the CIRC strengthen the consultative mechanisms in order for a more transparent and effective public consultation, which would in turn bring about clear rationales for supervisory requirements. The CIRC is expected to make public the comments received, the summary and resolution of the comments as well as an analysis of the necessity, practicality and impacts of the draft regulations.

In functional terms, supervisory transparency could be interpreted as the degree to which organizational, procedural and operational details are made public. The internal workings of the CIRC are found to be secretive to some degree since the way in which the supervisory authority is governed remains largely undisclosed. Its organizational information shall be made complete to include the objectives, composition and tasks of all the internal entities, in particular decision-making bodies, working groups and joint bodies. The rules of procedure for the decision-making bodies should be made public to allow the interested parties to understand the decision mechanisms at the highest level of the authority. Besides the internal workings, the supervisory activities conducted by the CIRC also have marked flaws in transparency. The completed supervisory activities are publicized in a partial and disorganized manner. The information about the ongoing and future supervisory activities is basically inaccessible. In the chapter, a practical approach is proposed that a specific unit could be established in the existing section 'working briefing' on the CIRC's electronic platform to assemble and thematically categorize the information about all types of supervisory activities and projects. The information should be publicly disseminated with such a level of particularity as to make available the time frame, actions, tools, products and outcomes involved in a supervisory activity. Certainly, products and outcomes are not immediately available at the time of the dissemination of information about ongoing and future supervisory activities. For the supervisory work in the long run, the releases will be rendered more informative providing the general facts about the substantive supervisory activities and deliverables planned for the pursuit of each operative objective in the coming years are made public. The CIRC's operative objectives, mostly qualitative, require further quantification in order for exact and transparent supervisory targets.

In terms of statistical disclosure, the weakness of supervisory transparency resides in the lack of granular data. Except for the disclosures about insurance undertakings' business conditions, the statistical facts are essentially published by the CIRC in the form of macro statistical data which shows the state of the supervised entities and the supervisory authority merely at a gross level. Particularly, the aggregate statistical data on the aspects of insurer solvency and supervisory work lacks granularity. On the aspect of insurance groups, the situation is even worse – the statistical data is unavailable. Broadly speaking, the insufficiency of statistical transparency could be resolved by breaking down the macro statistical data into multiple micro-level items. With an increased level of detail in the disclosed data, the interested parties will be enabled to have a broader perspective of the industry-wide conditions in a specific supervisory area. As proposed in the chapter, the statistical disclosure of solvency conditions should be aligned with the supervisory reporting made by solo undertakings to the authority with regard to data coverage on a best efforts basis. The use of median and quartiles to disclose capital adequacy ratios is put forward for the sake of accuracy and granularity. As for the supervisory activities that the CIRC conducts, the respective aggregates of the supervisory assessments, approvals and measures should be broken down according to type or circumstance. Statistical facts should be provided to summarize the essential findings of the integrated and theme-focused evaluations. When it comes to the statistical disclosure of Chinese insurance groups, it is absolutely necessary for the CIRC to make public the aggregate group-level data, which should at least contain figures for group business structure and solvency conditions. The figures for group business structure are supposed to reflect at an aggregate or average level the financial impacts of the subsidiaries in different business areas on an insurance group, the extent of interconnections between subsidiaries within a group, and the scale of exposures between insurance groups and financial market entities.

Summary of Findings, Conclusions and Recommendations

The essential findings, conclusions and recommendations in the dissertation are summarized in this final chapter. The subsequent parts encapsulate the main problems facing China's insurance supervision and regulation, and provide a synopsis of the approaches to these problems. In fact, there are additional problems and approaches being analyzed in the dissertation. It should be noted that the comparisons between the EU's insurance supervision and that of China, which are drawn to facilitate the identification of the problems and the formation of the approaches, are not recapitulated below for the sake of conciseness.

A. *Rule-making Legitimacy*

In China's insurance regulation system, the Insurance Act of China, as a legislative act enacted by the NPCC, is at the highest regulatory level. As statutorily defined, the legislative acts are supposed to stipulate essential principles in respective regulated areas, serving as the framework for further rule-making work. However, such principles are notably insufficient or unavailable for a large proportion of the regulatory issues in the Insurance Act of China. Numerous important regulatory issues are not even mentioned therein. Meanwhile, the implementing rules for the Insurance Act are delegated to the CIRC. The regulatory instruments of the CIRC include department rules and normative documents. Statutorily, the two types of legal acts are supposed to supplement the upper-level legal acts by providing implementing details, instead of laying down essential principles which should be determined through rigorous legislative procedures. Nevertheless, given the lacking of essential principles and the partial coverage of regulatory issues by the Insurance Act of China, the CIRC has to exceed the regulatory boundary by prescribing both framework principles and implementing details. Otherwise the regulatory framework would be unable to serve the needs of insurance supervision. All the department rules and normative documents, regardless of significance, are drafted and issued by the CIRC alone, without the involvement of other regulatory actors.

It will be ideal to have in place a regulatory system similar to the Lamfalussy Process adopted in the EU financial regulation which provides sufficient essential principles at the level of framework directive and a clear scope for the delegation of implementing acts to the lower regulatory level. But, it is impractical to apply the regulatory model to China's insurance sector, because such a transformation depends on legislators' willingness to introduce the model to financial sectors, entails extensive amendments to all legal acts related to insurance regulation and requires a redefinition of the roles of supervisory authorities. In light of the excessively high costs, a viable alternative is proposed in Chapter 2, namely establishing an independent committee reviewing the regulatory work by financial supervisors. According to the significance of a draft regulation, the reviewing process could be divided into two tracks: prudential procedures for proposed department rules and simple procedures for proposed normative documents. Under the prudential procedures, a draft regulation must be approved by the independent committee and should therefore take into account the revision opinions put forward by the committee. Under the simple procedures, a draft regulation could be put into effect without the approval by the independent committee, but the supervisory authority should make public the reasons in case it declines to accept the revision opinions of the committee.

B. *Rule-making Systematicness*

Unsystematic rule-making by the CIRC is identified as one of the major deficiencies in its regulatory and supervisory practices. The problem could be largely ascribed to the way in which normative documents are made. They are the regulatory instrument that is most frequently employed by the CIRC due to the less complicated rule-making process relative to other types of legal acts. The normative documents serve to implement all types of legal acts above them in regulatory status. For each supervisory area in the insurance sector, there usually exists a department rule accompanied by numerous discrete normative documents. The normative documents are intended to provide implementing rules applicable to the diverse aspects and circumstances related to a specific supervisory area on which the pertinent department rule is centered. For the clarity of supervisory rules, the interrelated normative documents supplementing the same department rule should be consolidated into a single implementing regulation so as to form a clear linkage between a department rule and its implementing details.

In practice, the use of normative documents is not confined to serving the purpose of implementation. They are also used by the CIRC to prescribe essential principles for some regulatory areas which are not involved in the legislative act and stipulate requirements on the supervisory areas which should have been dealt with in department rules given their significance. It is advisable to reclassify such normative documents as department rules, which is conducive to the methodological consistency in insurance legislation.

C. Supervisory Priority

As far as China's insurance supervision is concerned, there exist three parallel supervisory objectives with equal importance, including protecting policyholders and beneficiaries, promoting insurance sector development as well as safeguarding social and economic order.

The dissertation supports for a prioritization of policyholder protection over other objectives in the conduct of insurance supervision. There are several reasons for the prioritization. Firstly, insurance consumers, as members of the public, have a much weaker position in insurance contracting given the informational asymmetry between a normal consumer and an insurer about insurance products. Given the complexity of the pricing and other technical aspects of an insurance product, they can easily be subjected to unfair coverage terms or premium rate. Retail policyholders could hardly diversify their insurance exposures. They are not supposed to bear the losses resulting from the insolvency of an insurer as is the case with shareholders and creditors. However, policyholders are actually highly vulnerable to insurer insolvency. Policyholder protection should therefore be deemed to be the fundamental value of insurance supervision. Secondly, under the parallel arrangement of the supervisory objectives, the CIRC is expected to ensure the balance between the somewhat conflicting objectives. That is to say, in making supervisory rules, decisions and actions, it is legitimate for the supervisory authority to make compromises to preserve the collective interests of insurers at the expense of policyholders and beneficiaries. The need for compromises between the supervisory objectives, which stems from their equal status, is detrimental to the fundamental value of insurance supervision, i.e. policyholder protection. An explicit prioritization of policyholder protection in insurance legislation will underpin the prevailing of policyholders' interests under all circumstances by enabling the CIRC to legitimately give preferential treatment to policyholders in making and enforcing rules. Thirdly, with the parallel supervisory objectives in place, the insurance supervisors have to split the supervisory resources between them. The finite human, time and financial resources available to the supervisory authority could not be concentrated on the areas of activity which deserve more supervisory efforts.

Promoting insurance sector development is explicitly set as one of the main supervisory objectives pursued by the CIRC. However, there is no causal relationship between the development in insurance sector and the enhancement of policyholder protection. The boom in the insurance sector will neither lead to a change in the intrinsic nature of insurance contracts, nor reduce the degree of the risks inherent in insurance business. A sustained growth in premium income and asset scale cannot safely translate into the soundness of solvency position. The development in insurance sector will result in the increase of state-owned assets given the prevalent ownership structure of Chinese insurance undertakings, and meanwhile, more funding resources are available from the insurance sector to facilitate the fulfillment of the government's economic agenda. The promoting of insurance sector development is hence not of supervisory nature, but more of a macroeconomic policy. The task should no longer be performed by the CIRC on account of the conflict of interests present in the rule-making and oversight. For this reason, it shall be excluded from the scope of the CIRC's supervisory objectives and reassigned to a non-regulatory and non-supervisory institution of which the function is apt for its pursuance of the objective.

Apart from policyholder protection and the sector development promotion, there exists another supervisory objective: safeguarding social and economic order. For the sake of clarity and practicality, the general and obscure objective ought to be replaced by a specified one that fits into the context of financial supervision. The dissertation advises that the ensuring of financial stability shall be explicitly enshrined in the Insurance Act of China as a supervisory objective secondary to policyholder protection. The supervisory authority is expected to show sufficient regard for the cyclicality of their supervisory decisions and actions, in particular the potential adverse effects of the supervision on financial stability. Additionally, the supervisory authority is also expected to contribute to financial stability on its own initiative through rule-making and other supervisory activities. The establishment of the new supervisory objective is ascribed to the fact that the insurance sector is of high relevance to China's financial stability and there exists systemically important insurers. The fact is ascertained through a study of the systemic relevance of the largest Chinese insurance groups in diverse aspects, with evidence emerging in a range of aspects including shareholding in financial institutions, repo positions, debt market positions, exposures to the real estate market, credit and guaranty insurance business as well as reinsurance concentration.

D. Supervisory Specificity

Lack of specificity is the major weakness of the supervision by the CIRC. The weakness is found to exist in both of the two component stages of its supervisory review process.

At the stage of supervisory assessment, a larger proportion of the various supervisory assessments are aimed at classifying insurance undertakings into different level groups on the basis of the conditions of the undertakings in specified supervisory areas. However, the risk areas covered by the supervisory assessments are limited to those prescribed in the regulations. Emerging risk areas, which newly arise and merit focused analyses across the insurance sector, are overlooked or insufficiently assessed. There is an inconsistency between the predefined scope of supervisory assessment and the actual risk profile of the insurance sector. In addition, the level of the supervisory assessment is not adjusted in line with the risks and complexities inherent in insurance business. Insurance undertakings with business and financial discrepancies are assessed with the same level of particularity. The uniform particularity of the supervisory assessment across the insurance sector is liable to cause underestimation of the risk exposures of the complicated business and investment portfolios of some insurers, in particular those insurers with broad connections with the rest of the financial system.

At the stage of supervisory measures, classification outcomes, as the result of the supervisory assessments, serve as the basis for the decision as to what intervention shall be imposed. Regardless of the type of the supervisory assessments, each of the ensuing classification level is associated with several specified supervisory measures. An insurer with a risk of or an actual non-compliance would normally incur one or more supervisory measures specific to the classification level that the insurer is assigned. The close linkage between the classification outcome and the supervisory measures has a negative effect on the aptness of the intervention exercised by the CIRC. The classification outcome represents a general judgment by

Chinese supervisors of the conditions of an insurer in a specified supervisory area, in view of the uniform risk areas and particularity involved in the supervisory assessment of all insurance undertakings. The classification outcome itself does not contain detailed information about the risks, deficiencies or non-compliances that an insurer has. Distinct insurers assigned the same classification level are considered to have similar or equivalent degree of risks, deficiencies or non-compliances in a specified supervisory area. Nevertheless, the cause of the problems varies from one insurer to another. Given the reasons above, subjecting insurers to similar or identical supervisory measures on the grounds of a classification level they have in common could hardly bring about the supervisory measures apt to their respective situations.

The lack of specificity in the supervisory assessments and measures can be well mitigated by incorporating a detailed review stage into the CIRC's supervisory review process. It shall be positioned between the two existing stages. The results of the supervisory assessment stage will thus not be used directly as the basis for a decision on supervisory measures. Instead, the assessment results would be calibrated at the detailed review stage by theme-focused analyses across all insurers of the emerging risk areas that are exposed in the prior assessment stage and undertaking-focused analyses of those insurers with a complicated risk profile or severe deficiencies. The emerging risk areas mentioned herein are outside the scope of the predefined risk areas as are prescribed in the regulations. The undertaking-focused analyses serve to deliver an examination of the conditions of those insurers in specified or overall aspects according to the needs of the supervision.

As far as the formation of supervisory measures is concerned, the results of the detailed review activities are supposed to be used to adapt the supervisory measures associated with a classification level to the firm-specific factors of a particular insurer. The insurers with the same classification level would thus not be subjected to uniform supervisory measures designated for the classification level. The calibration made on the basis of the focused analyses with a better level of particularity could counterbalance the undue effects of the classification-based intervention to a large extent.

E. Intervention Intensity

A larger proportion of the supervisory measures are of restrictive or prohibitive nature. The CIRC is inclined to impose such supervisory measurers once a non-compliance with prudential requirements is reported or identified. An insurer failing to comply with the rules on solvency, governance and other prudential issues would usually encounter the mandate to restore compliance alongside restrictive supervisory measures. In fact, the restrictions would cause great pressure on an insurer which already faces difficulties in certain aspects, impeding its restoration to compliance to some extent. The insurer, in order for the revocation of the supervisory measures and the improvement in classification level, has to take such actions as to rectify its non-compliance within the shortest possible period. However, the actions serving the purpose tend to be short-sighted, because they might give rise to a recurrence of the previous non-compliance and the build-up of risks in other supervisory areas.

It is advisable to adopt a dual approach to the supervisory intervention by the CIRC. In case there is no deterioration in conditions after the initial non-compliance, the supervisory authority should refrain from imposing supervisory measures. The insurer concerned should instead be granted a time frame to rectify its non-compliance on the basis of a self-formulated plan. Where a deterioration in conditions occurs after the initial non-compliance or no progress is achieved after the lapse of two-thirds of the specified time frame, the supervisory authority is then expected to intervene in the situation by imposing additional supervisory measures. The supervisory response in a non-deterioration scenario does not mean the control over a non-compliant entity is absent, since the rectification process would be placed under the control by the supervisory authority through the approval of the rectification plan and the monitoring of the rectification progress. The differentiation in intervention between the two scenarios provides leeway for insurers to re-establish compliance as well as reserves the possibilities for supervisors to promptly react to the changing conditions of the non-compliant insurers. The balance between the legitimate needs of the supervisory authority and the supervised entities is conducive to the formation of supervisory intervention with due intensity.

F. Supervisory Transparency

The dissertation reviews the manner in which the CIRC functions and finds the weaknesses in its supervisory transparency. The weaknesses, characterized by the insufficiency of informational availability, particularity or orderliness, are found to exist in rule-making, internal workings, supervisory activities and statistical disclosures.

In regard to rule-making, the flaws in transparency arise from the unsystematic way of making supervisory requirements and the absence of rationales for important supervisory requirements. The unsystematic rule-making by way of issuing normative documents results in the requirements on a particular supervisory issue being separately stipulated in different normative documents. The disorder could be mitigated by a consolidation of interrelated normative documents into an implementing regulation corresponding to a specific upper-level legal act. As for the lack of rationales for important supervisory requirements, it has negative effects on the legitimacy and acceptability of the rules. Without the reasons given by rule-makers, stakeholders might interpret the motive and purpose of a supervisory requirement in a way that deviates from genuine supervisory considerations. The rationales for rules are expected to be made public before taking effect in the course of a public consultation during which explanatory and analytical documents accompanying draft rules could reveal the factors underlying specific requirements. The clarity of the rationale for rules and the transparency of public consultations are intrinsically interrelated and conducive to each other. The level of transparency of the consultation by the CIRC is nevertheless unable to serve such a purpose since the draft of rules is the only document published when comments are solicited from stakeholders and the wider public. It is advisable that the CIRC make public the comments received, the summary and resolution of the comments as well as the analysis of the necessity, practicality and impacts of the draft rules, in order to make explicit the reasons for the adoption, rejection or revision of policy options.

The internal workings of the CIRC are found to be secretive to some degree since the way in which the supervisory authority is governed remains largely undisclosed. The organizational information about the authority shall be made complete to include the objectives, composition and tasks of all the internal entities, in particular decision-making bodies, working groups and joint bodies. The rules of procedure for the decision-making bodies should be made public to allow the interested parties to understand the decision mechanisms at the highest level of the authority.

Besides the internal workings, the supervisory activities conducted by the CIRC also have marked flaws in transparency. The completed supervisory activities are publicized in a partial and disorganized manner. The information about the ongoing and future supervisory activities is basically inaccessible. A practical approach is proposed that a specific unit shall be established in the existing section 'working briefing' on the CIRC's electronic platform to assemble and thematically categorize the information about all types of supervisory activities and projects. The information should be publicly disseminated with such a level of particularity as to make available the time frame, actions, tools, products and outcomes involved in a supervisory activity. Certainly, products and outcomes are not immediately available at the time of the dissemination of the information about ongoing and future supervisory activities.

In terms of statistical disclosure, the weakness of supervisory transparency resides in the lack of granular data. Except for the disclosures about insurance undertakings' business conditions, the statistical facts are essentially published by the CIRC in the form of macro statistical data which shows the state of the supervised entities and the supervisory authority merely at a gross level. Particularly, the aggregate statistical data on the aspects of insurer solvency and supervisory work lacks granularity. On the aspect of insurance groups, the situation is even worse – the statistical data is unavailable. Broadly speaking, the insufficiency of statistical transparency should be resolved by breaking down the macro statistical data into multiple micro-level items. With an increased level of detail in the disclosed data, the interested parties will be enabled to have a broader perspective of the industry-wide conditions in a specific supervisory area. The statistical disclosure of solvency conditions should be aligned with the supervisory reporting by solo undertakings to the authority in regard to data coverage on a best efforts basis. The use of median and quartiles to disclose capital adequacy ratios is put forward for the sake of accuracy and granularity. As for the supervisory activities that the CIRC conducts, the respective aggregates of the supervisory assessments, approvals and measures should be broken down according to type or circumstance. Statistical facts should be provided to summarize the essential findings of the integrated and theme-focused evaluations. When it comes to the statistical disclosure of Chinese insurance groups, it is absolutely necessary for the CIRC to make public the aggregate group-level data, which should at least contain the figures for group business structure and group solvency conditions.

Bibliography

—— 'China Re Releasing 2016 Business Results: Stable Business Condition and Market Position' (*Xinhuanet,* 31 March 2017) <www.xinhuanet.com/money/2017-03/31/c_1120734513.htm> accessed 26 February 2018

—— 'Definition of Controlling Stake / Interest' (*the Financial Times Lexicon*) <lexicon.ft.com/Term?term=controlling-stake%2Finterest> accessed 9 March 2018

—— 'Scheme on Institutional Reform of the State Council (Release Authorized by the 2018 Annual Sessions of the NPCC and the CPPCC)' *Xinhua News Agency* (Beijing, 17 March 2018)

—— 'Shanghai Higher Court Issues 2013 White Paper: Insurance Disputes Tops' *Laodong Daily* (Shanghai, 4 April 2014)

—— 'The Dangers of Debt: Shadows Lengthen' *The Economist* (Hong Kong, 13 Apr 2013)

—— 'The Special Issue on Liability Insurance' *China Insurance News* (Beijing, 28 Oct 2014)

—— 'The Stock Market Shall Stop always Counting on Insurance Institutional Investors' *Beijing Times* (Beijing, 11 July 2014).

—— 'Yunnan Province to Launch Pilot Project of Small Loan Guaranty Insurance in 2014' (*Yunnan Express*, 15 January 2014)

——'Definition of Subsidiary Company' (*the Financial Times Lexicon*) <lexicon.ft.com/Term?term=subsidiary-company> accessed 9 March 2018

116319/3013637/3013645/index.html> accessed 16 February 2018

ABI, 'Business interruption insurance' (13 Nov 2014) <www.abi.org.uk/Insurance-and-savings/Products/Business-insurance/Business-interruption-insurance> accessed 22 June 2015

Alemanno A, 'Unpacking the Principle of Openness in EU Law Transparency, Participation and Democracy' (2014) 39(1) European Law Review 72

Alexandre Lamfalussy, 'The Release of the Committee's Final Report on the Regulation of the European Securities Markets' (opening comments to the Press, 15 February 2001)

Amri PD and Kocher BM, 'The Political Economy of Financial Sector Supervision and Banking Crises: A Cross-Country Analysis' (2012) 18 (1) European Law Journal 24

Anbang Life and Health, *2016 Annual Report* (Disclosure Document, 2017)

Anbang Property and Casualty, *2016 Annual Report* (Disclosure Document, 2017)

Anderson D et al., *Statistics for Business and Economics* (2nd edn, Cengage Learning EMEA 2010)

Arena M, 'Does Insurance Market Activity Promote Economic Growth? A Cross-country Study for Industrialized and Developing Countries' (2008) 75 (4) the Journal of Risk and Insurance 921

Armstrong E, 'Integrity, Transparency and Accountability in Public Administration: Recent Trends, Regional and International Developments and Emerging Issues' (2005) Publication of the Department of Economic and Social Affairs at the United Nations, August 2005

Australian Prudential Regulation Authority, Memorandum of Understanding between the China Insurance Regulatory Commission of the P.R.C. and the Australian Prudential Regulation Authority of the Commonwealth of Australia Regarding Insurance Regulatory Cooperation (Memorandum, 2015) <www.apra.gov.au/AboutAPRA/Documents/MoU-CIRC-of-China.pdf> accessed 10 August 2017.

Baranoff E, 'An Analysis of the AIG Case: Understanding Systemic Risk and Its Relation to Insurance' (2012) 31 Journal of Insurance Regulation 243

Bauhr M and Grimes M, 'What is Government Transparency: New Measures and Relevance for Quality of Government' (2012) The Quality of Government Institute at the University of Gothenburg Working Paper Series 2012

Blinder AS, *The Quiet Revolution: Central Banking Goes Modern* (Yale University Press 2004)

Board of Supervisors of EIOPA, *Decision of the Board of Supervisors concerning the Rules of procedure of the Mediation Panel pursuant to Article 41 of Regulation (EU) No 1094/2010 of the European Parliament and of the Council of 24 November 2010 establishing a European Supervisory Authority (European Insurance and Occupational Pensions Authority)* (Internal Procedure, EIOPA-BoS-12-032, 2012)

—— *Rules of Procedure* (Internal Procedure, EIOPA-BoS-11/002-Rev 2, 2015)

BoE, *The Bank of England's approach to resolution* (Publication, October 2014)

Borio C, 'Towards a macroprudential framework for financial supervision and regulation?' (2003) BIS working papers no 128

—— and Drehmann M, 'Towards an operational framework for financial stability: "fuzzy" measurement and its consequences' (2009) BIS Working Paper No. 284

Brewer E III and Jackson WE III, 'Inter-industry Contagion and the Competitive Effects of Financial Distress Announcements: Evidence from Commercial Banks and Life Insurance Companies' (2002) Federal Reserve Bank of Chicago Working Paper 2002-23.

Canadian Securities Administrators, 'Eight Canadian Securities Regulators Sign Regulatory Cooperation Agreement with China's Insurance Regulator' (Montréal, 10 November 2010) <www.securities-administrators.ca/aboutcsa.aspx?id=930> accessed 10 August 2017.

Carpenter D, 'Detecting and Measuring Capture' in Daniel Carpenter and David A Moss (eds), *Preventing Regulatory Capture: Special Interest Influence and How to Limit It* (Cambridge University Press 2013)

Central Committee of the Communist Party of China and the State Council, *The Implementing Framework for Establishing a Rule-based administration (from 2015 to 2020)* (White Paper, 2015)

Chen W, 'keynote speech' (meeting on comprehensively tackling misleading insurance sales, Beijing, 16 February 2012) <www.circ.gov.cn/web/site0/tab5212/info 194486.htm> accessed 26 September 2014.

China Central Depository & Clearing Co. Ltd., *2016 Statistical and Analytical Report on Bond Market* (Annual Publication, January 2017)

China Life Insurance Group, *2016 Annual Report* (Disclosure Document, 2017)

China Pacific Insurance Group, *2016 Annual Report* (Disclosure Document, 2017)

China Reinsurance Group, *Annual Report 2016* (Publication, 2017)

China Securities Depository and Clearing Corporation, *Statistical Yearbook* (July 2017)

Christian D and Lüdenbach N, *IFRS Essentials* (1st edn, Wiley 2013)

CIRC, '2016 Fact Sheet for the Primary Premium Income of Life and Health Insurance Companies' (22 February 2017) <www.circ.gov.cn/web/site0/tab5203/info 4060025.htm> accessed 16 February 2018

—— '2016 Fact Sheet for the Primary Premium Income of Property and Casualty Insurance Companies' (22 February 2017) <www.circ.gov.cn/web/site0/ tab5202 /info4060014.htm> accessed 16 February 2018

——'C-ROSS Formally Implemented: Positive Effects' (25 October 2016) <www.cir c.gov.cn/web/site0/tab6527/info4047909.htm> accessed 9 May 2017

—— 'Main Responsibilities' <www.circ.gov.cn/web/site0/tab5200/> accessed 11 September 2014.

——'Overview of Local Agencies' <www.circ.gov.cn/web/site0/tab5196/> accessed 23 April 2014

——'Policy Briefings' <www.circ.gov.cn/web/site0/tab5227/> accessed 4 May 2016.

——'Seeking Information on Insurance Institutions' <www.circ.gov.cn/tabid/5254/ Default.aspx> accessed 15 March 2017

—— 'Statistical Data' (monthly update) <www.circ.gov.cn/web/site0/tab5179/> accessed 15 March 2017.

—— 'The Catalogue of the Issues Subject to CIRC's Administrative Approval' (11 December 2014) <www.circ.gov.cn/web/ site0/ tab5177/> accessed 4 May 2016.

—— *Annual Report of the Activities about Administrative Information Publication 2015* (Report, March 2016)

—— *Annual Report of the Chinese Insurance Market 2015* (1st edn, China Finance Publishing House 2015)

—— *China Risk Oriented Solvency System Conceptual Framework* (Policy Paper, 5 March 2014)

—— *Notification of the General Framework of China's Second-generation Solvency Regulation and Supervision Regime* (Normative Document, No 42, 2013)

—— *Notification on the Consultation on the Draft Administrative Rules on Nuclear Catastrophe Reserves* (Notification No 506, 2015)

—— *Notification on the Draft Administrative Rules on the Capital Increase of Insurance Companies* (Notification No 422, 2014)

—— *Planning Outline for the development of China's insurance sector from 2011 to 2015* (CIRC Announcement No 47, 2011)

—— *Statistics on Insurance Consumer Complaints in the First Half of 2014* (Normative Document of CIRC Consumer Protection division, No 117, 2014)

—— *the Bulletin on Insurance Complaints in Q1 2016* (Notification, 2016) <www.circ.gov.cn/web/site0/tab5218/info4027855.htm> accessed 10 May 2016

—— *The Consolidated Budget of CIRC (2016)* (Financial Statement, April 2016)

—— *The Consolidated Outturn Accounts (2014)* (Financial Statement, July 2015).

—— *The General Framework of China's Second-generation Solvency Supervisory System* (Normative Document, No 42, 2013)

—— *The Notification on the Release of the Supervisory Rules on the Solvency Position of Insurance Undertakings (1 -17)* (Normative Document, No 22, 2015)

—— *the Outline of the Scheme for the Development of China's Insurance Sector from 2016-2020* (Normative Document No 74, 2016)

Cœuré B, 'Opening Remarks: Setting Standards for Granular Data' (3rd the OFR-ECB-BoE Workshop on Granular Data, Frankfurt am Main, 28 March 2017) <www.ecb.europa.eu/press/key/date/2017/html/sp170328.en.html> accessed 4 May 2017

Commission of the European Communities, *Review of the Lamfalussy Process Strengthening Supervisory Convergence* (Communication, COM(2007) 727 final, 2007)

Consumer Protection Bureau of the CIRC, *the Bulletin on the Evaluation Outcome of the Complaint-handling practice of Insurance Undertakings 2015* (Notification No 23, 2016)

Daley D, Haider-Markel DP and Whitford AB, 'Checks, Balances, and the Cost of Regulation : Evidence from the American States' (2007) 60 (4) Political Research Quarterly 696

Davies K, *Understanding European Union Law* (5th edn, Routledge 2013).

Davies PJ, 'China Approves HSBC's Ping An Stake Sale' *Financial Times* (Hong Kong, 1 February 2013)

Debbage S and Dickinson S, 'The rationale for the prudential regulation and supervision of insurers' (2013) Bank of England Quaterly Bulletin 2013 Q3, 218

Deighton-Smith R, 'Regulatory transparency in OECD countries: Overview, trends and challenges' (2004) 63(1) Australian Journal of Public Administration 66,

Dembeck J, 'Insurance Regulation in a Nut Shell' in *PLI's Course Handbook: Understanding Insurance Law* (Practising Law Institute, 2008) 5

Department for Accounting and Solvency Supervision of the CIRC, *the Bulletin on Solvency Supervision in the First Half of 2015* (Notification No 196, 2015) <www.circ.gov.cn/web/site0/tab5218/info3976555.htm> accessed 10 May 2016

Ding D, 'CIRC: 26,000 Insurance Sales Persons Involved in Misleading Selling in First Half Year' *China News Sevice* (Beijing, 27 July 2012)

Dreher M, Treatises on Solvency II (Springer 2015)

ECB, *Aggregated balance sheet of euro area credit institutions* (report, January 2018)

—— *Aggregated balance sheet of euro area insurance corporations* (report, December 2017)

EIOPA, 'EIOPA and the China Insurance Regulatory Commission Sign a Memorandum of Understanding' (Franfurt am Main, 10 August 2017) <eiopa.europa.eu/Pages/News/EIOPA-and-the-China-Insurance-Regulatory-Commission-sign-a-Memorandum-of-Understanding.aspx> accessed 10 August 2017

—— 'EIOPA Organizational Chart' (*Document,* September 2016) <eiopa.europa.eu/Publications/Administrative/2016%2009%20Organigram%20External%20USE.pdf> accessed 2 November 2016

—— 'Legal Framework' (*Website Section*, 2016) <europa.eu/about-eiopa/legal-framework> accessed 2 November 2016

—— *Annual Report 2015* (Publication, 2016) Annex III

—— *Consultation Paper on the Advice to the European Commission in response to the Call for Advice on recovery plan, finance scheme and supervisory powers in deteriorating financial conditions* (Consultation Paper, EIOPA-CP-14/062, 2014)

—— *Consultation Paper on the draft proposal for Guidelines on the extension of the recovery period in exceptional adverse situations* (Consultation Paper, EIOPA-CP-14/046, 2014)

—— *Cover Note for the Consultation on Implementing Technical Standards for Solvency II* (CP-14/011, 2014)

—— *EIOPA Multi-Annual Work Programme 2015-2017* (EIOPA-BoS-14/109, 2014)

—— *EU/EEA (Re)Insurance Statistics* (Database, EIOPA-FSI-16/025, 2016).

—— *Final Report on Public Consultation No. 14/016 on Guidelines on supervisory review process* (EIOPA-BoS-14/179, 2014)

—— *Financial Stability Report* (Publication, EIOPA-FSI-16-016, 2016)

—— *Single Programming Document 2017-2019 (AWP 2017)* (EIOPA-BoS-16/23, 2016)

European Commission, *Impact Assessment Board Report for 2013* (Government Report, 2013)

—— *Part III: Annexes to Impact Assessment Guidelines* (explanatory policy paper, 2009)

EY, *2016-2017 White Paper on Risk Management in Insurance Sector* (Publication, July 2017)

Fang Y, 'Ningbo Government to Purchase Catastrophe insurance Coverage at the Cost of 38 Million for Residents: Starting from 11th (*People's Daily Online*, 10 November 2014) <nb.people.com.cn/n/2014/1110/c365604-22864147.html> accessed 12 January 2015

Federal Insurance Office of U.S. Department of the Treasury, *Annual Report on the Insurance* Industry (report, September 2017)

Finance and Accounting Department of the CIRC, 'The Notification on the Transitional Requirements For the Implementation of C-ROSS' (CIRC Website, 13 February 2015) <www.circ.gov.cn/web/site0/tab5216/info3951934.htm> accessed 3 May 2017

Financial stability Analysis Group of the PBC, *China Financial Stability Report* (China Financial Publishing House 2017)

FSB, *2014 Update of List of Global Systemically Important Insurers (G-SIIs)* (Publication, 6 November 2014) <www.financialstabilityboard.org/wp-content/uploads/r_141106a.pdf> accessed 7 January 2015.

—— *Key Attributes of Effective Resolution Regimes for Financial Institutions* (Policy Document, 15 October 2014)

Gao G, 'Yidai Enters into O2O Market: Ping An Accelerating Strategic Deployment' *China Securities Journal* (2 December 2014)

Gao L, 'Analysis of China's Insurance Market Concentration' (2013) 1 China's Journal of Regional Financial Research 52

GDV, *Statistical Yearbook of German Insurance 2013* (Annual Publication, 2013)

Government Information Bureau of Macau, 'Signing of Co-operation Agreement between the Monetary Authority of Macau, China Insurance Regulatory Commission and the Office of the Commissioner of Insurance' (Macau, 18 December 2014)

Grimmelikhuijsen S et al., 'The Effect of Transparency on Trust in Government: A Cross-National Comparative Experiment' (2013) 73(4) Public Administration Review 575

Haas F, 'Current State of Play' in Decressin J, Faruqee H and Fonteyne W (eds), *Integrating Europe's Financial Markets* (International Monetary Fund, 2007) 58.

Haiss P and Sümegi K, 'The Relationship between Insurance and Economic Growth in Europe: A Theoretical and Empirical Analysis' (2008) 35 Empirica 405

Harrison TM and Sayogo DS, 'Transparency, participation, and accountability practices in open government: A comparative study' (2014) 31(4) Government Information Quarterly 513

Henisz WJ and Zelner BA, 'Interest Groups, Veto Points, and Electricity Infrastructure Deployment' (2006) 60 (1) International Organization 263

High-Level Group on Financial Supervision in the EU Chaired by Jacques de Larosière, *Report* (Brussels, 25 February 2009)

HM Government, *IA toolkit: How to Do An Impact Assessment* (Guidance Document, 2011)

HM Treasury, *The UK insurance growth action plan* (Policy Paper, 2013)

Hong Kong Insurance Authority, 'Equivalence Assessment Framework Agreement on Solvency Regulatory Regime signed by Office of the Commissioner of Insurance and China Insurance Regulatory Commission' (Hong Kong, 16 May 2017) <www.ia.org.hk/en/supervision/int_dom_cooperation/files/pr_20170516.pdf> accessed 14 August 2017.

Huang J, 'CIRC Poised to Permit Unit-linked Insurance Plans to Invest in NSDB Assets' *National Business Daily* (Beijing, 10 Oct 2014) 16

Hunter JR, 'Why is Regulation of Insurance Necessary' (Statement before The Task Force on Long-term Solutions for Florida's Hurricane Insurance Market, 14 November 2005)

IAIS, *Insurance and Financial Stability* (Paper, 11/2011)

—— Reinsurance and Financial Stability (Report, July 2012)

—— *Systemic Risk and The insurance Sector* (Note, 25 October 2009).

Impavido G and Tower I, 'How the Financial Crisis Affects Pensions and Insurance and Why the Impacts Matter' (2009) IMF Working Paper WP/09/151

Insurance Association of China, 'Annual Information Disclosure of Insurance Companies' <www.iachina.cn/hysj/ndxxplnew/rsxgsnew/> accessed 18 June 2015

Insurance Europe, *Solvency II: Understanding the Process* (Paper, February 2007)

Kaufmann C and Weber RH, 'The Role of Transparency in Financial Regulation' (2010) 13(3) Journal of International Economic Law 779

Khagram S et al., 'Overview and Synthesis: The Political Economy of Fiscal Transparency, Participation, and Accountability around the World' in Khagram S, Fung A and Renzio P (eds), *Open Budgets: The Political Economy of Transparency, Participation, and Accountability* (Brookings Institution Press 2013) 39

Kimball SL, 'The Purpose of Insurance Regulation: A Preliminary Inquiry in the Theory of Insurance Law' (1961) 45 Minnesota Law Review 471

Knot K, 'Granular Data and Macroprudential Policy: Examples and Challenges' (8th ECB Statistics Conference, Frankfurt am Main, 6 July 2016) <www.ecb.europa.eu/pub/conferences/shared/pdf/160705_8th_stats_conference/Knot.pdf?8c24351a2fc6add3c049e74e40f6f4ce> accessed 4 May 2017

KPMG, *2017 Survey Report on China's Banking Sector* (Publication, July 2017)

Kwon WJ, 'Economic Rationale for Insurance Regulation' in *Insurance Regulation Reflections for a Post-Crisis World* (Report, the Geneva Association, January 2012).

Leow J, 'Ping An to Test China Markets For Resilience' *The Wall Street Journal* (Beijing, 18 February 2008)

Levine ME and Forrence JL, 'Regulatory Capture, Public Interest, and the Public Agenda: Toward a Synthesis' (1990) 6 Journal of Law, Economics, & Organization 167

Li Y, 'Conjectures about the "Promotion" of the Big Four Insurance Undertakings' (2012) 14 China Economic Weekly 56.

Li Z, 'CIRC to Send Inspection Panel to Life Insurance Companies – Percentage of Stock Investment with Obligation of Disclosure by Insurance Companies Lowering to 9%' *21st Century Business Herald* (Beijing, 7 December 2016)

Liedorp F et al., 'Transparency of Banking Supervisors' (2013) 61(2) IMF Economic Review 310

Liedtke PM, 'What's Insurance to a Modern Economy?' (2007) 32 the Geneva Papers 211

Lu X, 'Detailed Rules regarding Investments of Insurers on Private Companies to Come Out This Month' *Shanghai Securities News* (Shanghai, 13 October 2009)

Ma YL and Pope N, 'Foreign Share, Insurance Density, and Penetration: An Analysis of the International Life Insurance Market' (2008) 11(2) Risk Management & Insurance Review 327

Management Board of EIOPA, *Rules of Procedure* (Internal Procedure, EIOPA-MB-11/002, 2011)

Meijer A, 'Understanding the Complex Dynamics of Transparency' (2013) 73(3) Public Administration Review 429

Mendes J, *Participation in EU Rule-Making: a Rights-Based Approach* (first published 2011, Oxford University Press 2011)

Mesquita BB and Root HL (eds), *Governing for Prosperity* (Yale University Press 2000).

Monetary Policy Analysis Group of the PBC, 2017 Financial Performance of Regions in China (Report, 2017) <www.pbc.gov.cn/zhengcehuobisi/125207/125227/125960/126049/3356630/3356459/index.html> accessed 4 May 2018.

Moss DA and Carpenter D, 'Conclusion: A Focus on Evidence and Prevention' in Carpenter D and Moss DA (eds), *Preventing Regulatory Capture: Special Interest Influence and How to Limit It* (Cambridge University Press 2013)

NAIC, 'NAIC Signs MoU Extension with China – Agreement Enhances Regulatory Cooperation' (Washington D.C., 28 March 2013) <www.naic.org/Releases/2013_docs/naic_signs_mou_extension_with_china.htm> accessed 10 August 2017

National Bureau of Statistics of China, 'Value Added (% of GDP) per Sector' (2017) <data.stats.gov.cn/easyquery.htm?cn=C01&zb=A0201&sj=2016> accessed 22 February 2018.

National Development and Reform Commission of China, 'Main Functions of the NDRC' <en.ndrc.gov.cn/mfndrc/> accessed 6 January 2015.

New China Life, *2016 Annual Report* (Disclosure Document, 2017) 22 <www.newchinalife.com/resource/11313/11329/11346/1695218/2406976/2407236/2407884/2412103/15051072101971364072785.pdf> accessed 6 October 2017

OECD, *Insurance Statistics 2013* (Annual Publication, 2014) Part I. <dx.doi.org/10.1787/ins_stats-2013-en> accessed 6 November 2014.

—— *Introductory Handbook for Undertaking Regulatory Impact Analysis (RIA)* (version 1.0, 2008)

Osiński J, Seal K, and Hoogduin L, 'Macroprudential and Microprudential Policies: Toward Cohabitation' (2013) IMF Staff Discussion Note 13/05

Ouyang X and Ye J, 'Tax-Deferred Endowment Insurance Looms: Pilot Scheme Launched in Shanghai This Year' *The Economic Observer* (Beijing, 4 May 2012)

Pan Y, 'Plan for Shenzhen Insurance Exchange filed to State Council possibly in future' *Securities Times of China* (Beijing, 3 February 2012) 5

PBC, '2016 Financial Market Statistics' <www.pbc.gov.cn/diaochatongjisi/116219/> accessed 16 February 2018

PICC Group, *2016 Annual Report* (Disclosure Document, 2017)

Ping An Insurance Group, *2016 Annual Report* (Disclosure Document, 2017)

Ping An Life, 'The Study of Insurer Overseas Investment' (China Insurance Asset Management Symposium, Beijing, May 2016)

—— *2016 Annual Report for Public Disclosure* (Disclosure Document, 2017) 101 <resources.pingan.com/app_upload/file/life/2016-nianduxinxipilubaogao.pdf> accessed 6 October 2017

PRA of the Bank of England, *The Prudential Regulation Authority's Approach to Insurance Supervision* (Introductory Report, June 2014)

Rejda GE and McNamara MJ, *Principles of Risk Management and Insurance* (global edn, 12th edn, Pearson 2014)

Rosenbluth G, 'Measures of Concentration' in Universities-National Bureau (ed), *Business Concentration and Price Policy* (Princeton University Press 1955).

Schaik L et al., *Policy Coherence for Development in the EU Council: Strategies for the Way Forward* (The Centre for European Policy Studies 2006)

Schaub A, 'The Lamfalussy Process Four Years on' (2005) 13 (2) Journal of Financial Regulation and Compliance 110

Secretariat of the CIRC, *Notification about the Consultation on the Supervisory Rules on Solvency Position of Insurance Undertakings (Public Consultation Version)* (Notification No 374, 2017)

Stigler GJ, 'The Theory of Economic Regulation' (1971) 2(1) The Bell Journal of Economics and Management Science 3

Stock J and Watson M, *Introduction to Econometrics* (updated 3rd edn (global edn), Pearson 2015)

Su P, 'Funds of Insurance Companies Shall be Free from Government Interventions' *China Business Journal* (19 July 2014)

Sun X, 'Warning Signal for China United Appears Again' *Investment & Finance* (22 June 2011)

Sun Y, 'New China Life Plunged into A Solvency Black Hole: Raising 15 Billion Debt only 50 Days after A Shrunk IPO' *The Time Weekly (China)* (9 February 2012)

Sun Y, 'Scheme to Establish Shanghai Insurance Exchange Reported to State Council' *Securities Times of China* (Beijing, 17 February 2011) 1

Tang Y, 'The Origin and Evolvement of NSDB Assets' *Securities Times* (Shenzhen, 22 Nov 2013) A5

The Center for Insurance Policy and Research at NAIC, *Market Conduct regulation* (Brief Abstract of Key Issue, 8 May2014) <www.naic.org/cipr_topics/topic_market_conduct_Regulation.htm> accessed 2 October 2014

—— *State Insurance Regulation* (Publication, 2014)

The Committee of Wise Men chaired by Alexandre Lamfalussy, *Final Report on the Regulation of the European Securities Markets* (European Commission Report, Final, 2001)

The State Council, *Opinions on Boosting the Development of Modern Insurance Service Industry* (Council Announcement No 29, 2014)

—— *Reply on the Approval of the Establishment of Regular Ministerial Joint Meeting Mechanism for Financial Supervision Coordination* (Council Notification No 91, 2013)

The State-owned Assets Supervision and Administration Commission of the State Council, 'Main Responsibilities' (official website, 3 November 2008) <www.sasac.gov.cn/n2506699/n7738060/n7738079/7738171.html> accessed 15 September 2014

The Technical Study led by Prof. Davis K, *Study of Financial System Guarantees* (Commissioned Report, 2004)

Tridimas T, 'EU Financial Regulation: Federalization, Crisis Management, and Law Reform' in Craig P and Búrca G (eds), The Evolution of EU Law (2nd edn, Oxford University Press 2011) 785

Tsebelis G, *Veto Players: How Political Institutions Work* (Princeton University Press 2002)

U.S. Federal Reserve, *Assets and Liabilities of Commercial Banks in the United States (Weekly)* (Statistical Release, H.8, June 2017)

UK Department for Communities and Local Government, *Multi-criteria analysis: a manual* (Guidance Document, 2009)

Vaughan TM, 'Financial Stability and Insurance Supervision: The Future of Prudential Supervision' (2004) 29 (2) The Geneva Papers on Risk and Insurance 258

Viñals J et al., 'The Making of Good Supervision: Learning to Say "No"' (2010) IMF Staff Position Note SPN/10/08

Wall LD and Eisenbeis RA, 'Financial Regulatory Structure and the Resolution of Conflicting Goals' (2000) 17 (1) Journal of Financial Services Research 223

Wandt M, 'Transparency as a General Principle of Insurance Law' (joint seminar by the Turkish and German chapters of AIDA on Transparency in Insurance Law, Istanbul, May 2012) 9 <www.aida.org.uk/pdf/Transparency%20book.pdf> accessed 26 July 2018.

— — and Bork K, 'Transparency in German Insurance Supervisory Law' in Noussia K and Marano P (eds), Volume I "Transparency in insurance law and regulation: the insurance undertakings, intermediaries and the supervisory authorities" (forthcoming).

— — and Sehrbrock D, 'Legal Aspects of the Solvency II Framework Directive' in Schoubroeck CV et al. (eds), Over Grenzen: Liber Amicorum Herman Cousy (Intersentia 2011), 923.

Wang Y, 'The Clarifications on Scheme on Institutional Reform of the State Council' (the First Session of the 13th NPCC, Beijing, 13 March 2018) <www.gov.cn/guowuyuan/2018-03/14/content_5273856.htm> accessed 9 April 2018

Ward D and Zurbruegg R, 'Does Insurance Promote Economic Growth? Evidence from OECD Countries' (2000) 67(4) The Journal of Risk and Insurance 491

World Bank, *Industry, value added (% of GDP)* (Data, World Development Indicators, 2014)

Wuhong L, 'Step up Efforts to Meet Regulatory Requirements on Loans to Small Business' (2014) 31 Caixin Century Weekly.

Xu W, 'Multiple Insurers Enter Personal Loan Guaranty Insurance Market' *Ningbo Evening News* (Ningbo, 26 February 2013)

Xu Y, 'Analysis on the Establishment of the Insurance Supervisory Objectives in China' (2009) 8 Journal of Shanghai Insurance 10

Xu Y, 'Junbo Xiang: The Reimbursements for Catastrophe Losses Less Than 1% of the Actual Loss Amounts' (*Xinhuanet*, 11 March 2014) <news.xinhuanet.com/politics/2014-03/11/c_119708822.htm> accessed 12 January 2015

Xu Z, 'Analysis of the Reform of Financial Regulation Based on the Scheme on Institutional Reform of the State Council' (*Caixin*, 13 March 2018) <topics.caixin.com/2018-03-13/101220637.html?sourceEntityId=101220731> accessed 9 April 2018

Xu Z, 'The Evolvements of Market Concentration in Insurance Sector and Resolution' (2006) 3 Journal of China Youth University of Political Studies 78

Yang Y, 'Shenzhen Begins to Implement Catastrophe Insurance Program' *Economic Daily* (Shenzhen, 10 July 2014)

Ye B (ed), *Administrative Law and Administrative Litigation Law* (3rd edn, China Renmin University Press 2011)

Yuan C, *A Study on the Insurance Supervisory Regime of China* (1st edn, Nanjing University Press 2011)

Yue D, 'Zhengjiang to Expand Provision of Small Loan Guaranty Insurance: Facilitating Credit Borrowing for Small Business' (*Xinhuanet*, 14 September 2014) <news.xinhuanet.com/fortune/2014-09/14/c_1112472523.htm> accessed 12 January 2015

Yue P, 'PBC, CIRC and Other Authorities Issue Policies to Support Tech Companies with Provision of Loan Guaranty Insurance' *Beijing Business Today* (Beijing, 16 January 2014).

Zhang C, 'Chongqing to Launch Pilot Project of Small Loan Guaranty Insurance: Maximum Three Million' (*Xinhuanet*, 2 June 2012) <news.xinhuanet.com/fortune/2012-06/02/c_112099800.htm> accessed 12 January 2015

Zhang Y, 'Successful Transition of Insurance Sector: Strengthening the Role of Risk Coverage and Achieving Rapid Developments' *International Financial News (China)* (16 October 2017)

Zhao J, Zhao C and Peng Z, 'The Measurement of the Contribution of Financial Industry to Economic Growth with the comparison between China and the U.S.' (2014) 4 Chinese Journal of Financial Regulation Research 77

Zhao X, 'An Analysis of China's Insurance Market in a historical period from the foundation of P.R.C.' (2003) 2 China's Economic History Research Journal 74

Zhao Y, interview with Xu X, deputy director of the department of fiscal and financial affairs of the National Development and Reform Commission, and Xiong Z, director of the department of policy research of the CIRC, *'Fostering the Development of Modern Insurance Sector'* (the website of China's government, Beijing, 28 August 2014) <www.gov.cn/wenzheng/wz_zxft_ft42/node_18486.htm> accessed 15 September 2014

Zhou D, 'How Do Chinese Insurers Invest Worldwide with Vast Amount of Premiums (Part I)?' (*Wallstreetcn*, 16 January 2017) <wallstreetcn.com/node/285216 > accessed 20 March 2017

Zhou F, 'Insurance History after the Foundation of P.R.C.' (2013) China's Journal of Insurance Intermediary

Zhou Y, 'Opening Remarks' (The Forum on the Globalization of China's Insurance Industry: Challenge and Future - How can Chinese Insurers Go Abroad, Beijing, 16 January 2017) <pit.ifeng.com/a/20170117/50589467_0.shtml> accessed 17 March 2017.

Zhu B, 'CIRC Further Relaxes Rules on Insurance Investments: Effective from 1 May' *China Securities Daily* (Beijing, 19 April 2014)

Table of Legislation

1. EU:

Commission Delegated Regulation (EU) 2015/35 of 10 October 2014 supplementing Directive 2009/138/EC of the European Parliament and of the Council on the taking-up and pursuit of the business of Insurance and Reinsurance (Solvency II) [2015] OJ L12/1

Commission Implementing Regulation (EU) 2015/2451 of 2 December 2015 laying down implementing technical standards with regard to the templates and structure of the disclosure of specific information by supervisory authorities in accordance with Directive 2009/138/EC of the European Parliament and of the Council [2015] OJ L347/1224

Consolidated Version of the Treaty on European Union [2012] OJ C 326/13

Consolidated Version of the Treaty on the Functioning of the European Union [2012] OJ C 326/47

Directive 2009/138/EC of the European Parliament and of the Council of 25 November 2009 on the Taking-up and Pursuit of the Business of Insurance and Reinsurance (Solvency II) (Recast) OJ L 335

EIOPA, *Guidelines on Supervisory Review Process* (Guidance, EIOPA-BoS-14/179 EN)

European Commission, *Impact Assessment Guidelines* (SEC (2009) 92, 2009)

Regulation (EU) No 1094/2010 of The European Parliament and of The Council of 24 November 2010 establishing a European Supervisory Authority (European Insurance and Occupational Pensions Authority), amending Decision No 716/2009/EC and repealing Commission Decision 2009/79/EC OJ L331/48

Regulation EU No 1092/2010 of the European Parliament and of the Council of 24 November 2010 on European Union Macro-prudential Oversight of the Financial System and Establishing a European Systemic Risk Board [2010] OJ L 331/1

2. China:

2.1 Legislative Acts by the NPCC

Basic Law of the Hong Kong Special Administrative Region of the People's Republic of China 1990

Basic Law of the Macau Special Administrative Region of the People's Republic of China 1993

Company Act of China 2005

Constitution of China 1982

Contract Act of China 1999

Criminal Act of China 1997

Insurance Act of China 1995
Legislation Act of China 2000
Maritime Act of China 1993

2.2 Administrative Regulations by the State Council

Provisional Regulation on the Supervision and Administration of State-Owned Assets of Businesses 2003
Regulation on Administration of the Establishment and Staffing of the Administrative Agencies of the State Council 1997
Regulation on Record-Keeping of Legal Acts 2001
Regulation on the Publication of Government Information in China 2007

2.3 Department Rules by the CIRC

Administrative Rules on Insurance Undertakings 2009
Administrative Rules on the Insurance Security Fund 2008
Administrative Rules on the Supervisory Responsibilities of CIRC Agencies 2004
Pilot Rules on Insurance Institutions Investing and Establishing Fund Management Company 2013
Provisional Rules on the Utilization and Management of Insurance Funds 2010
Rules on the Administrative Appeal at CIRC 2010
Rules on the Publication of Administrative Information at CIRC 2008
Rules on the Rule-making Procedures of CIRC Department Rules 2006
Rules on the Supervisory Responsibilities of the Local Agencies Affiliated to the CIRC 2016
Supervisory Rules on the Solvency Position of Insurance Undertakings 2008

2.4 Normative Documents by the CIRC

CIRC, *Administrative Rules on the Formulation of CIRC Normative Documents* (Normative Document, No 101, 2013)
—— and CBRC, *Supervisory Guideline on Commercial Banks Conducting Insurance Agent Services* (Normative Document, No 10, 2011)
——and PBC, *Issues Relating to Insurance Undertakings' Issuance of Capital-Supplementing Bonds* (Normative Document, No 3, 2015)
——*Administrative Rules on the Pilot Scheme: Indirect Investments of Insurers in Infrastructure Projects* (Normative Document, 14 Mar 2006)
——*Evaluation Methods for the Overhaul of the Misleading Sales in the Personal Insurance Sector* (Normative Document on Trial, No 105, 2012)
——*Notification of Certain Issues relating to the Investments of Insurance Undertakings in Equity and Real Estates* (Normative Document, No 59, 2012)
——*Notification of the Adjustments to the Provisional Rules on Insurance Asset Management Companies* (Normative Document, No 19, 2011)

——*Notification on Enhancement of the Supervision on Ratios of Insurance Funds Utilization* (Normative Document, No 13, 2014)

——*Notification on Insurer Investments on Financial Products Concerned* (Normative Document, No 91, 2012)

——*Notification on Issues Pertinent to Investment Risk Owner of Insurance Institutions* (Normative Document, No 28, 2013)

——*Notification on Issues Pertinent to the Improvement of Investment Management Capability of Insurance Institutions* (Normative Document, No 10, 2013)

——*Notification on the Issues about the Implementation of the C-ROSS* (Normative Document, 25 January 2016)

——*Provisional Administrative Rules on Infrastructure debt investment schemes* (Normative Document, No 92, 2012)

——*Provisional Administrative Rules on Insurance Holding Company* (Normative Document No 29, 2010) § 4

——*Provisional Rules on Insurance Assets Allocation* (Normative Document, No 61, 2012)

——*Provisional Rules on the Evaluation of Corporate Governance of the Insurance Institutions with Legal-Person Status* (Normative Document, No 112, 2015)

——*Rules on the Statistics based on the Consolidated Supervision of Insurance Groups* (Normative Document No 29, 2016)

——*Set-up of Metrics for Evaluating the Business Conditions of Insurance Undertakings* (Normative Document on Trial, No 80, 2015)

——*Supervisory Rules on the Evaluation of the Business Services of Insurance Undertakings* (Normative Document on Trial, No 75, 2015)

——*Supervisory Rules on the Scoring of Internal Control and Compliance of Insurance-Funds Allocation* (Normative Document, No 54, 2014)

——*Supervisory Rules on the Solvency Position of Insurance Undertakings No 15: Credit Rating of Insurance Undertakings* (Normative Document, No 22, 2015)

——*Supervisory Rules on the Solvency Position of Insurance Undertakings No 10: Integrated Risk Rating* (Normative Document, No 22, 2015)

——*Supervisory Rules on the Solvency Position of Insurance Undertakings No 11: Requirements and Assessments of Solvency Risk Management* (Normative Document, No 22, 2015)

——*Supervisory Rules on the Solvency Position of Insurance Undertakings No 2: MCS* (Normative Document, No 22, 2015)

——*Supervisory Rules on the Solvency Position of Insurance Undertakings No 16: Reporting on Solvency Condition* (Normative Document, No 22, 2015), §§ 7 – 69

——*Supervisory Rules on the Solvency Position of Insurance Undertakings No 17: Insurance Groups* (Normative Document, No 22, 2015)

Index